BOOK 22

For more O Canada Crosswords, go to

nightwoodeditions.com/collections/o-canada-crosswords

O CANADA CROSSWORDS

BOOK 22

75 *All New Themed Crosswords*

GWEN SJOGREN

NIGHTWOOD EDITIONS

1 2 3 4 5 — 25 24 23 22 21

Nightwood Editions
P.O. Box 1779
Gibsons, BC
VON 1V0
www.nightwoodeditions.com

Edited by Margaret Tessman
Proofread by Emma Skagen

Printed in Canada

ISBN 978-0-88971-357-4

The folk art on the cover is by Patricia Ryerson,
from the gallery Hubert and Belle's, hubertandbelle.com.

Contents

1 Landscape Architecture

Local landmarks – what's the city?

ACROSS

1. Originates from
6. _____ bean
10. Charged particles
14. Furniture retailer in Canada: _____ Allen
19. Physics lab device, for short
20. Nefarious
21. Waste allowance
22. _____ Farmers of Canada
23. Embarrass a partygoer?
24. So they allege?
26. Skeeter's kin
27. **Beacon Hill Park, in BC**
29. "The _____ of victory…"
30. Bread spreads
31. Dines at The Keg, say
32. Early Yucatán people
33. Ontario Nonprofit Network (abbr.)
35. Manitoba place: Île _____ Chênes
36. Graceful, in Greenwich
38. Rum-based beverage: Mai _____
40. Says
45. Chick's mama
46. Stands for hot pots
48. Rock band's crew member
49. Trimmed with lace
52. 1957 hit from Ottawan Paul Anka
53. Aircraft's tail assembly
55. Meander
56. Some allergens
58. Juno-winning Canadian band: _____ 41
59. Fellow FBI agent?
60. Italian appetizers
62. Lettuce type
64. Toronto Raptors league (abbr.)
66. GPS system
67. **Signal Hill National Historic Site, in NL**
70. Greek underworld god

75. Country music queen Tillis
77. 1975 Bachman-Turner Overdrive single: "Hey _____"
78. High-rise unit
80. Fraudster's scheme
84. Dirty rodent?
86. Conjuring up
88. Seasoned liver spread
89. Moves, in a CP rail yard?
92. Wield influence
93. Sharpen a razor
94. Feral feline
95. Turn coding into understandable language
97. Old Bryan Baeumler reno show: *Disaster _____*
98. Dad or mom
99. Lah-di-_____
100. Mass book
102. Early Canadian environmentalist: Grey _____
105. "_____ the season to be jolly"
107. Infatuate, old style
109. Private school student (var.)
111. Long-time Canadian Robin Hood product
115. Rage
117. **The Forks, in MB**
118. Book, in Bécancour
119. Canada's Silken Laumann, in the '80s and '90s
121. Genetic copy
122. Greek letter
123. Dandy
124. _____ of the above
125. Cosmetics colourant
126. "At Issue" group, on *The National*
127. Akita's irritant
128. Tarot card reader, say
129. Powerful horse

DOWN

1. Worked like a serf?
2. Leg bones
3. Passes legislation on Parliament Hill
4. Ship's spars
5. Educated
6. Deserves
7. This contains the iris
8. Sip of Scotch, say
9. Amino acid type
10. Repeat
11. Vertical axis on a graph
12. *The Old Curiosity Shop* heroine
13. Pen, in Pointe-Claire
14. **High Level Bridge, in AB**
15. Peacock's pride
16. Animal's skin
17. Ti-Cat rival in the CFL
18. TV "science guy" Bill, et al.
25. Lord's Prayer pronoun
28. Spoil
32. Ethical conduct
34. Nazi war crimes trial city
37. Circus performer's props
39. Abbreviated doctrines?
41. Tartness
42. Dutch cheese
43. Latvia's major city
44. Glimpsed
45. Surround a seamstress?
47. **Gastown, in BC**
49. Important historical periods
50. Mrs., in Madrid
51. CDA signed this trade agreement in 1947
52. Two, to 50-D
54. Play on words
56. Opera great Luciano
57. …Fah-_____-lah…
61. Dad's drivel?
63. Dangerous place for a herpetologist?
65. _____ Gallery of Nova Scotia

68. 20-year BC-born NHL star Sakic

69. Sudden gushes, in Greenwich

71. In need of a refill

72. Grin and _____ it

73. Golden rule preposition

74. A _____ in the right direction

76. Gymnast's pad

79. Pismire

80. Spill pigs' feed?

81. It precedes -Cola

82. Samsung competitor

83. Sauce made from chocolate and chili peppers

85. Kidlit Fly Guy books author Arnold

87. Jumbo shrimp and big baby, for example

90. **Mount Royal, in QC**

91. Conveyed via the ocean

93. Shushes

96. Early Joni Mitchell song: "_____ Morning"

97. "Shucks!" said the stitcher

101. Brent who played Data in *Star Trek: The Next Generation*

102. Vote no

103. Frankfurter, in Florida

104. Mythical story

106. Show scorn

108. Use a needle

110. Air Canada employee

111. Bomb on Broadway, say

112. South American Pacific coast capital

113. Cooking appliance

114. Strongly encourage

116. In 2020, this caused $1.3 billion in damage in Calgary

117. Abate

120. Harold Ramis *SCTV* character Green

SOLUTION ON PAGE 158

Breakfast Buffet

2

Eat this one up

ACROSS

1. Piers (var.)
7. Societal strife
13. Bends over
19. 1976 Joni Mitchell album
20. Oven part
21. Throat tissue
22. Language spoken in 30-D
23. **Italian serving with spinach**
25. Deck that includes The Magician card
26. Hollywood siren West
27. Askew: Off-_____
28. Listen to the voice of experience
29. Weasel's relation
31. Optical device
32. Movies character played by Canada's Mike Myers: Austin _____
34. Aerodynamic
38. Warsaw residents
39. Kyoto carp
40. Body art image
41. US org. whose motto is "Fidelity, Bravery, Integrity"
43. Tanzanian port: Dar es _____
47. Third-largest ocean
49. Narrow-minded
52. Liturgical invocation
53. Variegated in colour
54. C&W queen Lynn
56. Media moments: Photo _____
58. Some pages in *Canadian Geographic*
59. Vamoosed
62. Commentator MacLean of *Hockey Night in Canada*
63. Patchy horses
65. **Mexican morning meal**
69. Released prisoner
72. Rogers Cup line umpire's call
73. Blinks of an eye
77. Alberta Bowhunters Association (abbr.)

78. Language course for a new Canadian, for short
79. Journal writer
82. Lummox
83. Laptop battery, for short
85. Backer
87. Rectangular gaming piece
89. Surgeon's instrument
91. Typography dashes
92. Here and there (Lat.)
95. Equinox mo.
96. Sloped, in Southampton
98. Verses containing five metrical feet
100. Everest expedition mountaineers
102. Daily Canadian paper: *Toronto _____*
104. Church passageway
105. 2012 Carly Rae Jepsen EP song: "Just a Step _____"
106. Small firearm
108. Weathered
109. Community's cultural values
113. **French cuisine serving**
116. Pulsating light
117. Inequitable, at the CNE?
118. Smaller
119. Slanted type style
120. Semi-precious gemstones
121. Painter's stands
122. Turns back the clock?

DOWN

1. Former Global show: _____ *Will They Think of Next?*
2. Mythology queen goddess
3. Not fully closed
4. Simple sugar
5. **Crustless Italian version of 113-A**
6. Amniotic pouch
7. Itch or instinct
8. Carollers' quaff

9. Took a chance
10. Sprightly, maybe?
11. Vends on eBay.ca
12. Colt's gait
13. Waxy, insoluble substances
14. Slew of stuff
15. Furtively
16. Willow tree type
17. Yearns to plant a yew?
18. Toboggan
20. 1983 Michael Jackson hit
24. Vehicle seized for non-payment
26. Brewer's barley
30. Middle Eastern country
31. Freetown nation: Sierra _____
33. Vulnerable place?
34. Tim Hortons Brier team leaders
35. Canada Dry product: _____ water
36. Saskatchewan CFLer, for short
37. Film _____
38. National airline of Pakistan (abbr.)
41. Mattress for a Japanese pad?
42. Laurentians resort: Mont _____
44. Central Asian sea
45. Assistant
46. CFB dining hall
48. BC shares a small border with this state
50. Canadian opera singer Teresa
51. Chinchilla or coypu
54. Tiers
55. Operational Duty Officer (abbr.)
57. Average scores, for Canadian golfer Brooke Henderson
60. Western Canada mammal
61. Canadian hip hop singer Michie, et al.
64. Song sung in church
66. Biblical city of sin
67. Archaeological dig sites
68. Part of HRH, for Edward VII
69. Gives a chef one star?

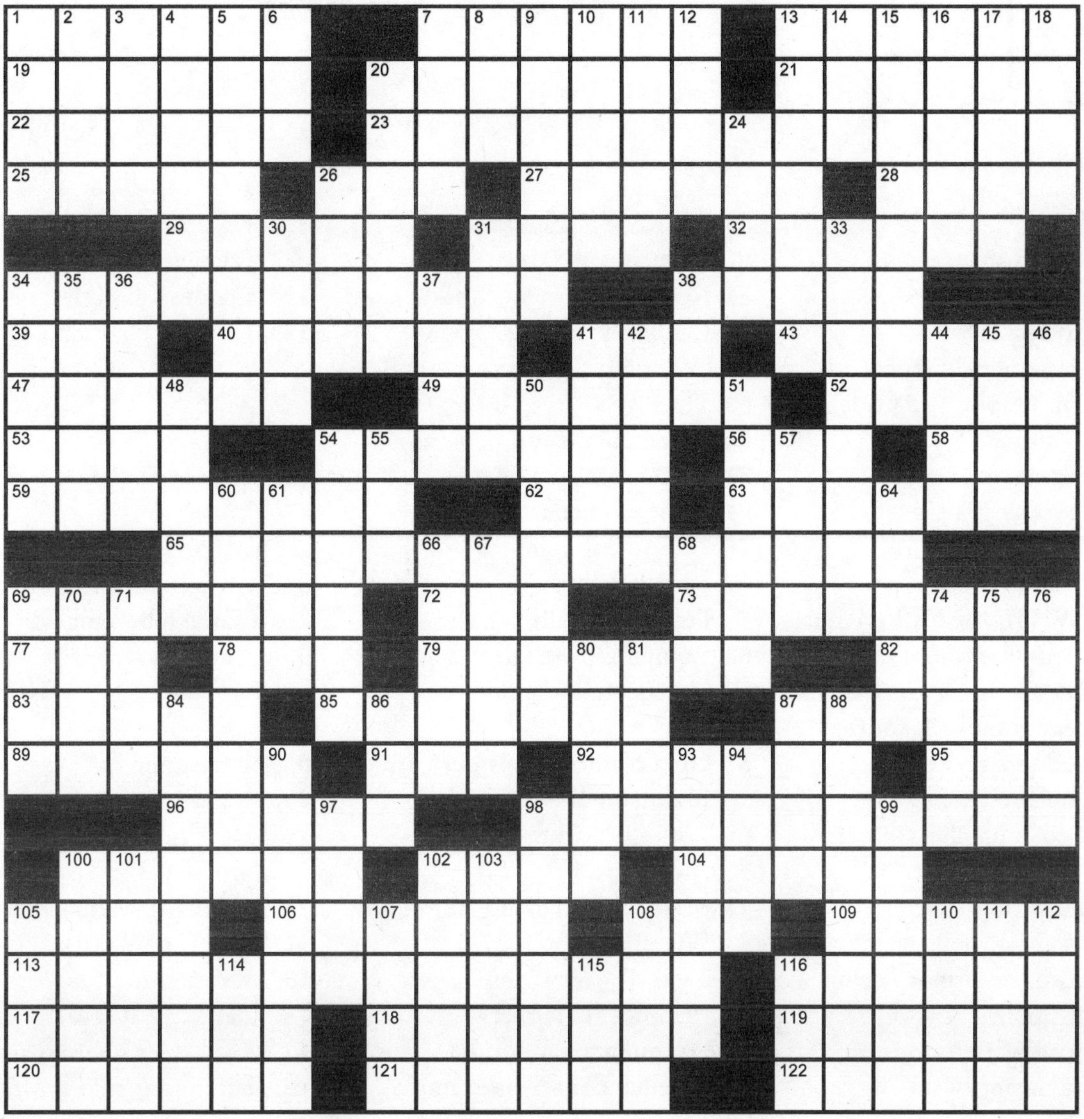

A crossword puzzle grid with numbered cells (1–122).

70. "This won't hurt _____!"
71. Risqué, at Honda Indy Toronto?
74. Boom or bang
75. Piano upkeep professional
76. Ceases
80. Calgary Stampede rodeo participant, at times
81. Tehran country
84. Kitty in the back lane?
86. Initials of a 1970s Canadian prime minister

87. Loses lustre
88. **A western one contains peppers**
90. Noisy dancers?
93. More banal, at the bakery?
94. Uttered
97. Clinch, like the carpenter?
98. Roof of the mouth
99. Aquarium fish
100. Took a turn at the plate, like a Blue Jay
101. Israeli city

102. Groove on a glacier
103. Wrongs, legally
105. Aftershave product: _____ Velva
107. Foot bottom
108. Loonies, say
110. _____ in the wall
111. In memoriam notice, for short
112. See 73-A
114. Move quickly
115. Unhealthy
116. _____ John A. Macdonald

3 Trivia Pursuit

Are you game?

ACROSS

1. Ottawa performance venue: National _____ Centre
5. Italian coastal city
10. *Dark Angel* actress Jessica
14. Ottoman Empire VIP's title (var.)
18. Hens' home
19. Middle Eastern VIPs
20. Gloat
22. Muddy a river's waters
23. **After WWII, the Netherlands sent 100,000 of these in thanks to Ottawa**
25. **Canadian James Naismith invented this sport**
27. Car sound systems
28. Nova Scotia hamlet: Garden of _____
30. Weakness
31. There was no room at this?
32. Ontario-born former Boston Bruin O'Reilly
34. Tim Hortons treat
35. Personal histories
38. Shred cheese
39. Raptors city, for short
40. Annoying
44. Postings at YYC
45. Mountainous Indian ox
46. Pack away
48. Fine wool type
49. Yank's Civil War opponent
50. Long-time Canadian bookstore chain
51. **In 1988, Edmonton's Palm Dairies created the world's largest this**
53. Supper serving
54. Device that throbs
56. End of a pen
57. Poses at the studio
59. Late '90s Nickelodeon sitcom: *Kenan &* _____

60. Piece of asparagus
61. Crunchy pesto seed
64. Newfoundland pine marten and Canada lynx, for example
66. "Winning _____ everything"
68. Thief
70. Prevaricates
71. Bacon slices
74. Mended once more
76. Old Athens coins
79. harbourpublishing.com, for ex.
80. Puppies' mouths?
82. Common pronoun
83. Unsafe building, say
85. Char
87. **Only country Elvis performed in outside the US**
89. Without a cloud in the sky
90. Shoshonean
91. Most compos mentis
93. Unseat a despot
94. Table d'_____
95. Reminder of surgery
96. Of yesteryear
97. Newfoundland, for example
98. Brainstorms
100. Some Labatt libations
101. Recced the joint
103. SW Ontario place: _____ Pelee National Park
104. Luau serving
105. Thrill, in Tunbridge Wells
108. Canadian singers Thomas and Tyson
109. Like freezing cold temperatures
113. **The world's highest tides occur here**
115. **Ontario is home to this largest freshwater island**
118. People-eating giant
119. Swindler who stays straight?
120. Cancel a space mission
121. Old letter, in Germany
122. Glasgow refusals

123. Feminine pronoun, in Frontenac
124. Creates a need for a cane
125. National charitable group: _____ of Canada

DOWN

1. These are passed on Parliament Hill
2. Drub, on the playing field
3. Lacquered metalware
4. Halloween beverages?
5. African country
6. Large Australian birds
7. None
8. Rob anagram
9. Postulate
10. Saskatchewan Benedictine monastery: St. Peter's _____
11. You might arrange this at BMO
12. Some U of T degs.
13. Make a request
14. They settle disputes
15. Objective for Steven Stamkos?
16. Haft
17. Friend to our nation
21. Gull's relative
24. Writes with a Montblanc?
26. Hosiery hue
29. First aid place at the Front
32. Actual bone attached to the sternum?
33. Rabbits have pointy ones
34. Frumpy females
35. Cops put them in a lineup
36. Devoured
37. **"Graveyard of the Atlantic" in Nova Scotia**
38. Lively dance in 2/4 time
39. "It hit me like a _____ of bricks"
41. **This tallest tree in the nation stands in BC's Carmanah Valley**
42. Get on your patellas to pray
43. Cat calls

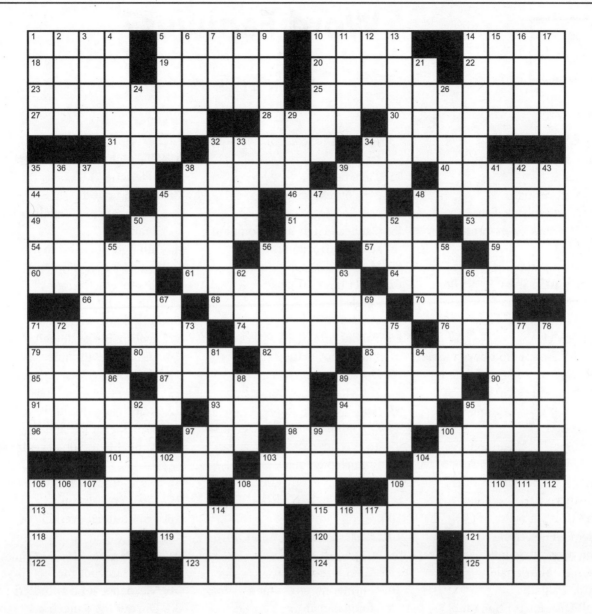

45. Michael Bublé cover: "I've _____ You Under My Skin"
47. Hollow bodily cylinders
48. Titanium or tin
50. Bank of Canada governor Mark (2008–13)
52. Prepare to shoot an arrow
55. This holds panes in place
56. Mythological sea nymphs
58. Pearly whites displayer
62. Only, in Offenbach
63. Game of marbles piece
65. Gather for a conference
67. Land parcel
69. Salvage a grounded ship
71. *Ransom* star Rene

72. Beatles lyric: "He's _____ nowhere man"
73. Luxury condo amenity
75. Weight-loss programs
77. Turkic language (var.)
78. They mimic monkeys?
81. Old-fashioned hairnet
84. Former Ontario premier Bob
86. Reverberates repeatedly
88. Civic Holiday mo.
89. *Big Brother* host Julie
92. Consume quickly, colloquially
95. Epilepsy episode
97. Ritzy
99. Gloomy
100. He clowned around circuses for almost 50 years

102. Rogers Centre ump's call
103. "Band of Gold" singer Freda
104. Canada's Mike Weir sinks lots of these
105. Black, to poet Blake
106. Hindu myth serpent
107. A Brit stores this in the boot
108. Favourite of teen fans?
109. Foal's papa
110. Jewish month
111. Skating milieu
112. Bills in California but not in the Great White North
114. New Canadian Library (abbr.)
116. Grp. US lawyers belong to
117. _____ *de plume*

SOLUTION ON PAGE 158

4

Word Families?

They're all relative

ACROSS

1. These systems bring rainy weather
5. Scrape covering
9. Shredded cabbage dish
13. Sneak attack on ex-president George?
19. Creative notion, in Quebec
20. Afghanistan area: _____ Bora
21. Australasian bird
22. Kent or Kings, in New Brunswick
23. **1992 Whoopi Goldberg movie**
25. Warrior pose exercise regime
26. Delay at the Royal Bank?
27. Larger ape description
29. **Jackpot**
31. In 2019, TELUS announced it would buy this alarm service co.
32. New Zealand fruit or bird
34. Northern African capital city
35. Soft Scottish rolls
39. EDM CFLer, formerly
41. For years, these bills featured Sir John A. Macdonald
43. Pride or sloth
44. Full Disk Encryption (abbr.)
47. Currency for a Continental vacation
48. Nicaraguan politician Daniel
50. Philippines tongue
52. **Group of frat buddies**
56. "_____ never work!"
58. Nailed a picture to a wall
59. Have lunch
60. Movie rating category
61. Atlantic icefield
62. Canadian coin birds
63. Wielded a sword
65. Blue Jay's mistake
67. Orderly display
68. **Legal contract proviso that retains pre-existing conditions**

73. A hunter follows this type of trail
75. Tie type
76. Mrs. Shrek, for one
78. Metric weight unit
79. Canada's High Liner company sells this frozen product
80. Healthy diet component
82. Pool player's stick
84. Landed
85. Painful
86. **Partial title of a 1971 Paul and Linda McCartney single**
89. Horse show prize
91. Hit with a sense of awe?
93. Go _____ length
94. Direction on a Quebec compass
95. To this time
96. Emulated golden Canadian Olympian Penny Oleksiak
97. As written, to Hadrian
100. "_____ girl!"
101. Easternmost point in Canada: Cape _____
103. Clerics' garments
105. Former acronym for a Canadian airline
107. **Country of origin**
111. Not first-rate, say
117. Like some Verdi pieces
118. Old Rick Mercer sitcom: _____ in Canada
120. **British fairgrounds game**
121. Former Canadian culinary show: *What's for _____?*
122. 1995 Alanis Morissette album: *Jagged Little _____*
123. Sharon, Lois & Bram, for years
124. Den for a bear
125. Falls as icy rain
126. Children's winter toy
127. These tick by quickly (abbr.)
128. _____-Aryan

DOWN

1. CTV nightly news anchor LaFlamme
2. Norse war god
3. Manitoba, directionally from Ontario
4. Cain and Abel's brother
5. Walked with confidence
6. Joins together, surgically
7. With the bow, musically
8. Cloth dying technique
9. Devilish, like Stallone?
10. Ominously imminent
11. Lion rival
12. Old West lawman Earp
13. Adjective for a sunflower seed
14. Securing, at the dock
15. Annual Pamplona event: Running of the _____
16. Word processing command
17. Virile equestrian?
18. Promotional overkill
24. Equal Rights Amendment (abbr.)
28. "The same for me!"
30. '70s dance for a swindler?
33. Dig out the dandelions
35. Infant, in Joliette
36. Atmospheres
37. Anne, in *Anne of Green Gables*
38. Heavy toper
40. Mulroney's German contemporary
42. NL folk song: "Jack Was Every Inch a _____"
44. Like bright overhead lights
45. Prima _____
46. *Kingsman* comics character: Gary "_____" Unwin
49. Spoil, like overripe fruit
51. "I need to see a man about _____"
53. Zimbabwean city

54. Biblical paradise
55. Ant-Man portrayer Paul
57. Celtic collar
61. Worry excessively
62. Hardy's comedic partner
64. *Jane Eyre* author Charlotte
65. _____ A Sketch
66. Greek letter
69. PNE, for one
70. Take stock
71. Ear part
72. Taj Mahal city
73. Gaze impolitely
74. T-shirts for Marco?
77. India's eighth-largest city

79. Of the unborn, in Britain
80. CRTC's American counterpart
81. Varieties
83. Jazzy American singer James
85. Helmsmen, say
86. Range or river in Russia
87. Deadens with novocaine
88. S. Amer. snake
90. Prepped for a run on the printing press
92. Poppycock
98. Like Terry Fox, to Canadians
99. Epic poem sections
101. Gleamed
102. Skateboarders perform McTwists on these

104. Chairs in provincial parliaments?
106. Drivers' licences, for ex.
107. Trendy crazes
108. Seed's sheath
109. Spike on an antler
110. Fingertip part
112. Annual event: CIBC Run for the _____
113. Island east of Java
114. Zesty attitude
115. Moved smoothly
116. Trainee
119. Antiquity, old style

Rockin' Since the '70s

5

Stalwart stars

ACROSS

1. North American shrubs
7. Squadron on the seas
13. Hospital worker (abbr.)
16. Offbeat
19. Acknowledgement
20. **Cummings of The Guess Who**
21. Northern seas diving bird
22. Landscaper's tool
23. Francisco Franco title
25. Accusing of wrongdoing
27. Have some grub
28. Escape one's pursuers
29. Open-toed shoe style
31. Second-person pronoun
32. Decadent
34. Crime techs' milieu
35. Bleach, like a plant
37. Potential source of danger
39. Wellsprings
41. Harvest whale skin
42. See 28-A
43. Related through mother
45. Tries again on eBay
47. US "Losing My Religion" music group
48. Signs up for classes
50. Uses a blender
51. US terr. that split into two states in 1889
54. Test at Trent University
56. Protection (var.)
57. Square dance group, for example
58. Ready to eat
59. Lyric poem
61. 1984 Bryan Adams album
64. **Rush member Lee**
65. "We stand _____ for thee"
69. **Emmett of Triumph**
70. Rough-and-tumble girls
72. **Jay who led Crowbar**
73. Brown who was Canada's first black female MLA
78. School fundraising team (abbr.)
79. Angry crowd's ruckus
80. Rounds in the ring
81. Seep out slowly
83. Tirade
87. Swiss peak
88. Classical composers' lodgings?
89. Erode
91. US gov. medical research grp.
92. Baby's noisy toy
93. 1983 Romantics hit: "Talking in Your _____"
94. Toronto lakeshore entertainment venue: Ontario _____
96. *Teenage _____ Ninja Turtles*
99. Makes a confession
101. Pasty-faced
102. Conservatory, in Victorian times
104. Stop _____ dime
105. South Texas city
107. Showy trinket
108. Raised platforms
110. Drab
111. Aquamarine or emerald
114. Loosening string
116. Simultaneously
119. Tell a whopper
120. Expected, like baby
121. **Rough Trade singer Pope**
122. São Paulo country
123. _____ Diego
124. Canada's capital (abbr.)
125. Drags nets on the sea bottom
126. Stout swords (var.)

DOWN

1. Stuffing seasoning
2. Iris part
3. Aztec emperor
4. Astonishment
5. Gordon Lightfoot hit: "_____ Highway"
6. _____ over a hot stove
7. Put up with
8. Tricky manoeuvre
9. _____ *Doubtfire*
10. *The National* political panel
11. Realm
12. Erelong, to a poet
13. Moroccan city
14. Voided
15. Felon's fake name abbr.
16. Presidents Hayes or Harrison, by birth
17. Treats from Calgary's Glamorgan Bakery
18. Lakehead University B.A., for example
24. *Obiter dictum*, e.g.
26. **April Wine singer Goodwyn**
30. Abandons, in the Sahara?
33. Short-lived rage?
34. Barracks beds
36. Former US car brand, for short
37. In this spot
38. **Rush member Lifeson**
39. Not true
40. Armistice
43. Physics energy unit
44. Black, in Baie-Comeau
46. Ogre or animal
49. _____-do-well
50. Musician Walter Ostanek: Canada's _____ King
51. Extinct bird of old
52. **"Rock Me Gently" singer Kim**
53. A minor and B major
55. Shed fur
58. Oust from the CBA?
60. Canada _____
62. Salad green
63. **Max Webster front man Mitchell**
64. British time standard (abbr.)
65. Creole cooks' ingredient
66. **"Cinnamon Girl" singer Young**
67. Mushy meal
68. Right, in Rivière-Rouge

71. Newspaper column type
74. Expenditures
75. Hussar's equine
76. Coronation garments
77. Bygone days
80. Squash type
82. Stun with a taser
84. Make a comparison
85. **Sweeney Todd singer Gilder**
86. Third-person pronoun
88. Carolled or yodelled
89. Old-style abbreviation for Calgary's province

90. Postcards, to a collector
92. **Guess Who and BTO member Bachman**
93. Frank who sang Paul Anka's "My Way"
95. Little fellow
96. Ski hill bumps
97. A Greek Muse
98. Remove slack
100. Cement mixture
101. Bits of bread
103. First thesaurus creator

105. Misplaces
106. Interjection expressing satisfaction
109. Diplomat's forte
110. Paul Martin autobiography: _____ or High Water
112. Arabic title
113. Actors Gibson and Brooks
115. Single woman's final words?
117. By what means
118. Coke can opener

6

Scary in the '70s

Get your popcorn ready

ACROSS

1. Pleads
5. Promiscuous puss?
11. Some Keats poems
15. Chunk of granite
19. Canada's Clara Hughes won Olympic speed skating bronze in this state
20. Melodious
21. _____ Major
22. South American balsam
23. **Head-spinning Linda Blair horror film**
25. Alpine plant gardens
27. Mosaic artist
28. On the ball
30. Pain in the you-know-what
31. Euphoria
34. Indicated with an asterisk
36. Actress Spacek who had the title role in 70-D
37. 2002 album: *O _____! Ultimate Aerosmith Hits*
39. The _____ is cast
40. **Gregory Peck picture (with "The")**
42. Ron MacLean, on *Hockey Night in Canada*
46. Tim Hortons breakfast sandwich roll
50. Jitters
54. Piste sword
55. Positive battery terminal
56. You shouldn't wash these with lights
58. Streets, in Saguenay
59. Milk-curdling enzyme
61. Set aside
63. Overly gory
65. Tit for _____
66. Angle-measuring instruments
68. Sigh of contentment
69. Beverage initially made in Canada in 1906

71. Travellers' nightly lodgings
72. **Long-running seasonal slasher franchise**
76. Winnipeg, say (abbr.)
77. Expressing a past action, in grammar
80. Brief snooze
81. Attribute to a writer?
85. *Star Wars* Solo
86. Make merry
88. Prepare for a confrontation
90. Motorcycle giant: _____-Davidson
91. West Coast waters mammal
93. Greek mythology nymph
95. "There you have it," in Trois-Rivières
97. Former BC Lieutenant-Governor Campagnolo (2001–07)
98. Donald Sutherland/Kate Nelligan spy film: *Eye of the _____*
100. Olden days nanny
102. Shawinigan summers
103. **Scary shark film**
105. Received
106. Vientiane nation
108. Brock who died in the Battle of Queenston Heights
111. Parched, in yore
115. Kigali citizen
120. Get pregnant
122. Chops onion
124. Girl who leads?
125. Hospital professional
127. **Donald Sutherland/Julie Christie thriller**
130. Biblical garden
131. Handout, in Harrogate
132. Came after
133. Canada's Governor General (1904–11): _____ Grey
134. The wicked don't get this

135. Spoken
136. Ranked, at Wimbledon
137. Squirrels' nest

DOWN

1. Southern Alberta town: Picture _____
2. Moral value
3. Some highlanders
4. Mattress linen
5. Toronto retailer: _____ Tea Leaf
6. Famed Boston Bruin Bobby
7. Dam on BC's Columbia River
8. Cobras' shapes
9. CIBC RRSP, for example
10. Foursomes
11. 1867 celebratory song: "_____ Dominion"
12. Plane without a pilot
13. Old Spanish coin
14. H.H. Munro pseudonym
15. Kitchen sieve
16. Meat counter cuts
17. Guinness and Baldwin of acting fame
18. *The Buddy Holly Story* lead Gary
24. Medical diagnostic "picture"
26. City in Germany
29. Musical chord
32. Trigonometric ratio
33. Knitting class supply
35. Kidney related
38. Peter Pan's nemesis
41. The Vancouver Symphony Orchestra makes this
42. Brave one's favourite sandwich?
43. International grp. of oil producers
44. Consciousness
45. **Final film in Roman Polanski's "Apartment Trilogy" (with "The")**
47. Perfect
48. Flower part

49. State of peace after hostilities
51. Jet's navigational device
52. Six species of this are found off Canada's Atlantic coast
53. This, in Tijuana
57. Swedish banknote
60. Victoria landmark: _____ Harbour
62. Summer shoe type
64. Former spelling of Bangladesh's capital
67. Jewish period of mourning
70. **Stephen King book-turned-movie**
73. Dined at home
74. Relinquish rights
75. Flash drive predecessor

77. Unit of loudness
78. Highly unusual
79. Order more *Maclean's*
82. Here's hoping Wiarton Willie doesn't see this
83. *Nota* _____
84. Bird world newborn
87. Enjoy a Russell Peters performance
89. Radio knob
92. Next to
94. Bot
96. Tall tale teller
99. She secures your corset
101. Long steps
104. Rescuer, in Reno
107. Starch from a palm tree

108. More emotionally distant
109. Probe affixed to a balloon
110. Pays to play, in poker
112. American electric carmaker
113. Biscuit served with clotted cream
114. 77-A, for example
116. Zapped in the micro
117. Kuwaiti currency
118. Go gaga for
119. _____ minted
121. _____-Canadian
123. Earring type
126. It precedes Aviv, in Israel
128. US film director Spike
129. Roulette wheel bet

7 Going the Distance

Place to place in provinces

ACROSS

1. Famed Scottish loch
5. Hoarder's disorder (abbr.)
8. Pierce
12. Barbaric
18. Honolulu home
19. Annual natural Canadian event: Spring _____
21. Tramp
22. Pens, like Margaret Atwood
23. **About 95 km, in Nova Scotia**
26. Consecrate
27. Prohibited by law
28. Door prize draw
29. Highlands hunting aide
30. It has a handle and a spout
32. Serving no practical purpose
34. Provide reception hors d'oeuvre
35. Sullied, in *Henry VIII*
40. Kagawa currency
41. "Eureka!"
43. Event in Montreal (1967) and Vancouver (1986)
44. Contaminate
46. Nasal membranes
48. Sailors' yeses
52. Spanish devil
54. Innocent or inexperienced
56. Sleazy sort
58. Nudists' runs of luck?
60. Ban anagram
62. Class of molluscs
63. Seasoned rice dish
66. Math discipline, for short
68. Liberal politician, in Leeds
69. Dressed in
73. Patriotic Canadian, say
76. Assignment
77. Destroying, in Dulwich
79. Greek goddess of youth
80. Harvey's burger topping
82. Pariah, in India?
84. Philosophy area, for short
86. Nighttime noisemakers

91. Positioning with a compass
93. Dissenting religious group
96. Cause to fall?
97. Old-style ointment
98. Sign at a Global TV studio
100. Drug cop
102. Iced anagram
103. Bitty bug
104. Quebecer Gilbert who played only for the Rangers during his NHL career
106. Excel document
108. Toronto nickname: The Big _____
112. Spicy dances?
115. Piste match
116. Austrian composer Wolfgang Amadeus
118. German songs
120. Smelled
125. Weather map line
126. **Around 380 km, in British Columbia**
128. Bar over a musical note
129. _____ of Wight
130. Golden _____
131. Duck breed in Canada: Green-winged _____
132. Metal slot on a shoe
133. Air Transat arrival times, for short
134. First Japanese–Canadian MP Bev
135. Shaft under a car

DOWN

1. Lamb's reply to the Little Red Hen
2. Coast guard Canadian icebreaker: _____ *Grey*
3. Synagogue
4. Absolutely positive
5. **Nearly 200 km, in Ontario**
6. Infectious disease
7. "Zip-a-Dee-Doo-_____"

8. Evasive
9. Made in Canada Kerr's product (var.)
10. Cold water gastropods
11. Canada Post delivery items
12. Decorative drape
13. See 97-A
14. Desmond depicted on Canada's $10 bill
15. Slanted
16. Canadian cinematic award (1980–2012)
17. Glyceride, for example
20. _____ of 1812
24. Moulding shaped like an "s"
25. 1964 Tony Randall film: *7 Faces of Dr. _____*
31. Horse handling strap
33. Kitchen style
35. Sleep Country Canada sells these
36. Highway 400 off-ramp
37. Pole on a ship
38. Cultured pearl type
39. Genealogy testing swab substance
42. **About 1,845 km, in Ontario**
45. East Kemptville NS used to have a mine that produced this
47. Canadian car owners do this a lot in winter
48. Toward the stern
49. 1945 Allies conference meeting site
50. Stojko who was seven-time Canadian figure skating champ
51. Streamlined
53. Racetrack loop
55. Obesity
57. *Brady Bunch* actress Plumb
59. Patty Hearst's abductors (abbr.)
61. Women's lingerie wear
64. Parthenon goddess

65. *King Lear* line: "_____, foh and fum…"
67. UN labour standards agency (abbr.)
69. Sing like Michael Bublé
70. Former US first lady Bush
71. In motion
72. Cut carrots into cubes
74. *Star Wars* franchise first name: _____-Wan
75. Sue Grafton mystery: _____ *for Silence*
78. Bert Bobbsey's twin
81. Oslo nation (abbr.)
83. Temporary hair colours

85. Cape Breton choir: _____ of the Deeps
87. Canada's "Man of a Thousand Voices" Little
88. Weapon for 115-A
89. Obnoxious
90. Pig roast rod
92. Most feminine
94. Harsh crow's cry
95. Stepped all over
99. Vivid Australian parakeet
101. Like chicken Kiev, say
103. Use a milk frother
105. Decorative wall panels (var.)
107. Travelled by toboggan

108. Hit hard, old style
109. Saunter
110. _____ layer
111. Afghanistan city
113. Excessive tippler (var.)
114. Stitch like a tailor
117. Pace around the paddock
119. Medical care aide (abbr.)
121. Greek cheese
122. _____ one's muscles
123. Latin footnote abbr.
124. 2001 Hockey Hall of Fame inductee Hawerchuk
127. Art aficionados' stop in TO

8

Wonder(s)ful

Awesome engineering from around the world

ACROSS

1. US org. that employs CDN astronauts
5. Foe of CONTROL, in *Get Smart*
9. Mediterranean Sea island
14. Vancouver landmark: Stanley _____
18. Molecular particle
19. Esteemed First Nations person
21. Fencers' swords
22. Succulent plant
23. Newfoundland waterway: Strait of Belle _____
24. Dorothy, to Uncle Henry
25. Vagabond
26. May or June?
27. **Italian wonder that tilts**
31. Crusades opponents
32. *Five Gates to Hell* BC-born actress Patricia
33. Summarizes
37. Tries to buy on eBay
38. Don an evening gown?
39. Football pass type
40. _____ face
43. Wanders
44. Collapsible bed
45. Whiteheads and blackheads
46. Divisions on the Trans-Canada
47. Little bitty food bits
48. Huntington's _____
51. Canadians Tapp and Harron acted on this show: *Hee* _____
52. Participate in a play
53. Number of Canadian territories
55. Erect
56. Cruddy coating
58. Sigh of relief interjection
60. Incomplete Mozart opera: *L'_____ del Cairo*
61. Sculptor's partial body of work?
62. Lock opener
63. Expression of disgust
64. Without a rival, in excellence
67. European economic grp. created in 1957
68. Elf's kin
70. 2013 Justin Bieber track: "I _____"
71. Mononymous Australian singer
72. In 1977, Héctor Torres scored the first this for Blue Jays: Grand _____
74. Sparkling topper for a princess
75. Salves that soothe
76. Ants and gnats, say
78. "A rose by _____ other name"
79. Tenth mo.
80. Sack material
82. Sulky expression
83. One of golf's greats: Ben _____
85. LSD, for example
87. None, in Nottingham
88. Semester at McGill
89. Western Canada crop
90. 2008 Bryan Adams single: "I _____ I'd Seen Everything"
92. Supply, but sparingly
94. Reynolds of *Smokey and the Bandit* fame
95. Weekend treat?
96. Begat
97. Lumpy puddings
101. **Pharaoh Khufu commissioned this Egyptian wonder**
104. Indian chef's butter
107. Cuts from the team, say
108. Alice Munro won this prestigious prize in 2013
109. Diabolical deeds description
110. Walk the dog trick toy
111. Insect world colony builder
112. Subarctic forest
113. Number of ladies dancing
114. One end of a hammer
115. Groups of two
116. Labels
117. Theoretical Big Bang substance

DOWN

1. Carpentry fasteners
2. On the Atlantic
3. It precedes eclipse or energy
4. In agreement with
5. Sheldon who won *Battle of the Blades* with Kaitlyn Weaver in 2019
6. Straightens things out?
7. *The Country Girl* US playwright Clifford
8. Dry, to a Spaniard
9. Length measurements
10. Cooks' coverings
11. Toronto NHLers, for short
12. Not perm.
13. Make an "h" sound
14. Greek goddess's cure-all?
15. Pie _____ mode
16. Toronto museum for over 100 years (abbr.)
17. Muskoka concertgoers' venue: _____ to Bala
20. Edits
28. Most aloof
29. Some moms in the meadow
30. Congeal
34. Northern Canada landmark: Arctic _____
35. **This wonder connects the Atlantic to the Pacific**
36. Turned sharply
38. Romantic outing
39. New Brunswick premier Bernard (1999–2006)
40. _____ on the wrist
41. **Iconic Incan civilization wonder**
42. Process of combining
43. **Lengthy Chinese landmark**
44. **"Wonderful" Roman amphitheatre**
47. Predatory whale
48. Healed

49. Sound like a snake?
50. Grow
54. Long-time Canadian retailer: _____ Hardware
55. Cotton capsules
57. Some loaves
59. Propellers' sound
61. Pound, like a heart
62. Myanmar money
65. Carbonated beverage
66. Harris/Talbot show: *Love It or _____ It Vancouver*
68. Small, carnivorous mammals
69. Keyboard's indentation key

73. Talkative avian
75. Will, by birth
76. Ontario place: _____ Dover
77. *Doctor Zhivago* actor Omar
81. Like ignored advice
82. Necklace adjunct
84. Process of organism development
86. Intense indignation
88. Arena seating level
89. Roof toppers
91. Sharp-toothed fish
92. Drank slowly
93. Secret rendezvous

94. Disreputable poultry farmer?
96. Leaf pore
97. Leg bone
98. Canada's Bill C-38: _____ Marriage Act
99. Nitrogen compound
100. City name in Oregon and Massachusetts
102. CFBs house this type of personnel
103. Water-filled ditch
104. Swindle
105. Gardener's tool
106. Ophthalmologist's orb

SOLUTION ON PAGE 159

9

Sons of Canada

Mcs and Macs

ACROSS

1. Like a cushy couch
5. Reticent
8. Makes like Michael J. Fox
12. Soda since 1911: Orange _____
17. Colourful aquarium fish
18. Weeding implement
19. As white as a _____
21. *Wuthering Heights* scribe Emily
22. Army newbies
24. White wine from Verona
25. PEI's official animal
26. Give the right to
27. **Famed Canadian peacekeeper Lewis**
29. Ribonucleic Acid (abbr.)
30. Mistaken premise
32. It's often set in Canada: *Ice _____ Truckers*
33. Old-style reward
34. Soup type: Scotch _____
37. Scraped by (with "out")
39. Ex-Leafs Tie Domi and Tiger Williams, for example
41. Surname of two *Schitt's Creek* stars
42. Bullfighters
45. Lacking emotion
46. Bard's composition
47. Quebec area: Gaspé _____
49. Footwear cushions
53. Like a bad apple?
55. With 115-A, a former CBC comedy–drama
57. Wear away a levee
58. Alberta cloud formation: Chinook _____
59. Burning
61. Axilla
62. One way to buy: On _____
65. United Empire Loyalist (abbr.)
67. Gun the engine
68. Beseech
70. Far from land
71. Pre-workout activity
73. Flowery headgear
76. Reserved Officers' Training Corps (abbr.)
78. Flu type from the birds?
79. Chameleon's kin
80. Indigenous Americans' SUVs?
85. Canada _____ Plan
87. Neutrinos are produced by this process
89. Scrooge catchphrase word
90. Took in revenue, like a provincial government
92. Makes seawater potable
93. Bouquet holder
94. Occasionally
98. Jumped off the springboard
99. Proclivities
100. In need
101. Primatologist Fossey
102. National Gallery of Canada display
105. On the sick list
106. **Actor and stand-up comedian Norm**
109. In an icy manner
113. Spoiled _____
115. See 55-A
116. Capital of South America's largest nation
117. Biased against pensioners
118. Ignited once more
119. Mandela's pol. party
120. Valcourt Christmas visitor: Père _____
121. Long-time Canadian correspondent and columnist Charles
122. 1958 Frankie Avalon hit: "_____ Dinah"
123. Inquire
124. American jazz drummer Krupa

DOWN

1. Causing pain
2. 1994 Alice Munro collection: _____ *Secrets*
3. Accurate datum
4. Car rental company in Canada
5. Con artist's decoy
6. Vancouver's Pacific Rim, for one
7. Affirmative answer
8. Minerals analysts
9. Bit from a Purdys box
10. Durable furniture wood
11. Like intense thunderstorms
12. Indigenous Canadian group
13. Retired Ottawa-born NHLer Brind'Amour
14. Deprived of liberty
15. High mason?
16. Groups of six witches?
20. These slot into mortises
21. Bridle snaffle
23. Golden state for Canadian Olympic hockey teams
27. **Former New Brunswick premier Frank**
28. Pleasingly plump
31. Nest on a cliff
33. *Will & Grace* **star Eric**
34. "_____ the Man Down"
35. Word software command
36. Hovering above
38. Enjoyed an outing for two couples
40. Platform for a performer
42. China piece used at the Empress in the afternoon?
43. Brando movie: _____ *Waterfront*
44. Separate into filaments, old style
47. Pay-_____-view
48. Sniper's requisite ability
50. Cuts off
51. *The Sopranos* star Falco
52. _____ bad example

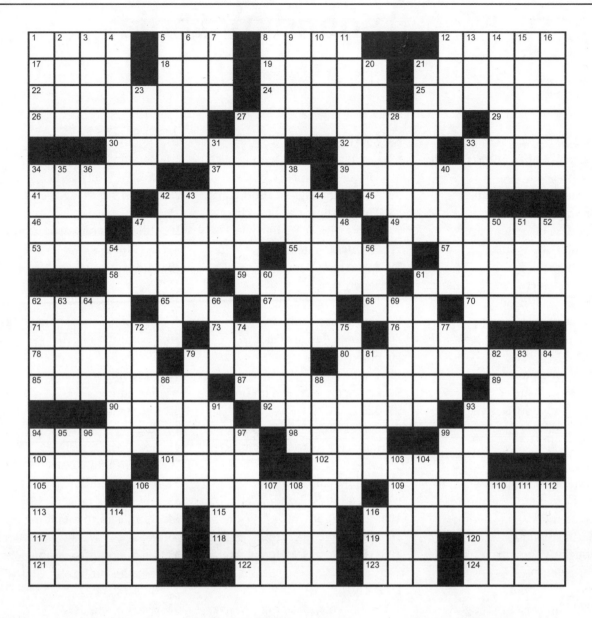

54. East Coast fiddling great Buddy

56. National Energy Board (abbr.)

60. Planted false evidence

61. Plazas in ancient Greece

62. Switch

63. Tar

64. Karpluk who starred in 55-A/115-A

66. Jet _____

69. Upright

72. Member of an Eastern Christian church (var.)

74. Capture a felon

75. Edmonton Oilers star Connor

77. Little poodle's plaything?

79. Lacking red blood cells

81. Canadian poet and novelist Humphreys

82. Former Israeli foreign minister Abba

83. Saskatchewan, directionally from Alberta

84. Hall & Oates hit: "_____ Gone"

86. This causes rust

88. Recently

91. _____ than a doornail

93. Rejecting, like a US president

94. Rockies National Historic Site: _____ Tunnels

95. The study of eggs

96. Lava description

97. Made nighttime noise

99. Drew, Jonathan and JD Scott

103. Makes wages

104. Old-style regret word

106. Gell

107. Cairo's river

108. _____ reflux

110. Ice sheet off Newfoundland

111. Legal claim on property

112. Bill met Hillary here

114. Involuntary contraction

116. Lea bleat

SOLUTION ON PAGE 160

10 Legendary Ladies

Roman goddesses

ACROSS

1. Recurrence of an ancestral trait
8. Stave off
13. Canadian military rank
18. Driving forces?
19. **Goddess of agriculture**
20. Oranjestad's island
21. Irons
22. Like a crunchy chip in Chelsea?
23. Unpleasant encounter with a jogger?
24. Ann M. Martin teen series: *The Baby-_____ Club*
25. _____-A-Roni
26. Not more than
27. Have antipathy for
28. EEG indicator line
30. Rock reef
32. Some classical compositions
34. **Goddess of wisdom**
39. Chef's measure, for short
41. Sound units
42. Marine mollusc
43. Douglas/Close thriller: _____ *Attraction*
45. *The _____ Couple*
46. 1970 Poppy Family single: "That's Where I _____ Wrong"
47. Pickle variety
48. Oscar Peterson played this
50. One under par, at Fairmont Jasper Park Lodge Course
52. Skilled in deception
53. Kids' racing vehicle
56. Bogart/Bacall movie: *Key _____*
58. Traumatic experience
60. Ontario Veal Association (abbr.)
61. Head of the Huns
63. Jessica who played Patsy Cline in *Sweet Dreams*
65. Clumsy one's interjection
67. Canadian calling need: _____ code
68. Low land tract
69. Canadian Morley who was a *60 Minutes* stalwart
73. More napped, like a soft fabric
75. Tim Hortons meal purchase
77. Herr's "three"
78. **Goddess of good luck**
79. August birthstone
81. Stately tree
82. Like a tinny sound
84. Customary ceremony
86. Rabbinic Judaism text
90. Good chums
91. See 13-A
94. Common Second Cup order?
95. Slang
96. Spanish Renaissance painter
97. Indigenous group in southern Africa
98. **Goddess of the hunt**
99. Gratuitously gazing
100. Petty arguments
101. Jazz singer Fitzgerald, et al.
102. Herbal teas for Hercule

DOWN

1. National organization: The War _____
2. Riot anagram
3. Official mineral of Ontario
4. **Goddess of the hearth**
5. Atlas page boxes
6. Hi-fis
7. It's celebrated at St. Joseph's Oratory
8. Grew together, botanically
9. **Goddess of truth**
10. Canadian actress Durance, et al.
11. Hem once more
12. See 39-A
13. Boots for Brits: Doc _____
14. Calla lily, for example
15. **Queen of the gods**
16. Dojo belts
17. Harangue
26. WestJet pilots' milieu
28. Soldier's cartridge belt
29. Edit
30. Cdn. taxation advocacy grp.
31. Org. for US lawyers
33. Midday
35. Cease
36. Lift your glass
37. Luxurious country lodgings
38. Chemical radical
40. Daddy
42. Description of some blood lab procedures
44. Old Italian currency
46. Rug
49. Reached a target
50. La Senza purchase
51. Saharan landforms
53. _____ on a tangent
54. Architectural moulding type
55. Pickled flower bud for cooking
57. Tuscaloosa state (abbr.)
59. Fourth album from Canada's Billy Talent: _____ *Silence*
62. Fido's biscuit, say
64. Old cheddar adjective
66. Workplace for Canada's Atom Egoyan
68. Starbucks Canada employees
70. Equestrian's latitude?
71. Sushi bar fish
72. You might win at Timmies by rolling up this
74. Globular cloud type
75. **Goddess of war**
76. Marilyn played her in *Gentlemen Prefer Blondes*
79. Type of cadence that ends a hymn
80. Traces of colour
83. Canadian Cancer Society fundraising month

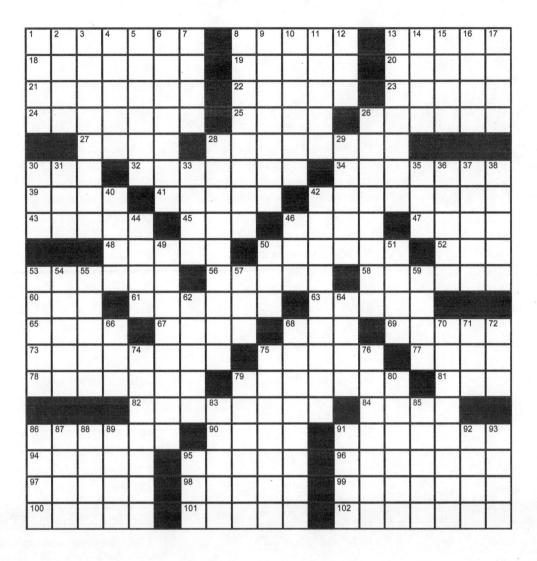

85. Goddess of the earth
86. Bathroom fixtures
87. ER acronym

88. Goddess of the moon
89. Governor General's Award-
   winning writer Cohen
91. Yiddish "bread"

92. Pimples problem
93. Foresters saw these?
95. Suffix with lemon or orange

Who Am I? 1

An iconic NHLer

ACROSS

1. They pick up passengers at YYZ
5. Bassist's break?
9. Beanie Babies, in the '90s
12. Dashboard gauge (abbr.)
15. 2009 Nickelback single: "If Today _____ Your Last Day"
18. Everly Brothers classic: "_____ Have to Do Is Dream"
19. London landmark: Marble _____
20. Royal Society of Edinburgh (abbr.)
21. CFL playing field gain
23. Lucy _____ Montgomery
24. Liver secretion
25. **His jersey number**
27. Former Alberta premier Jim, et al.
29. Canadian singers McLachlan and Harmer
30. Safari sighting
31. Clear the broadleaf
32. Impetuosity
34. Old-style cemetery pillar
35. _____ alcohol
37. Biblical Hebrew king
38. Match segment of 75-A
39. Swiss _____
40. US intel org. since 1947
41. Back muscle, for short
43. Fans' cheer word
45. Uninterrupted transitions
47. Ship's steering spot
49. Acts of pillaging
52. Post-it piece
53. Circle curve
56. Arboreal area demarcation
58. These dispense beer in bars
60. **NHL trophy he's won three times: Ted _____ Award**
62. Loonie denomination
64. Ottawa River rafting spot: Champlain _____

66. Physics resistance ratings
67. Mallard's kin
70. Battery component
72. Romantic meeting
73. Shelves beside hearths
74. Jim Carrey movie: *Me, _____ & Irene*
75. Sport for Canada's Milos Raonic
77. **His major junior team: Rimouski _____**
79. Song for a pair
81. Troublemaker
85. Stenographer's notebook
86. Burden
88. Flower
90. Social gathering on 83-D
91. Catch in a falsehood
93. Famous Egyptian king
94. Cause of a death on the Nile?
96. Movie theatre patron's interjection
97. Fortified defensive ditches
99. Beagle's baby
101. Prisoner's place
103. Take place
105. Canadian athletic excellence award: Lou _____ Trophy
106. Astronomer who discovered Uranus
108. When said three times, a 1970 film
109. Anagram for Ares?
110. Competed at the Tim Hortons Brier
111. Woodbine competitor
115. **His Nova Scotia hometown**
117. Midget buffalo
118. Unaccompanied
119. Gin-based cocktail: Tom _____
120. Words heard two times at the altar
121. Baby talk syllables
122. Kellogg's cereal: All-_____
123. Some amount

124. Tax not paid by Albertans (abbr.)
125. _____ *de guerre*
126. Latin 101 verb
127. Swerves, on the sea

DOWN

1. Spend the night outdoors
2. Orchard spray in bygone days
3. You might see this mammal in the Gulf of St. Lawrence
4. **He is… (with 104-D)**
5. Like a diseased Dalmatian
6. Olympic gold-winning Canadian equestrian Lamaze
7. Eyeball membrane
8. Roget's books
9. Just off the vine, say
10. Thais and Vietnamese
11. U of C awards these
12. Legendary literature?
13. Settles up with Visa, say
14. Time units (abbr.)
15. More undulating
16. Like some customs
17. Medicinal plant
22. River mouth areas
26. Move quickly
28. Tattle to William?
33. Tilt
34. Glossy coating
35. Not ersatz, in Dortmund
36. Theatre level
37. **Leading the Penguins, he's won this three times**
39. 1973 hit from Canada's Keith Hampshire: "The First _____ the Deepest"
42. Rail anagram
44. Like a cardiologist's sincere comment?
46. **He scored this at the 2010 Olympics**

48. Gorgon who turned onlookers to stone
50. Bell tower sounds
51. Joust, verbally
53. Greyish, facially
54. Male sheep
55. Abnormal bodily sac
57. Slice (off)
59. On the _____
61. Shark's fin description
63. Clarinet mouthpiece component
65. Think tank output
67. M&M Food Market, for one
68. South American shrub
69. Still in the sack
71. Sierra _____ Canada
72. _____-for-tat

74. Little cars, in Lancashire
76. National Incident Management System (abbr.)
78. Arctic airline: Canadian _____
80. One of five senses
82. Southern Ontario Indigenous group
83. Pearl Harbor place
84. German industrial region
87. Excellent
89. Section for third-class *Titanic* passengers
91. Fez accoutrement
92. Steal, old style
95. Hundred Acre Wood bear
97. Abandon on an atoll

98. How some prescription drugs are taken
100. Fake
102. Grasslands for gauchos
104. **See 4-D**
105. Muslim holy site
106. Long-time CTV news team member Robert
107. Data storage medium
108. Provoke on the playground
110. Preserves
112. Doves' sounds
113. KFC serving, for short
114. Notable time periods
116. Long-time Canadian band: The Tragically _____

Du You Know the Way...

To these cities

ACROSS

1. Recipe starch
5. Jacket fasteners
10. Some British noblemen
15. Not yet up
19. Under-the-hood gunk, say
20. Discomfiting
21. Eastern Christian church member (var.)
22. Newfoundland-set musical based on 9/11: _____ *from Away*
23. Grew more mature
24. Canadian polling firm since 1986
25. Region's flora and fauna
26. Frequent Ucluelet BC precipitation
27. **North Rhine-Westphalia capital**
29. Blue
30. Toronto's Shay Mitchell starred in this: _____ *Little Liars*
32. Collection for Bianca Andreescu?
33. Young horses
34. Achieves through trickery
36. Swerve (var.)
37. Lasagna dish
38. Not "nope"
39. Manulife product (abbr.)
42. Man's formal headgear
45. Settled a bill
47. **Adriatic Sea city in Croatia**
50. Painting style that boggles the eye
51. Long-running TV comedy: *The Big _____ Theory*
52. Early Germanic letter
53. Refuse to react
54. Habitual imbiber of Beaujolais?
55. Banting shared his Nobel Prize money with this Charles
56. Cold cuts store section
57. Gradually absorb
58. Software customers
60. Like 9-to-5 employees
62. Without any hesitation
63. Is consistent with
64. Eyelash cosmetic
69. Abuse
71. Harshly criticizes
72. Dilapidated Dodge, say
76. It plays LPs
77. Phuket resident, for example
78. Swiss Chalet meal choice
79. *Carousel* tune: "This Was _____ Nice Clambake"
80. Venus de Milo is missing these
81. Tori's Canadian-born husband McDermott
82. Military school frosh
83. **French name for city known for a WWII battle**
85. Former Canada–US agreement: Auto _____
86. Use a Crock-Pot timer
87. Northwest Germany river
88. Greek letter
89. 1980s Alberta premier Getty
90. Citadel Hill gives you a good one
91. Terrible, to an Apostle?
94. Ottawa landmark (with 42-D)
96. Baden-Baden, for one
99. Wasaga Beach wear
102. That woman
103. **Sichuan province city**
105. Folic or formic
106. Harsh, in tone
108. Starts a tennis tournament?
109. Pressing need
110. Email, say
111. Canadian-born, Oscar-winning actress Shearer
112. Honda Indy Toronto events
113. Lender's claim
114. Not relaxed
115. You might raise this glass at Kitchener's Oktoberfest
116. Subway, in Montreal
117. 1971 Pierre Berton book: *The _____ Spike*

DOWN

1. Umpteen fish?
2. Engage in debate
3. Wedding attendee
4. Bookies' numbers
5. Most Blue Jays games do this
6. Hypodermic syringe component
7. Slangy language
8. Docks
9. Employee on 60-D
10. **Ireland's largest city**
11. You can catch a train at this Toronto station
12. Great Plains Indigenous tribe
13. Sup
14. You can buy one at Grand & Toy
15. Crop fields
16. *Bluenose*, for example
17. Send forth a signal
18. Refuse to acknowledge
28. Public panache
31. Take back due to a defaulted payment
34. Temporary trend
35. Swing a boom on board
36. _____ of Turin
37. Sty sow
39. Stephen Sondheim musical: _____ *the Woods*
40. Licorice treats
41. _____ terrier
42. See 94-A
43. Share your opinion
44. Chinese mammal sometimes loaned to Canadian zoos
45. Kicking Horse _____
46. Aesop fable: *The _____ and the Grasshopper*

47. Becomes less shiny
48. Hospital ward
49. Household cleanser brand
51. Green gemstone
52. Find a replacement tenant
55. Fasten a rope while climbing
56. **United Arab Emirates city**
57. Muscat resident
59. Description of a certain Simon?
60. Feudal estates
61. Parental edict: "_____ it!"
63. Dirt
65. Shorebird with a long bill
66. Sign of the ram
67. Hasidic leader
68. BMO GIC, for example
70. Drive-_____ window

71. Talk over the Net?
72. BC-set reality TV offering: _____ *Fever*
73. Lily variety
74. Microscope part
75. Famed Nova Scotia island
77. PI
80. Bluish-green colour
81. *Schitt's Creek* star Levy
82. Dress with elaborate care
84. Angle measurements
85. House of Commons personage (abbr.)
86. Cubism icon Pablo
89. **South Africa's third-largest city**
90. More prideful
91. Happily hyper

92. 1997 novel from Ontario's Nino Ricci: _____ *She Has Gone*
93. Nobel-winning physicist Enrico
94. Chrysalises
95. Expel
96. Damascus country
97. Leafs through a book at Chapters?
98. Concerning, old style
99. CFB word
100. Frosted, at the bakery
101. Three-time Canadian prime minister
103. Res at U of T
104. Aquatic bird
107. Foldable bed

13 Historic Canadian Hotels

Putting out the welcome mat

ACROSS

1. Scored on a serve at the Rogers Cup
5. Hawk's baby
9. *Little Big Man* Oscar nominee from BC: _____ Dan George
14. "Vamoose!"
19. Italian resort town
20. Alaskan city
21. Every 60 minutes
22. 1986 #1 Heart hit: "_____ Dreams"
23. **St. Andrews resort originally opened in 1889**
25. Eliminate all traces
26. Willie Mitchell wore this jersey number as a Canuck
27. Noisy outcries
28. **Quebec City stalwart since 1893: Château _____**
30. Canadian tennis pro Bouchard
31. Flying mammals
32. Decorated cupcakes
33. Sue Grafton mystery: _____ *for Lawless*
36. Ceremonial Jewish dinner
37. Bar
38. Road construction pylons
40. Pulteney Bridge British city
41. Of the soft palate
43. Psychological state
44. Silent film successor
46. Putting gear on a horse
50. Garden pest
52. Adolescents
53. Nut in a squirrel's stash
54. Impale
56. Capable of being heard
58. Layered breakfast casserole
60. Filthy coating
61. Calgary landmark: _____ Christie Park
62. Eyeball, in old literature
64. Neat
65. **Saskatoon hotel that opened its doors in 1935**
70. Thickening agent: _____ gum
71. Far away
72. Borrow from a vagabond?
73. Calgary or Cranbrook, properly?
74. Thin layer of bone
76. Like favouritism in a family business
79. Wickerwork material
81. Moisten the turkey
82. Greeting from Pooh
83. It follows tea or paper
85. May is this in Canada: Celiac _____ Month
87. Ridiculous
89. *King of Kensington* co-star Fiona
90. Catlike carnivore of Africa
91. Drain blockage
92. Batman's buddy
94. Roadside hazard for the military (abbr.)
95. 1935 Hitchcock movie: *The 39 _____*
99. 1970s Canadiens goalie Dryden
100. Stable mama
101. Son, in Saguenay
103. Small pianos
105. **Toronto hotel that first welcomed guests in 1929**
107. Wear for a dreary day
108. Sporting event: Canada Winter _____
111. BC ex-premier Christy
112. **Winnipeg hotel named a National Historic Site in 1981**
113. Came up in the morning?
114. From now on, old style
115. Anger
116. Dust bug
117. Glasgow residents
118. Manicured the lawn, say
119. They're mined and refined
120. Kootenay or Crowsnest, in the Rockies

DOWN

1. "_____ only a mother could love"
2. Thick skin on your heel
3. Fascinate your fiancée?
4. Ill-fated
5. Gossipy tabloid since 1926: *National _____*
6. 1998 Shania Twain hit: "_____ Still The One"
7. Papineau pals
8. Parliament Hill politician, for short
9. Fine-grained sedimentary rock
10. It gives you a sign of the future?
11. Tehran nation
12. British trading business founded in 1600: _____ Company
13. Swindle a sheep farmer?
14. Suffix with home or farm
15. Fashionable
16. Type of 108-D, for short
17. _____ Wednesday
18. Convened
24. Much ado about nothing
28. The _____ Four
29. Home for a heron
31. Harvey's fare
33. **Banff National Park landmark for 100+ years: Château _____**
34. Mobile labourers
35. Canada's Anka wrote this Tom Jones hit: "_____ A Lady"
37. Gets overwhelmed with anxiety
39. Sound of surprise
40. Little blister
42. Sass
43. **Edmonton hotel named for our first prime minister (in 1915)**
45. Persevere: Keep _____

46. Too quick to judge or act
47. Giving grounds for a lawsuit, perhaps
48. **Halifax hotel since 1927**
49. High chair part
51. Manure
55. Abrade
57. Roald who created Willy Wonka
59. Alberta and Saskatchewan do this
63. Highlands landforms
66. Release light, say
67. Go bad
68. Hydro-Québec power problems
69. Not impressed

70. Male FBI agent
72. Rude person
75. Assisting in wrongdoing
77. Electrical socket insert
78. Fitted with architectural brackets
79. Strengthen an army again?
80. Alternate name for gramma
82. Breach computer systems (with "into")
84. Journalist Chen who appeared on CBC and CTV
86. Temporary pauses
88. Heavy cart
93. Saltbush
94. Sort

96. Live in a tent
97. Illinois city
98. Commences
100. American artist: Grandma _____
102. Annoyed
103. Military rank moniker
104. Eyelid infections
105. Take a siesta
106. Yin's opposite
107. Lion's bellow
108. Petro-Canada product
109. _____ de Triomphe
110. Bovine sound
112. To and _____

14 National Nicknames

...also known as

ACROSS

1. Vena _____
5. Write a cryptic message
11. Misfortunes, like measles?
15. Not kosher (var.)
19. Ontario place: _____ Sound
20. Monies used in Freetown
21. Uncluttered
22. Garden weeder
23. Residents of Quebec's largest city
25. Like a House of Commons motion?
27. Tankard beverage
28. Fashion designer Reem
29. Canadian army rank: _____-General
31. Overly fastidious
32. Grates a lemon
34. Casual "hello"
35. Jewish congregation's gathering place
36. Awaken
38. Beauty treatment
41. Shish kebab kin
45. Greetings from Gaius
46. Dummy
48. Rajah's other half
49. Noise in the night
50. Cabbage-family vegetable
51. Tower above
53. Saskatchewan city: _____ Battleford
55. Russian parliamentary assembly
56. Lively spirit
57. Soluble salt
59. Portable electronics battery type
61. Romaine lettuce
62. Coral reef isles
64. Baby beds, in Brighton
66. Jerk (var.)
67. Canadian restaurant franchise: Pizza _____
68. American young adult fiction author Horatio

71. **Breadbasket of Europe**
73. _____ board
75. Behold
76. Service at Edmonton's St. Joseph's Basilica
79. Musical clef
80. Canadian senator Peter (1977–1998)
82. _____ Clemente
83. Located at
85. *The Mikado* character
87. The CSA sends astronaut trainees here
91. Nights before some holidays
93. Daniel who wrote *Robinson Crusoe*
95. Docks for sitting by the bay?
96. Serving two purposes
97. Newfoundland seacoast area: _____ Nova National Park
99. Cleanse, spiritually
101. Scotland Yard stool pigeon
102. "_____ stupid question…"
103. Edible gastropod
104. Royal Alexandra Theatre attendee
106. Canadian made aircraft: Twin _____
107. Take off weight
109. Dixie dish
110. Candle
112. Tilting
115. Espresso-based beverage
117. Plunge into the pool
118. TikTok or Spotify
121. More comfy pub area
123. 90-degree corners
126. Converse
127. Em, to Dorothy
128. Noble standards
129. Affectations
130. Kin of an auk
131. Janitorial cleansers

132. Shipping platform
133. Fishing lure

DOWN

1. Prolonged sleep
2. Off the base without a pass
3. **Land of Grace**
4. Tan anagram
5. Vote in
6. Gets closer to
7. Coca-_____
8. It follows fast
9. Skin related
10. He tries to write a term paper?
11. Prefix with Aryan or European
12. Salacious ogle
13. Popular pooch, for short
14. Type of infection
15. **Land of Smiles**
16. Sticks up
17. They wriggle in water
18. Eagles singer Glenn
24. Demolish, in Derbyshire
26. Roof support
30. **Land of the Rising Sun**
33. Core
34. Place to hang your homburg
35. *CODCO* offering
36. Casino table tool
37. Egg shaped
38. _____ jacket
39. Erelong
40. Cherry, in Chambly
42. Fencing hit acknowledgement
43. Knight's combat wear
44. Like dough on the rise
46. When Canadian soldiers stormed Juno Beach
47. Birds that hoot
52. Clark government federal cabinet minister MacDonald
54. Sandwich meat
58. **The Boot**

60. Bucks' partners
63. House of Commons official: Sergeant-at-_____
65. Work those abs, say?
68. TFSAs and RRSPs
69. Robertson Davies 1955 Leacock Medal winner: _____ of Malice
70. Biological groups
71. Practical
72. Canadian Screen Award candidate
74. Order from that fellow?
77. Provide assistance
78. Treeless tract in 71-A
80. Canadian-born Ironside star Raymond

81. Southwestern Siberia city
84. Children's TV character: _____ the Explorer
86. 1989 Peter Mayle bestseller: A _____ in Provence
88. **Land Down Under**
89. Japanese rice wine
90. Daminozide
92. **India's Teardrop**
94. **Gift of the Nile**
98. 1966 The Association song: "_____ Comes Mary"
100. Narcissist's trek?
105. Ontario Six Nations reserve people
106. Annual golf event: RBC Canadian _____

108. Take without authorization
110. Governor General or Lieutenant-Governor
111. "Halt!" to a sailor
112. Some keyboard keys
113. Douse
114. "To Sir, with Love" vocalist
115. *Superman* character Lois
116. UBC faculty
117. Stewed Indian serving (var.)
119. Persian folklore being
120. Almost silent interjection
122. Make a purchase at Leon's
124. This holds hair in place
125. Chatter's gift?

15 | *Schitt's Creek* Cleans Up...

At the 2020 Emmy Awards for comedies

ACROSS

1. Rascal
6. HGTV Canada offering: *Family _____ Overhaul*
10. Small piece of paper
15. Redblack rival at TD Place Stadium
19. Large Vietnamese city
20. Alpine goat
21. _____ acid
22. Gymnast's floor or balance beam jump
23. **Best supporting actress winner (with 78-A)**
24. Recipe amt.
25. Western Canada groceries chain: Save-On _____
26. Canada's has the *Bluenose*
27. Sirloin tip and prime rib products
29. Relax restrictions, say
31. Matured, like melons
33. Add drops, in Islington
34. Mini map in an atlas
35. Disclose details
36. Emulates Canada's Shawn Mendes
38. Newspaper reporters used to bang out copy on these
43. Hearty soup type
47. Locker room fungus
48. Solitary band type?
49. Teems
50. Carve into
52. Like a stray shot
54. Ontario Camps Association (abbr.)
55. Moonfish
56. **Dan Levy shared the Emmy for this with 13-D**
58. Ladder rung
59. **Winning comedy category for *Schitt's Creek***
62. Trading partner of CDA
63. Some SAR personnel
66. Explosion
69. 2003 Will Ferrell holiday film
71. Hang a curtain?
72. Dignity
76. Abbr. for BC's largest city
78. **See 23-A**
82. Sobbed
83. **Best actress winner (with 120-A)**
87. _____ *Geste*
88. Pharaohs' snake symbol
89. Sacred Indian fig plant
91. Bit of evidence for Miss Marple?
92. Shell for a seed
93. Metalworker, of sorts
95. Do additional research: _____ into
97. Sired by Adam in Eden
99. The Brick staffers
101. Fire starter's crime
102. Boring
103. Game played on a 16 × 16 board
105. Yiddish scandal spreaders
110. Convention attendee's badge
113. Some teeth
114. Election winner's oration
115. Arabic dignitary
116. One side of Everest is here
118. Former Ontario premier Harris
120. **See 83-A**
121. Common credit card
122. Accustom to (var.)
123. And others (abbr.)
124. Was incorrect
125. Barbara who played TV's Jeannie in the '60s
126. Opposite of assets
127. Like a clammy cave
128. Rumpled

DOWN

1. Juno-winning female vocalist Ulrich
2. Clergyman's camera brand?
3. Actresses Camp and Kendrick
4. Like Lysol disinfecting wipes
5. Pastry loving 17th-C. German Lutherans?
6. Top 40 topper
7. Elaborate motifs some musicians must play?
8. Quarks, for example
9. Former Montreal MLBers
10. Social security protection, say
11. 2006 Red Hot Chili Peppers song: "_____ Girl"
12. Canada's Derek Drouin won high jump Olympic gold here
13. **Co-winner Cividin for 56-A**
14. Elementary particle
15. Like slightly undercooked penne
16. Riding strap for a monarch?
17. Keen to play?
18. *Toronto Sun* commentary
28. See 10-A
30. Relative of Ramses I
32. Lake Erie spit: Long _____
35. Gained knowledge
37. State of penury
39. Persian spirits
40. Act histrionically
41. Canadian Grand Prix entrant
42. Opens pea pods
43. Sold-out shows (abbr.)
44. Toronto Bloor-Danforth line TTC station
45. Untruthful person
46. Repress
47. Guess Who hit: "_____ Eyes"
51. Vineyard, in France
53. Petri dish substance
57. Have a hippo?
58. Cold dessert

60. Antiquity, old style
61. _____ Antonio
64. Batter?
65. PC's "guts"
67. Church offshoot group
68. Domain of former Russian rulers
70. *Royal Canadian Air* _____
72. Exchanges Scrabble tiles, say
73. Electromagnetism pioneer Nikola
74. Disgust (var.)
75. Brew some Earl Grey
77. Zero, at an FC Edmonton match

79. Annoying exterminator?
80. Loathe
81. Chinese dynasty or currency
84. Punishing places for sinners?
85. Omaha resident
86. Lambs' mothers
89. Dazzle a drunkard?
90. Like Little Annie of comic strips
92. Orchestral composition
94. Iranian capital (var.)
96. _____ scaloppine
98. Christians, as opposed to Jews
100. **Best actor winner Levy**
101. Nectar for Hindu deities

104. Caused limping
106. Indian leader who lent his name to a jacket style
107. 1985 Canadian fundraising song: "_____ Are Not Enough"
108. Eva Gabor sitcom: *Green* _____
109. Sheltered from the sun
110. Church part
111. During
112. _____ *en scène*
113. Long-time pharmacy chain: Shoppers Drug _____
117. Darts players' place
119. Rockies animals

Drink Up

Put some puns in your potables

ACROSS

1. ROC: _____ of Canada
5. Montreal neighbourhood: _____-des-Neiges
9. CANDU reactor's centre
13. Annual Nova Scotia event: _____ Rogers Folk Festival
17. Nabisco cookie
18. Tempt a trout?
19. Geological age (var.)
20. Conceal
21. Drill type
23. Abandon at the altar
24. 2002 short story collection from Canada's Lisa Moore
25. **Beverage for those on the go?**
26. **Tipple for thoughtful folks?**
28. Bonaparte's favourite brandy?
30. Trek
31. Popular tree in Colorado?
34. *National Post* front page piece: _____ story
35. Like the most overgrown fen
39. Fermented beverage
40. Badger's burrow
41. Officer responding to Calgary's Canada Olympic Park?
42. Actresses Blair or Diamond
43. Disinclined to do anything
45. John A. Macdonald was born one
47. Clinch a victory at Canada Life Centre?
48. Congo capital
51. Major US river
53. Property ownership papers
54. **Belfast bar beverage?**
57. Incurred debts
61. Shoe design star Jimmy
62. Old Canadian insurance company: _____ Life
67. Some medical procedures
68. Some South American tubers
70. Audiophile's equipment
71. Legume family climbing plant
72. Cause exasperation
73. Clone
76. Duct
77. Slip out of place, medically
79. Contented kitten's sound
80. This makes waste
81. Aquarium fish
82. 2018 film shot in BC: _____ *at the El Royale*
84. **Soda jerk's dairy serving?**
88. **Drink for chilly speed skaters?**
92. Canada earned 17 Olympic medals in this state
93. Title granted to Canadian opera star Emma Albani in 1925
94. CFL quarterback, for example
95. _____ *Like It Hot*
96. Green acres?
97. Give a critique
98. Went too fast on the Trans-Canada
99. See 98-A
100. 1958 film: *Desire Under the _____*
101. Extraordinary thing
102. Conclusions, to curling teams?

DOWN

1. Canada Cordage sells this
2. Beach birds (var.)
3. Trickle
4. Beefy fillets
5. Grab onto your necklace?
6. Sports shoe part
7. Eight-line verse form
8. Post-WWII European economic org.
9. Tangy Louisiana cuisine style
10. *Trompe l'_____*
11. Desk type
12. Records data in Excel, say
13. Highlight of an art exhibit?
14. Cone-shaped tent (var.)
15. Red Sea port city
16. *The Real Housewives of Atlanta* star Leakes
22. Unkind
26. Like a '60s TV squad?
27. Nonconformist
29. Snacks
31. Frenzied
32. Org. that searches for extraterrestrial life
33. Aleve relieves this
35. Recurring themes
36. US Civil War general Robert
37. Former Oiler and Flame Ladislav
38. Makes lace
40. Anagram for 64-D
41. BC salmon
44. In good order, on the boat?
46. **Designer Chanel's favourite beverage?**
49. Command to a protective canine
50. "Michael, Row the Boat _____"
52. Frequently, to an old poet
55. Leave at the pawnshop
56. 2010 Sarah McLachlan song: "Loving You Is _____"
57. Acronym on an invitation
58. Maple genus
59. Alliance Canada joined in 1949
60. Naked as the day you were born?
63. Overwhelm, emotionally
64. Mars' Greek counterpart
65. Monthly payment for some
66. Lavish with love (with "on")
69. Soviet-developed ballistic missile
72. Cast-out son of Abraham
74. Old World bird
75. House of Commons option: _____ Member's Bill
78. Row
79. Asiatic green: _____ choi
80. Ships are steered from here

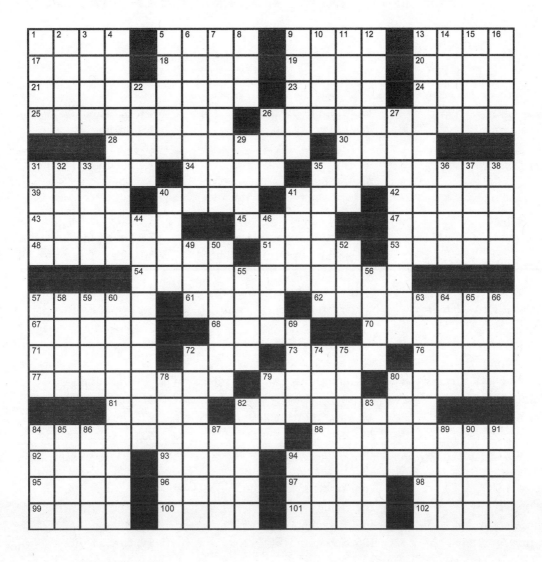

82. Macdonald-Laurier Institute online offering: Pod _____ Canada

83. American media company: Metro-Goldwyn-_____

84. Tousle a coif

85. At the apex

86. Metallic fabric

87. Mosque officiant

89. Holy relic (var.)

90. Egghead

91. You are, in Spain

94. Stamkos or Crosby, e.g.

SOLUTION ON PAGE 161

In the Merry Month of May

Canadians celebrate

ACROSS

1. Broad bean type
5. Former Ontario premier Rae
8. Vancouver Symphony Orchestra section
13. Parasite on a Pomeranian
17. Set on fire again
19. "The mouse _____ the clock"
20. Poetic foot
21. Very bright lamp
22. Tropical lizard
23. Nova Scotia-born *42nd Street* star Keeler
24. Rich dessert cake
25. Monarchs' domains
26. Stats for Blue Jays pitchers
27. Forehead
29. River in Hesse
31. Escapist excursions?
33. Head adjunct
34. Water balloon-hitting-the-ground sound
35. Source of fleece
36. Influenza description
38. Showy flower variety
40. Top of Canada area: Arctic _____
44. Church layman
46. Descriptive of a Greek singing group?
48. Coil of yarn
49. Long-time Canadian band: _____ Test Dummies
51. Within the bounds of the law
53. Croat, for one
54. Hog enclosure
57. Catch some sun
58. Kidney beans container
59. Some scale notes
61. 1987 Blue Rodeo hit
62. Rose anagram
64. Vagabond
66. African carnivore

68. Brings in the harvest
70. Study of plants
72. Kick out of the CBA
76. On _____ of
78. Toronto's John Tory, et al.
80. Crepe de _____
81. See 64-A
83. Fabric dying technique
85. Health care provider (abbr.)
86. Observer
89. Every word in a language
90. Ontario paper: *Windsor* _____
91. Wicked deeds
92. Necessitate
94. Calendar component
96. Indigenous art piece: Totem _____
97. Make more beautiful
98. Taxonomic group
101. Concert bowl level
102. Béchamel, for one
103. Written work theft, old style
104. Tallies
105. Canadian singers Sylvia or Ian
106. Show, on CBC
107. Funereal fire

DOWN

1. Monk's title
2. Alberta Energy Regulator (abbr.)
3. **A special day is named after her**
4. Radiant
5. Circus tent
6. Shakespearean protagonist
7. Woodbine wager
8. Scottish slopes
9. Sitar player's music style
10. Pain relief drug
11. **A May long weekend marks the unofficial start of this**
12. Afflicted by involuntary muscle movements
13. **Celebratory display**

14. Canadian history figure Secord
15. Shelter in a cove
16. Vast chasm
18. Northern Ireland Railways (abbr.)
25. Gag
27. Bit of sweat
28. Give a great review
30. Charitable organization: _____ of Dimes Canada
32. Tropical cuckoos
34. Porcine guffaw?
35. Japanese rice wine
37. Alpine Club of Canada (abbr.)
39. **It's a festive stat for many Canadians**
41. Breton or Gael
42. She commits perjury
43. Covetous feeling
45. Bread for grandma?
47. Halifax or Hamilton
50. Arrogant person
52. Neck and neck, at a Canucks game
54. Gritty fruit
55. Nursery purchase
56. "Sure," slangily
58. Central Asian people (var.)
60. Small cut
63. **Miniature versions of 13-D for kids**
65. Of great significance
66. Small African animal
67. Grate bit
69. _____ gin
71. In 1957, Canada's Lester Pearson won this prize
73. **Reason for the celebration**
74. *Winter Studies and Summer Rambles in Canada* author Brownell Jameson
75. Fanny's buttocks?
77. China, Japan, Korea, et al.

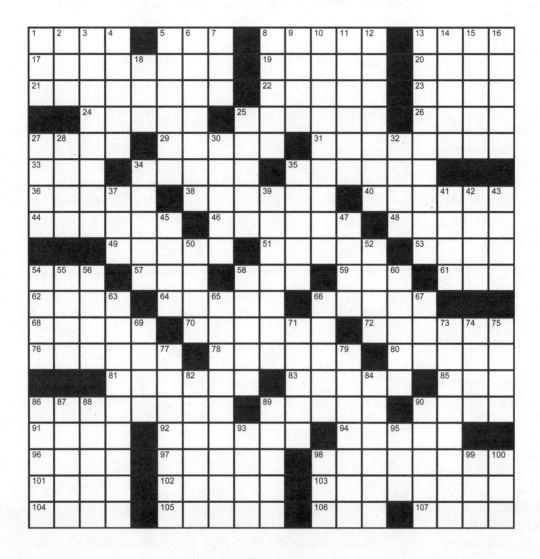

79. Sensory inputs

82. 39-D always falls on this

84. Weather forecasting barometric line

86. Greek pennies, in olden days

87. Shaped like an egg

88. Took care of the Tin Man?

89. Tablecloth fabric

90. Prepare furniture for refinishing

93. With the bow, to a viola player

95. Yuletide beverage

98. Hot spring

99. Muff

100. Canadian Club alcohol

SOLUTION ON PAGE 162

18 Ladies & Gentlemen

A couple of silver screen stars

ACROSS

1. Dadaist artist Jean, et al.
5. Mortarboard adornment
11. Decorative urn
15. Work units
19. *Made in Canada* actress Pinsent
20. Have _____ of a time
21. See James Bond?
22. Swanky fundraiser
23. Flowering plant type with two seed leaves
25. Famed American jockey Willie
27. Sometimes submerged sandbar
28. Plastic surgery procedure, for short
29. Property owner's legal document
30. CBS drama with multiple spinoffs
31. Long-time *Coach's Corner* commentator Cherry
33. Racy cellphone message
35. Attitude of eagerness
36. Dynamite detonator
38. Snooze
40. Long-eared animals
42. Skippy played this *Thin Man* series pooch
46. **1941 *That Hamilton Woman* co-stars**
50. 1960s US singer Bobby
52. Film starring 91-A: *Adam's _____*
53. Ancient wind instruments
55. Article of food
56. Political autonomy desired by colonists, say
60. Ontario place: Sault Ste. _____
61. Santa Claus facial feature
62. Like a baby yet to be born
63. Parcel delivery co.
64. Sonata's final passage
66. Cease
68. Theatrical light sheet
69. Canada Post purchases
71. Vancouver NHL player
73. Paltry sum, in Paris?
74. Golf green cup
76. 1985 Loverboy hit: "Lovin' Every Minute _____"
77. Possesses
78. WestJet pilot and Air Canada flight attendant
80. 37th US president Richard
82. More mature, like fruit
84. Mythical utopia
85. Commandeer
86. Be a third wheel
88. Started a fire
89. Red-orange dye obtained from a tree
91. **1942 *Woman of the Year* pair**
96. Step anagram
97. Hardy perennial
99. Coat with plaster
100. Season for drinking eggnog
101. Luke Skywalker, for one
102. Scruff of the neck
105. Ben Mulroney, to Brian
107. Intimidate, in the pasture?
108. Bulgur-based salad
113. *Degrassi: The Next Generation* star Dobrev
115. You'll see these in the Rockies: Mountain _____
117. 2/2 time score notation
118. Highlanders' caps
121. Of hearing
122. Attendee, for short
123. Canadian charitable organization: _____ Seals
124. Singer/actress Falana
125. Second-year student
126. He trained 101-A
127. Potato variety grown in Canada
128. Chalcedony type

DOWN

1. Municipal electee (abbr.)
2. Print *The Handmaid's Tale* again
3. National board game of India
4. Easy winner: _____-in
5. **1963 *Cleopatra* couple**
6. Tool that comes to a point
7. US children's poet Silverstein
8. Like an infamous marquis?
9. Run off to wed
10. US bone china maker since 1889
11. Three-piece suit piece
12. More washed out, in complexion
13. 2004 Jim Carrey movie: *Eternal Sunshine of the _____ Mind*
14. Bat an _____
15. "My goodness!"
16. Disreputable landscaper?
17. Group that sings en masse: _____ club
18. See 128-A
24. Bit of difference
26. Popular '80s Canadian band: _____ Without Hats
30. Winnipeg Blue Bombers league (abbr.)
32. Prefix that means "new"
34. "…all snug in _____ beds"
37. Long-necked white bird
39. Wild plum type
41. Old-style healing ointments
42. Maureen Forrester operatic offerings
43. Former Canadian women's clothing chain
44. Indian culinary dish
45. Canadian singing sisters: Tegan _____ Sara
47. Takes on a trainee
48. Dracula's lascivious ladies?
49. Levin and Gershwin
51. TV series starring Canada's Sandra Oh: *Killing _____*

54. Geological period (var.)
56. _____ River AB
57. Tête-à-tête, say
58. Window bars
59. Loiter at the bakery?
61. 1948 *Key Largo* lovers
63. Tense
65. HVAC system conduit
67. _____ in Boots
70. Cetus constellation star
71. Substitute for chocolate
72. Venomous Asian snake
75. Canadian living overseas, say
77. Provide aid
79. Draw ballot

81. Peace Tower city (abbr.)
83. Song of praiseful joy
84. Popular tourism site in India
85. Fredericton, for short
86. "Ta-ta!"
87. State of undress, old style
90. Supernatural influence on human affairs
92. Some Greek letters
93. Sell on eBay
94. Nearabout
95. Boxwood brethren
98. Used a ricer
101. Occupation
103. Rage

104. Rice dish (var.)
106. Lillehammer Olympics country (abbr.)
108. Town northeast of Albuquerque
109. Jann Arden's vocal range
110. It lights up a radar screen
111. Glenn Gould favoured this classical composer
112. Mount Olympus goddess
114. Bugs that plague your picnic
116. Singer Guthrie
119. "_____ whiz!"
120. Royal Canadians musician Victor Lombardo played this

Lyrical Words...

Decipher the link between theme answers

ACROSS

1. Islam god
6. Louvre part
10. *The Graham Norton Show* broadcaster (abbr.)
13. *Baroness von Sketch Show* group
17. Innocent
18. Sharpen a knife
19. *The Stepford Wives* author Levin
20. Midget buffalo, in Indonesia
21. They snitch to the cops
23. Family member, for short
24. **Plots on the prairies, say**
25. Swerve or distort
26. Star in Perseus
27. Like a smooth transition
29. Former Afghani currency
30. California wine region
32. Sound of the crowd at McMahon Stadium
33. Scientific study of tissue structure
38. Golden principles?
40. _____ Age Security
43. Canada's Monty Hall hosted this show: *Let's Make* _____
44. It's got the beat?
46. Encouraging words to a lad?
48. Most regretful
50. Jack-in-the-pulpits, e.g.
52. Gamblers roll these
53. **Destination Canada website: For Glowing** _____
54. Shaw Festival play milieu
55. Bags
56. Little dog's cry
57. **BC municipality:** _____ **Vancouver**
58. Swiss mountain
59. Spicy entree jelly
62. Finish for early photos
63. **Resident born in Edmonton, say**

67. Yellow veggie
68. Subway, in Paris
69. Lotion emollient
71. 20th-C. French writer and philosopher Henri
73. Compensate for wrongdoing
75. Whales' food source
76. Dawson City airport code
77. _____ a positive note
79. Moments of achievement
81. Pub match projectile
83. Spectators' sounds of contempt
85. Amy who wrote *The Joy Luck Club*
86. Ozzie and Harriet slept in these
89. Melds
91. Actors Knight and Danson
95. **1984 Juno single of the year: "**_____ **Up"**
96. Lobster eggs
97. German temperature scale developer Daniel
99. Middle Eastern seaport
100. Dorothy's aunt, et al.
101. Rein anagram
102. Lay out in logical order
103. Aphid, for one
104. Ouija board answer option
105. Scandinavian carpets
106. Ottawa-born ex-NHLer Dan

DOWN

1. South American cuckoos
2. Lean
3. Louise Penny Inspector Gamache mystery: *Still* _____
4. Openly declare
5. 2006 Canadian film: *Away from* _____
6. Scallions
7. Lengthy
8. "Short" is this to 7-D
9. Magnetic flux density unit

10. African country: Guinea-_____
11. Soft cheese type
12. Nightclubs liked by Liza?
13. _____ spade a spade
14. Type of exercise
15. **They're now "us"**
16. Bits for young boys?
22. Long-handled hammer
28. Largest amount
29. Like a shrewd MP?
31. Equitable, to Tiberius
33. Chopped meat meal
34. Indiana Department Of Education (abbr.)
35. Blood fluids
36. Dilly-dallying
37. Cole Porter composition: "I _____ a Kick Out of You"
39. Limping
41. National Historic Site: Peterborough Lift _____
42. Goes from brunette to blonde
45. **Loyal Canadian**
47. Electronics connectors
49. Extra special ability, for short
51. "Gross!"
54. Winnipeg's Tracy Dahl is this: Coloratura _____
55. Release tension
57. Soccer pitch structure
58. _____ minute now
59. Advice column since 1956: Dear _____
60. Tennis tournament top player
61. Utopian places
62. Outlook email button
64. Quebec floral symbol: Blue flag _____
65. Meadow rodent
66. House add-ons
68. Cheese type: _____ Jack
69. Wildebeest's relative
70. Dalhousie professors' podia

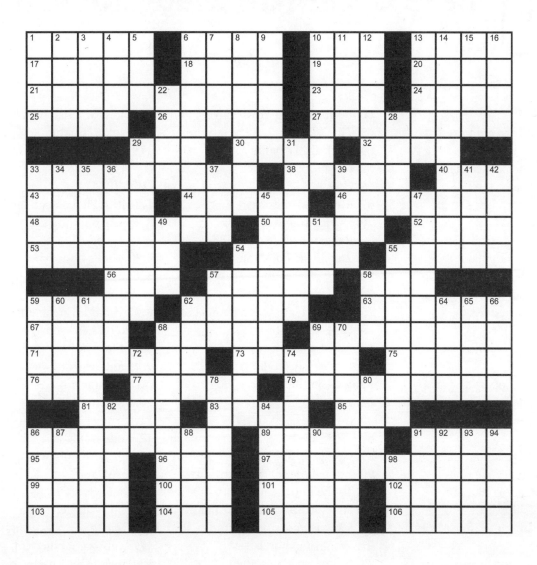

72. Hungarian's southern neighbour
74. Bygone days bone repository
78. Become compulsive in behaviour
80. Defence attorney's attaché?
82. With regard to, in olden days
84. Bid on a house
86. Bunker at Glen Abbey: Sand _____

87. **Broad, like the St. Lawrence**
88. Rogers Centre roof feature
90. Islam branch
91. Variation of via
92. Mysterious (var.)
93. Knob
94. Eyelid infection
98. Catch a criminal

Record theme answers here:

24-A: _____
53-A: _____
57-A: _____
63-A: _____
95-A: _____
15-D: _____
45-D: _____
87-D: _____

What is the link between the theme answers?

_____

[20] These Boots Are Made for Walkin'

Get in step with this one

ACROSS

1. English actor Guinness
5. Crack, like dry skin
9. WestJet low-cost carrier
14. Fit for a queen, say
19. '60s dancer's boot style
20. Ring of light
21. United _____ College Fund
22. Lively, in Longueuil
23. With 111-D, he shared top billing with Secret Squirrel
24. Historical periods
25. Tree type
26. Canadian environmentalist Suzuki
27. Delicately dots with liquid
30. These ding when baking is done
31. Trigonometric ratios
34. Linkage
35. Toronto attraction: Bata _____ Museum
36. Not romantic, like some relationships
38. "The Fall of the House of Usher" author
39. Construction site boot type
43. Broadcast, on CTV
44. Clear minded
46. Currency and magazine distributors, say
48. Intact product (abbr.)
49. Object named after Canadian astronomer John Stanley Plaskett
51. Canada's Wonderland ride effect?
53. Employ
54. Officiates Flames games, for short
55. Doled out
57. About, in estimating
58. Silent
59. Powder used in glass polishing
60. Be enrolled at York University
63. The Keg, for one
64. Neck artery name
67. Not hidden
68. Guts
69. Mountain ridges
70. Having rounded bends
72. Religious service bread disc
73. *The Jungle Book* song: "The _____ Necessities"
74. 1492 ship
75. Calgary Flame Monahan, et al.
79. Long-legged bird
80. Rowing crew's equipment
81. Vigorously, in the army?
83. Spill, in the sty?
84. Zero
85. Colleges, collectively
87. _____ and go
89. Golf pro's fib?
90. Boots type for a stormy day
92. To the utmost, for short
94. State that borders the Atlantic
96. Canada goose, for example
97. Wool shop purchase
99. Passed on a message
100. Midland ON landmark church: Martyrs' _____
103. Beat-up
105. Raccoon's relative
106. Canadian government payment, colloquially: Baby _____
107. Vast Asian desert
108. Canadian media personality Levant
112. Colorado skiing mecca
113. English empiricism philosopher
114. Hugged
115. See 90-A
116. Length measurement
117. Braid or pigtail
118. Joni Mitchell debut album song: "Cactus _____"
119. Eye

DOWN

1. British kitchen appliance
2. House building site
3. _____ ideal
4. Soldier's boot type
5. Something to roast on an open fire
6. Keyboard instrument
7. Old orchard spray
8. Put forward a concept
9. Medicine from a smarmy salesman?
10. 90-A, to Brits
11. US poet Nash
12. Lode jackpots
13. Spaniard's polite phrase: _____ favor
14. Calls via a CB
15. Tooth surface coating
16. Donate
17. Arab world chieftain
18. Digital clock parts, for short
28. Hydroxyl compound
29. Quick sip
30. 2011 Avril Lavigne track: "Stop Standing _____"
31. Painful twitch
32. Cream of the crop, say
33. Diamond weight measurement
35. Around a quarter of a cord
37. Wispy clouds
39. Room type at the Royal York
40. Like a layered wedding cake
41. 1974 April Wine song: "I'm _____ for You Baby"
42. Assignments for U of T English majors
45. Extended dialogue in class?
47. Travelling between airport terminals

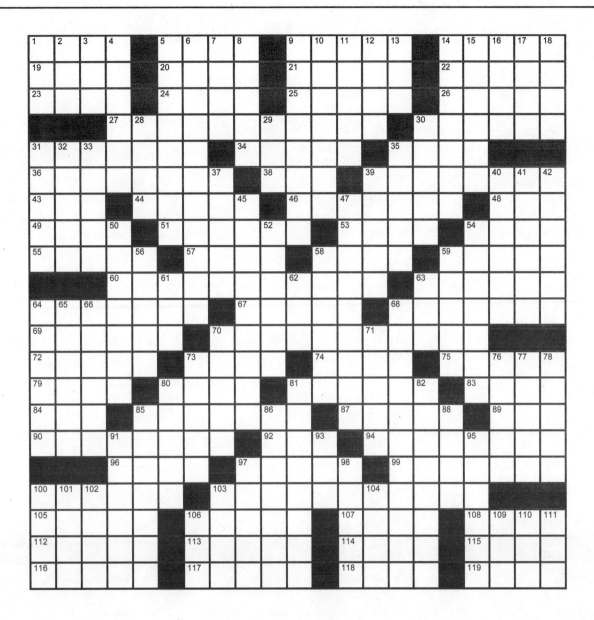

50. Hand-held TV channel changers
52. Paris attraction for art aficionados
54. Goes to bed
56. Post office machine
58. 1978 Marc Jordan hit: "_____ del Rey"
59. Hidalgo houses
61. Christmas carol contraction
62. Chaim Potok novel: *My Name Is Asher* _____
63. Compass pt.
64. Racket in a rookery
65. Film starring 1-A: *Lawrence of _____*

66. Shoppers Drug Mart pharmacy purchase
68. Not capable of being changed
70. Chapters sells these
71. Signed on the dotted line, say
73. Bleated, in the meadow
76. Calm fears, say
77. *Bête* _____
78. Canadians excel at this Olympics sport: _____ skating
80. Earthy pigment
81. Frees from Springhill Institution
82. Holiday season
85. Inane
86. **Animal skin boots**
88. Labatt Bass _____ Ale

91. _____ *dictum*
93. _____ of the iceberg
95. **These cover fishermen's feet**
97. From that time forward
98. 1985 Bryan Adams hit: "One _____ Love Affair"
100. Defraud
101. Garden watering device
102. Fully absorbed in
103. Way in or out
104. Busy ex-premier Gary?
106. Lunch counter order, for short
109. Nuke
110. _____ de Janeiro
111. See 23-A

SOLUTION ON PAGE 162

21 Shiny Stuff

Provincial symbols

ACROSS

1. Most wise
7. March astrological sign
12. Growing grey
17. River in Nebraska
18. Modifies text
19. *Antiques Roadshow* piece
20. Provider of bonds, say
21. Save from an unsafe situation
22. Clarinetist's rapidly alternating note
23. Spaghetti strand
24. Moral principle
25. Woke
26. Signified
28. More rash
30. Alice Munro offering: *Who Do You Think You _____?*
32. Distinct local species
34. Layered Italian dish
39. Doggie docs
41. Delete computer files
42. Yukon community: _____ Crow
43. Pelican's pouch
44. Clumsy
46. Cathode Ray Tube (abbr.)
47. Gamete
48. Salon stylist's favourite musical?
49. On the _____ and narrow
51. In a unilateral manner
53. **NL's official mineral**
55. Sailor's time on land?
59. Palliative care facilities
64. Manage okay
65. Running behind schedule
66. Red Chamber member, for short
67. Jewish religious text
68. You can see these at the Toronto Zoo
69. Lode find
70. Prim, and proper too
72. *I, Claudius* role

73. Government of Canada stationery supply?
75. Agitates
77. Egyptian cobra
78. Sedative for two Shakespearean gentlemen?
80. Fortune teller's calling card?
82. National park in Alberta
86. Makes easy: _____ down
88. Old-style cuirass
91. Really loathe
92. Noisy crow family bird
93. Encroachment, on an avenue?
94. Distributed cards for canasta
95. Baby bird hooters
96. Like a smelly sot?
97. Distinctive cultural spirit
98. Quebec municipal official
99. Rock garden greenery

DOWN

1. Rotate
2. *The Sun _____ Rises*
3. Laboratory measuring device
4. Chopin piece
5. Ancient cemetery pillars
6. *The National* correspondent McKenna
7. **Official gemstone of ON**
8. Mould again
9. Cut into
10. Filtered chemical solution
11. Fredericton-to-Saint John dir.
12. Canadians Gosling and Reynolds, for example
13. Yogi
14. Canadian optometry chain since 1990
15. World's longest river
16. **NWT's official mineral**
18. Before, in days of old
25. Lets a ticket holder back into a venue

27. Wayne Gretzky served as this at Vancouver 2010
29. Canada's Darcy Oake, for one
30. Hertz competitor
31. Airbnb owner's income
33. Chemical salt
35. Reason to take Aleve
36. McMaster alum
37. Hit with a hammer
38. Off-kilter
40. Luxury hotel feature
42. Eavesdrop
45. Scrabble player's square
47. Yoko _____
50. Speedy equestrian
51. Provincial tune: "_____ to Newfoundland"
52. Canadian Heritage, for example (abbr.)
54. "_____ Maria"
55. *The Lion King* villain
56. Optimism
57. *Vancouver Sun* column type
58. Remaining amount
60. Lithium-_____ battery
61. Craft projects, say
62. Corn units
63. Take a trip to The Bay
66. **NS's official mineral**
70. Post office worker who uses an ink pad?
71. Principle of Chinese philosophy
74. Prevents
75. Baby carrier brand
76. On the double
79. Manitoulin Island people
81. Rootstock used in perfume
82. **BC's official gemstone**
83. Help a wrongdoer
84. Former Iranian hereditary monarch's title
85. National sports organization: _____ Canada

87. His or her, in Hull

89. Bakery purchase for a birthday party

90. Hullabaloos

92. Children's nurturer

22 Down Under Denizens

Aussie animals

ACROSS

1. Middle school subj.
5. Funky US singer Khan
10. Overly pleased with oneself
14. "Jabberwocky" opener
18. YCJA, and others
19. He wrote many fables
20. Note taker, for short
21. Go on a tirade
22. Rate again
24. **Eucalypt eater**
25. Plankton piece
26. Some UBC degs.
27. Mount Etna output
28. Arabian Nights chap
30. Red Skelton character Kadiddlehopper
31. Enzyme type
33. Remove moisture by squeezing
34. Blasting crew's explosive
36. Matterhorn, for example
37. Change a password
38. Palindromic "What?"
40. *The Kids in the Hall* segment
42. A320-200 jet flown by Canada's national carrier
44. Description of verses by a famous British poet
47. Celebes and Celtic
49. Canadian retailer since 1984: Mastermind _____
50. Long flower stalk
52. Hero's poetic saga
54. Parts of spurs
56. Former federal government ministry: _____ of Women
57. "Beat it!"
59. Eroded
63. Jackrabbits
64. Mini motorbike
66. Irate
67. Lea anagram
68. Coleridge poem, say
69. **Horned lizard**

71. Pork product
72. _____ in the sky
73. 2010 Johanna Skibsrud Giller Prize winner: _____ *Sentimentalists*
74. Originates from
75. *Three's Company* actor Richard
77. Spanish punch
79. Bioweapon toxin
80. Catch up to a competitor
81. Deposed a leader
84. Bats' dwelling
85. Let the dogs loose
86. Use a juicer
88. Former federal Liberal cabinet minister Gray
90. 1984 hit song from Canada's Luba
92. Remove a cat's weaponry
94. Sets a trap, say
96. Fishing pole
97. Gather parishioners together?
101. Blonde shade
102. Leonard Nimoy autobiography: *I Am _____ Spock*
104. Has on
106. Otitis symptom
108. Canada's Michael J. Fox starred in this '90s sitcom: _____ *City*
110. Gruesome
112. Alliance Canada joined in '49
113. Maine Coon or Manx
114. Secrete
115. **Rabbit-eared marsupial**
116. Least deep
119. Seabirds (var.)
120. Nimble
121. Electric car brand
122. Well aware of antics
123. Fly by the _____ of one's pants
124. VCR insert
125. Neuters
126. Greek letters

DOWN

1. Boston Tea Party place
2. Mount Logan climber's equipment
3. Inactive time
4. Small dosage of liquid medicine (abbr.)
5. Canadian Academy of Recording Arts and Sciences (abbr.)
6. The boot, say
7. Tibet's continent
8. Kingston Online Services (abbr.)
9. "…partridge in _____ tree"
10. More old-fashioned
11. Noted US anthropologist Margaret
12. In darkness
13. **Predatory lizard**
14. Gillette Canada razor blades brand: _____ II
15. **Kin of 75-D**
16. Prayer said three times a day by Catholics
17. Team that plays at 50-D
20. Reggae music dances
23. **Semi-aquatic mammal**
29. Lily, in Lachine
32. MPs do this in Parliament
33. Braided rope fabric
35. Dubbed a duke, say
39. It's headquartered in Montreal: _____ Institute for Statistics
41. Chinese philosophy principle
43. First name in US civil rights
45. Dalhousie dorm, for short
46. Ontario autopsy agency: Office of the Chief _____
48. Indian gurus
50. Commonwealth and McMahon, in Alberta (var.)
51. Walk unsteadily
53. Like a facetious faun?
55. Space-saving footnote abbr.

56. Goes to Real Canadian Superstore
58. Physicians' group: Canadian _____ Association
60. Polynesian woman
61. Addiction recovery program founded in 1951
62. Middle Eastern country
64. Carving knife holder
65. They give CPR
69. Shania Twain song: "From _____ Moment On"
70. Northeastern Italian region
73. 1998 Jim Carrey movie: *The _____ Show*
75. **Hopping marsupial**
76. Fatty tumour
78. Scoring play at 50-D: Field _____
80. Completely demo a kitchen
82. Unagi
83. Like an art class poser
86. Take a breath
87. **Spiny anteater**
89. 1989 Canadian film: _____ *Blues*
91. In theory, if things are perfect?
92. Runs like a reindeer?
93. **Burrowing marsupial**
95. Cagliari is the capital of this island (abbr.)
98. Emphasize
99. California mountain
100. Rogers Cup brawls?
103. Boreal forest, in Canada
105. Musicians' snoozes?
107. Mythological strongman
109. Birds' digs
111. Holder for hair
112. Quebec's Marc Garneau flew with this US org.
117. Cool, once
118. "_____ is me!"

23

Monumental...

In Canada

ACROSS

1. Holier-than-thou
5. Cause annoyance
9. Door slot for mail
13. Encircled, old style
18. Young salmon
19. Wings, in Latin
20. Canadian C&W pioneer Heywood
21. Bubbly
22. 1995 Colin James "best of" album: *Then _____...*
24. **Parliament Hill monument commemorating Confederation**
27. Bathroom fungal growth
29. Guys-only bash
30. _____ inept
31. Male kid
33. Dismounted
35. Eastern Canada mammal: Harp _____
36. They have taxing jobs?
41. Stage of enlightenment for a Buddhist
43. Seize (with "on to")
47. Khaki fabric
48. Potato chips brand popular in Canada
50. Brillo's brethren
51. Score with a stylus
53. In a convincing manner
55. _____ the fat
57. Isn't a brat
58. Cheering crowd's syllable
59. "O _____ can you see…"
60. Dull hog?
61. Impolite behaviour
62. Launch wartime hostilities
64. McGill reunion attendee
65. _____ Canada
66. Bees' sweet stuff
67. **Sole equestrian statue in Montreal**

71. Carrot flower cluster
74. "_____ la la!"
75. Bar from inclusion
76. Partially cook vegetables
80. Lisbon's country
82. Glance over the headlines
83. Queen Victoria's successor: King Edward _____
84. "Aha" alternative
85. Toronto CFL team, colloquially
86. Warm or chilled Japanese beverage (var.)
87. Some grammatical voices
89. Find oneself in Japan?
90. Drake has won four Junos for this: _____ Recording of the Year
91. Bird on Canada's $1 coin
93. Mainland BC region: Sunshine _____
94. Meander along
95. Neighbour of California
98. Pastry chefs make these
100. Regina's Victoria and 11th, for short
101. Whitewater activity float
103. Pair
104. Cuts into thirds
108. Kennedy family matriarch
110. Cape Verde money unit
115. **Montreal religious monument**
118. Abruptly took notice
119. High and mighty people
120. Humerus neighbour
121. Chump
122. Rational
123. Justin Bieber's voice type
124. These grow in pods
125. "Come Sail Away" US band
126. Not now

DOWN

1. Desktop junk folder contents
2. Biblical bringers of gifts

3. Eurasian range
4. HGTV Canada show: *Sarah Off the _____*
5. Hamilton university, briefly
6. Quebec place: Sept-_____
7. 1982 Aldo Nova hit
8. _____ position
9. Wetland
10. Networks that connect computers (abbr.)
11. Classical music vocal pieces
12. Mineral deposit in a stream
13. Butcher shop waste
14. Turn at the craps table
15. Ancient Semitic deity
16. EGOT component
17. Hair colouring
23. **Montreal monument erected for a famed British admiral**
25. Support (var.)
26. Served as an intermediary
28. Richler classic novel: *Solomon Gursky _____ Here*
32. 1969 movie musical: *Hello, _____!*
34. Weapon that temporarily paralyzes
36. Ghana city
37. Young pig
38. A _____ for sore eyes
39. WSW opposite
40. Former Rideau Hall resident Hnatyshyn
42. Haul behind you
43. Crunchy cereal
44. Spice up the proceedings
45. Carrying too much weight
46. Unkempt
49. Use 50-A, say
52. **Vancouver Celtic monument commemorating a shipwreck**
54. Old CBC show: _____ *30*
56. Hanging bed

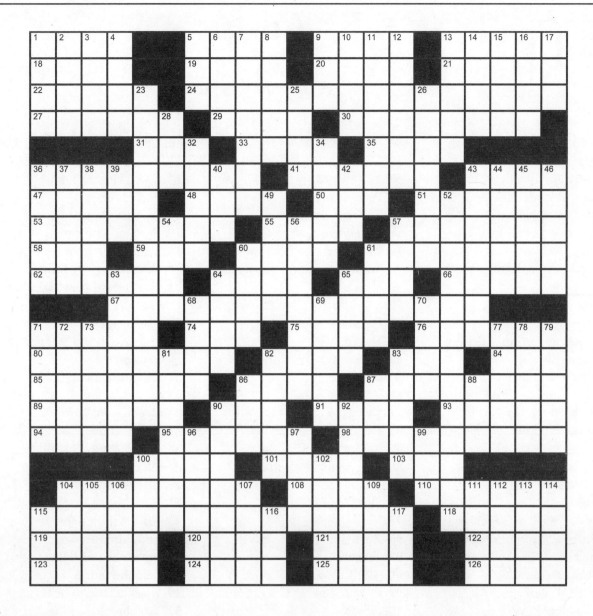

57. *Hamilton: An American Musical* character Aaron
60. Humdrum
61. Mob's scene?
63. Helped commit a crime
64. Like a missing marine, say
65. Ugandan ex-dictator Idi
68. Soft sheepskin leather
69. Form of 1-D, often
70. Wading bird
71. Violinist's stroke
72. Three-time Giller Prize nominee Lisa
73. The Scarecrow lacked this
77. Chevrolet ceased production of these in 1988
78. Place to put treasures

79. Graham and Edwards, on CTV's *ETALK*
81. Come to grips with a disappointment
82. Sweetness or sourness
83. Like a windmill or a feather
86. Lose tautness
87. Hawaiian foodstuff
88. Note promising payment, for short
90. Design anew
92. Withdraws
96. Make back, after a loss
97. Drug pusher's nemesis
99. Feed an actress her lines
100. Flower for John Jacob?
102. Cars made in Oakville

104. Enamelled metalware
105. Destroy an archaeological dig?
106. Common preposition
107. Yemeni city
109. Perceive, old style
111. *Schitt's Creek* ensemble
112. Golden Olympic state for Canada's Catriona Le May Doan
113. Sandy ridge
114. 2002 nominated book by 72-D
115. Bumped into, in passing
116. _____ Vegas
117. XX or XY chromosomes indicate this

SOLUTION ON PAGE 163

Au *Jus*

A letter pattern puzzle

ACROSS

1. Wintry rime
6. "Hurry up!"
10. An envelope's adhesive is on this
14. Old Testament task?
17. Iconic American highway: _____ 66
18. Canadian Medal of Bravery recipient
19. Rule anagram
20. Actress Thurman
21. Covering for Canada's Lynn Crawford
22. Anti, to a hillbilly
23. Like some dancers' potential?
25. BC-born NHLer Barrie
26. Books' innards
28. Attack
29. Man's biographical tale?
32. List component
34. Fitting
37. Destroyed, like the Jabberwock
38. Quebec-born Bourque who won the Norris Trophy five times
39. Rockies' ridge
40. _____ Flakes
42. No longer in
43. **Burlap fibre**
44. Bodily joint sac
45. **Old diner music maker**
47. Vagrant's behind?
48. Size for 52-A
50. Alberta political group: _____ Conservative Party
51. Taxi for jazz great Calloway?
52. La Vie en Rose undergarments
53. Drop the ball, say
56. What 59-A pays for
57. Ethiopian emperor Selassie
59. Tenant
61. Unit of work
62. Canadian _____
64. Contemporary of Bela
65. Servings for Suzette?

66. Bit of dust
67. Unagi
68. **YCJA word**
69. Pear variety
72. **Thomas Hardy novel: _____ the Obscure**
74. Camp bed
75. "Father of nuclear chemistry" Otto
76. Supreme _____ of Canada
77. Famed Fabergé piece
78. Slogan
80. Homebuyer's new subdivision purchase
81. Windshield finish
82. New York state city
85. Ocean floor "carpet"
87. Toronto hospital: Mount _____
88. Disney movie elephant
92. Dukes and earls
94. Slender
95. Heir
96. Australian bird
97. "Encore!"
98. _____ around the collar
99. Of base eight
100. Plead
101. Prince Edward Island, directionally from New Brunswick
102. Miners find these
103. Like a dapper dresser

DOWN

1. College grp. for guys
2. Shoddily made, in Shropshire
3. Pronoun for a duo
4. Ottoman
5. Sport for Canada's Bianca Andreescu
6. Hats, in Hull
7. 16-D, for example
8. Source
9. Fifth canonical hour

10. Chimney sweep's malady?
11. 12 full cycles of moon months
12. Like a chi-chi painter?
13. Pod contents
14. **Largest planet**
15. Frittatas' kin (var.)
16. 2005 single from BC's Daniel Powter: "_____ Day"
24. Get together, like Canadian skaters Duhamel and Radford?
27. Play a guitar
30. Like McMahon Stadium night games
31. Multi-grain bun flake
33. _____ *culpa*
34. Renounce a formerly held belief
35. Tree trimmer, say
36. 2007 Céline Dion album: _____ *Chances*
39. Maltreaters
41. Bottom-line earnings, in Britain
43. **Auditorium name in Calgary and Edmonton**
46. Pip at the finish line
47. Lamb's sound
49. Kolkata used to be this
51. 1969 biopic on Guevara
52. Canadian media personality Mulroney
53. Observation, old style
54. Bounce back again, in a canyon
55. Hold a grudge
58. Texter's chuckle abbr.
60. BC-born *This Is the End* actor Rogen
63. They rebuff or eschew
66. Popular video game franchise: _____ Kombat
67. Borders
68. Scrawled notes
69. Play a role on stage
70. Offensive
71. **Scarab beetle**
73. "That's disgusting!"

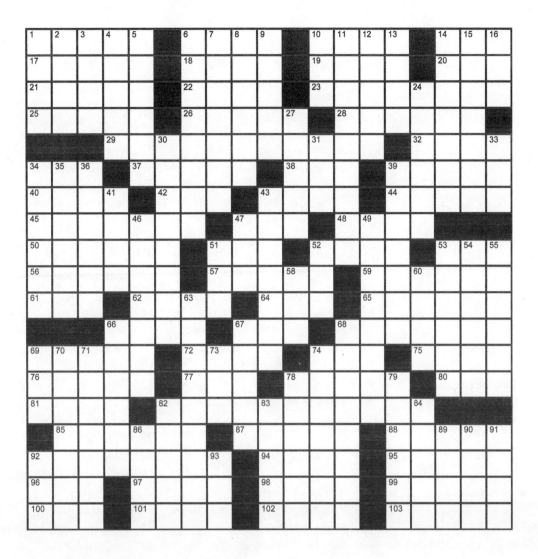

74. Addictive recreational narcotic
78. Western Europe ancient standing stone
79. _____ favourite
82. It's midway between Hawaii and Australia
83. Funny car fuel
84. Lily family plant
86. Popular social media posting
89. Rogers Centre glove
90. Ship or schooner
91. Shania song: "It _____ Hurts When I'm Breathing"
92. Canadian energy sector regulator (abbr.)
93. Fish-catching trap

Eventful in the '80s

Moments that shaped our nation

ACROSS

1. Prices
6. Gush out
10. Gaiters
15. Planetary neighbour of Earth
19. Make steak in the oven
20. It parallels the radius
21. Coiled snake
22. Grey _____
23. Type of lily
24. *SCTV* "newsman": _____ Camembert
25. Orbital point
26. Extremely attentive
27. **Global sports event (1988)**
30. With great skill
31. Coercion
32. Think about Terpsichore?
33. Jet-black
34. Level
35. "Put _____ on it!"
36. Marlo Thomas sitcom: _____ *Girl*
38. Old-style weight allowances
40. Talks about felines in Frontenac?
41. It precedes upsilon
42. Babbled on and on
44. Lit cigar end
45. Glimmered
46. Cold War competition
48. Deer type
50. Dirty spot
52. Golfer's moment of glory: _____-in-one
53. This US corporation invented Dubble Bubble
55. Give dignity to a duchess?
59. Titan who shouldered a heavy load
62. 1997 treaty city in Japan
64. *National Post* piece
66. Dart like a dove
67. Ecosystems

69. **Anthem officially adopted in 1980**
71. Largest desert in the world
73. Middle Eastern leader's title
74. Canned fish variety
76. All thumbs, say
78. Paltry amounts, in Patras
79. Indicates
81. Score instruction to play slowly
83. Farrier's file
85. Inexpensive
87. Flower necklace on Lanai
88. Place for posting: _____ board
92. Heated coal for a fuel source
94. Engine speed, in brief
96. Pure
98. Compass pt. for Toronto to Kingston
99. Backs, anatomically speaking
100. Singer's vocal cord malady
102. _____ Minor
103. You might do this at TD?
104. Language spoken in Islamabad
105. _____ good example
106. Participant in 46-A
108. Line that indicates barometric pressure
110. Prickly part of a rose
111. **Constitutional amendments document drafted in 1987**
114. Jets or Canucks
115. Up for the day
116. Victoria or Vancouver
117. Didn't go to The Keg
119. Caribbean citrus fruit
120. Fix frayed seams
121. Network of nerve cells
122. Former PEI premier Campbell
123. Bothersome bug?
124. Convenes at athletics competitions?
125. Mighty mythological Olympian
126. Papyrus or bulrush

DOWN

1. National network (abbr.)
2. Like a prophet's message
3. Sunny room in your home
4. Used a harrow
5. Criticizes, in Canterbury
6. Civil court plaintiff
7. Childhood pal
8. Air Canada's magazine
9. The Romans and Chinese built these
10. Con's ruse
11. Canadians wear these on November 11
12. Green liqueurs
13. Magicians' illusions
14. Pert
15. **Terry Fox began this in 1980**
16. High-spirited horse
17. Filled with
18. Mythology libertines
28. _____ projection
29. Until this time
31. Excel document contents
37. Diacritical mark
39. Gather the leaves
40. Pointy face part
42. Work by Robertson Davies, say
43. Surrey neighbour in BC
45. Northeastern Alberta area: Athabasca oil _____
47. **Mulroney/Reagan meeting in 1985**
49. Like Lahr's *Wizard of Oz* character
51. Golfers start from here
53. _____ point
54. Long-time Canadian chart-toppers: Blue _____
56. Sound of a honking horn
57. Currency for purchases in Turkey
58. WJ arrival times
59. Opposite of 115-A

60. 1973 Jim Croce hit: "_____ in a Bottle"
61. Butcher shop cut
63. Way over there
65. Twaddle
68. 16-D, for example
70. Zany stunt
72. Cineplex Odeon theatre part
75. See 106-A
77. Bridge support
80. 1980s show starring Mr. T: _____-*Team*

82. Like some verdant parks
84. Turkic language family
86. Enzyme type
88. Hair clip
89. Afternoon meal serving
90. Aggressively taking territory
91. It precedes "-do-well"
92. Funeral procession
93. Trying times
95. Garment slit
97. More robust, in build

99. Contretemps between cleaners?
100. Little-leaguer descriptive
101. Currency once used in Kabul
103. Calm with a balm, say
105. Glibness
107. Bones that connect hips
109. Leaves like Ella?
112. Cuts down trees
113. Easy anagram?
118. Maiden name preceder

SOLUTION ON PAGE 164

26

Elegant in the '80s

Supermodels strutted their stuff

ACROSS

1. Ump's call a Blue Jay is happy to hear
5. Early Eire alphabet
10. Dirty kids need these
15. Genesis brother
19. Lira anagram
20. TIFF trailer, for example
21. Indigenous group in Alaska
22. _____-European
23. **She was CoverGirl's main model**
26. Time for a midday meal
27. Schwarzenegger catchphrase: "_____ la vista, baby!"
28. Schnauzer's saliva
29. Permissive answer
30. Confuse
31. Puts duds on
33. Held fast to
35. Most wily
36. Beaufort, in northern Canada
37. Wine descriptive
39. Beat Generation writer Jack
41. Brooke Henderson's best shot?
46. Markedly different
50. Music's Yoko
51. Lascivious stare
52. Crustacean type with seven sets of legs
54. In the calm, at sea
55. Håkan from Calgary's Stanley Cup-winning team
57. Founder of scholasticism
59. Roller coaster rider's interjection
60. Made fabric using a loom
61. Snares
63. Like a task that can be completed
65. Frequently
66. Dawning
68. Spaniard's cheer
69. Former Governor General LeBlanc

72. Abbot's helper
75. Turn up
78. Gets a loan from Scotiabank
82. Colonel or captain, in the Canadian military
83. Start of a magical incantation
85. Took a diagnostic picture
87. Michael Bublé sang one with Dolly Parton on her 2020 album
88. Multiple Juno winner Murray
89. Chinese fruit (var.)
91. Real Canadian Superstore department
92. Standard American English (abbr.)
93. Montana city
95. Surprise
99. Of the shoulder
101. Canadian para-swimming record-setter Nikita
102. Sumptuous Empress repast
103. Access to a second storey
106. Sound at a paintball session
108. Skip Cheryl who led Canada's curling team to silver at Vancouver 2010
112. Ottawa-based website and paper: *The Hill* _____
113. Maple syrup source in Quebec
114. Composed, like Canada's Kit Pearson
117. River in Rome
118. Ester or ketone
119. **She signed a $6 million contract with Estée Lauder**
122. Wander
123. Bowed, like a ceiling
124. Put off decision-making
125. The same, in ancient Rome
126. Drops or droops
127. Tries to slim down
128. Ancient Italian shields
129. Grand Banks fish catchers

DOWN

1. *Borat* actor: _____ Baron Cohen
2. Worthy one, in Buddhism
3. Assembly of _____ Nations
4. Aristocrat, maybe
5. Decide upon
6. Crossword formats
7. Garden digger
8. Early church lectern
9. Rabat country
10. Outlaw
11. Acetylene is one
12. She used to send cables
13. Tints
14. Sows' enclosure
15. **She's known for her non-airbrushed beauty mark**
16. Positive end of a battery
17. Canadian reality show winners for six seasons
18. Group of nine
24. Variant of 113-D
25. Song by 88-A: "_____ Be Seeing You"
30. Old pesticide
32. Winter weather cap parts
34. Mandolins' kin, for short
35. Gloves fabric
37. Honoured French holy women (abbr.)
38. Was mistaken
40. Hamilton Philharmonic Orchestra instrument
41. Beauty mark of 15-D
42. Ever's phrase partner
43. Flue detritus
44. 1811 Jane Austen novel: _____ *and Sensibility*
45. **She became the "exclusive face" of Revlon Ultima II**
47. Commonly
48. Canadian-born *Scream* actress Campbell
49. *Tiger Beat* fan

53. Canadian children's magazine since 1976
56. **Nothing came between her and her Calvins**
58. Circlet of thread
62. Antwerp airport code
64. Great _____ Lake, NWT
65. "_____ the ramparts we watched…"
67. Sole condiment?
70. Marks on old manuscripts
71. Posh dressmaker or hatmaker
72. Baby buggy, to a Brit
73. She wears 113-D
74. Overnight lodgings
76. Arcade favourite: _____-Man

77. Harmful gas
79. River in Yorkshire
80. Withdraw from mother's milk
81. "Don't change," says the editor
83. UBC grads
84. Ill humour, in olden days?
86. Cravings
90. 1990s CBC show: *The Kids in the _____*
94. Belonging to the two of us
96. Quartets
97. US rental car company in Canada
98. Artist's anatomical model
100. Small computing program
103. Chili con carne, et al.

104. Fungal infection
105. Honour _____ thieves
107. Bristly bit on barley
108. Chic chapeau for Chantel
109. Home
110. Fortify with masonry
111. Wee shots for a Scot
113. Wraparound dress style
115. This org. impacts Canadian oil prices
116. Vegetarian dietary staple
119. Hippies' home
120. Points out a perp
121. US novelist Levin

SOLUTION ON PAGE 164

27

A Mixed Bag

...of territorial and provincial potpourri

ACROSS

1. Famed London gallery
5. Jean de Brunhoff's children's stories elephant
10. Determining principle
15. Tater
19. Old Turkish VIP (var.)
20. 1987 Tom Selleck comedy: *Three Men and* _____
21. Vote for your MPP
22. Region of Italy known for wine
23. Boisterous bash, Down Under
25. Gradually diminish (with "off")
26. Switchblade, for one
27. Sean _____ Lennon
28. Burial places
29. Allies' official understanding
30. New York city
32. **Its motto is *Gloriosus et liber***
34. **Canada's highest ever temperature was recorded here in 1937**
36. Gala anagram
37. Platform for a queen
39. Mayberry's town drunk
40. Head nurses, in the UK
44. Gone bad
47. Thanksgiving Day mo.
50. Most streaky, like some cheese?
53. Lower, to Lord Tennyson
54. Swami
55. Bard's creation
56. _____-relief
57. Speak indistinctly
58. Pop music pair: Hall & _____
59. Not any place, colloquially
62. Canadian _____ of Postal Workers
63. Expose Zorro?
64. Fair, to a Toronto Raptor?
65. Driveway surfacing substance
66. Some gaits
68. Beach house supports

69. Rhythmic pattern in Cuban music
71. Blew up a photo, say
73. Brightly coloured bird
74. Parachute attached to a boat
75. Predatory fish
76. Tony-winning actress Hagen
77. Hails from Hadrian
78. Tap
79. Online store, say
82. French pronoun
83. Call to the courthouse?
84. Sound of a sneeze
85. Tesla or Volt
86. Sea in Uzbekistan
87. Go down, in a card game
91. **Canada's oldest English-language university was founded here in 1785**
97. **This part of a provincial name was added in 2001**
101. HB pencil end
102. Compass point
103. YouTube upload
104. Non-Jew
105. Stanley Park art installation: Totem _____
106. Like a perfect paradigm?
108. Like most engagement rings
110. Port city in Yemen
111. Full of charm
112. Argentinian city: Buenos _____
113. Sarnia-born 2003 Masters champion Mike
114. "_____ we forget"
115. Church music piece
116. "I _____ see that coming"
117. Eros anagram

DOWN

1. Puget Sound city
2. Pertaining to severe pain
3. Tightly gathered crowd

4. A muff can cover this
5. Respectful Hindu title (var.)
6. Weapon of mass destruction
7. Bridgetown's Caribbean island
8. Harlem Globetrotters founder Saperstein, et al.
9. *The Catcher in the* _____
10. Some Greek consonants
11. Word of woe, in olden days
12. Nasal partitions
13. Frozen mass
14. Less lenient
15. Miss Canada pageant contestants' ribbons
16. "Poppycock!" to a famed playwright?
17. See 30-A
18. Sofa lacking a back
24. NHL Sens city
29. _____ de deux
31. Skinny
33. Metrical foot
34. Bro's sibling
35. Bellhop or skycap
38. Minute bug
41. **Canada's oldest national park is here**
42. Crowns for royal ladies
43. Adjust an alarm clock
44. CPP recipient
45. *Beetle Bailey* dog
46. Consequently, old style
47. Win a debate, say
48. Old-style torch toppers
49. Warthog's weapon
50. My, in Magog
51. Like parents of SPCA-acquired pets
52. Significantly alters a script
53. **It's Canada's largest territory**
54. More willing to play Trivial Pursuit?
57. Radiation, e.g.

58. **This province has about 250,000 lakes**
60. Otters' lairs
61. Pelvic bone
63. Remove a binding
67. Sobeys burger beef type
68. Petty argument
70. Mad, in Madrid
72. 1981 film: _____ Boot
74. *Good Will Hunting* actor Matt
78. Forward-thinking 20th-C. Italian art movement?
79. Greek letter
80. It's covered in baize: _____ table

81. Long-time Christmas lights brand
83. Absolutely certain
84. Boat for Noah's menagerie
85. Preoccupied during roll call?
86. Emulate Canada's Ryan Reynolds
88. More avant-garde
89. Coin unique to Canada
90. Some GE appliances
91. Neighbour of Tibet
92. Abrade the shoreline
93. Cardiff country
94. Perspire
95. Work on a loom

96. Coral reef atoll
98. Fellow jingle writers?
99. Céline Dion duetted on this soundtrack song: "Beauty and the _____"
100. Jockey Turcotte inducted into Canada's Sports Hall of Fame in 1980
103. King Henry who had six wives
107. Twosome
108. Father
109. In 1985, the Canadiens retired this Doug Harvey jersey number

28 On the Mat

A twist on gymnastics

ACROSS

1. Bishopric titles in the Coptic church
6. Ova pouches
10. Orange potato
13. Eastern Europe citizen
17. **Gymnast's safe storage space?**
18. Former Italian currency
19. Art Gallery of Ontario (abbr.)
20. Not feral
21. Pens and cages
23. **Gymnast's easy victory?**
25. Bunk
26. "Fast" acronym
28. Most hopeless
29. 13 of these border Canada
31. Angina drug: _____ nitrite
32. Tree type with needles
33. Former Saturn car model
34. Gaze with intensity
36. Muses' mountain
41. Seven-time Wimbledon winner Steffi
43. Sinus cavities
45. Brotherly band: The Bee _____
46. '60s cartoon character: Atom _____
47. Skittles players' targets
49. Process of putting things back together
52. Sin or taboo
53. Newborn narwhals
54. Anagram for 18-A
55. Neighbour of a Yemeni
58. **Glass for a gymnast?**
60. Minos ruled here
61. Roadwork pylon
62. Unique dialect
63. Flip or flop?
65. Accordion-like instrument
67. Like shifts and sheathes
71. Chicken _____ king
72. Baroque-era instrument
73. Nigerian money unit
75. Sea-to-Sky Highway off-ramp
76. Bloodbaths, at BMO Field?
79. Woodworking files
81. Weekly earnings
82. Anagram on the side?
83. Important "chapters" in history
85. Bey known as "Canada's First Lady of the Blues"
87. Lavender or lilac shade
90. Set of skill-testing questions
91. Juan or Evita, of Argentina
92. **Turn type that tricks gymnasts?**
94. Newspaper since 1889: *The _____ Journal*
98. Short stride
99. CRV, for example
100. In _____ of
101. **Male gymnasts' jewellery?**
102. Mortar troughs
103. 1987 Dan Hill/Vonda Shepard song: "Can't We _____"
104. Bathtub scrubber's target
105. Legalese for "bar"

DOWN

1. Jasper, in downtown EDM
2. Censor
3. Nova Scotia's 20th premier John
4. Dole out
5. Canadian table- and kitchenware chain
6. Area of urban blight
7. _____ Transat
8. Second Cup coffee additive
9. Audacious
10. Hoarse cry
11. Somerset stove
12. Sign of bread gone bad (var.)
13. Moores and Mark's
14. Wash
15. PGA Tour Champions pro Stephen from Canada
16. Green, in Granby
22. Suffer an injury, say
24. Enzyme type
27. Yodeller's peak
29. You'll see "ARRÊT" on a red this in Quebec
30. Eight-time Grammy Award nominee Amos
31. Some UBC studies
32. They keep peaches?
35. They document the details
37. Mojave plant
38. 1970s weapon for Tim Horton?
39. Lacking light
40. Flair for fashion
42. African fox
44. **Middle Eastern gymnastics move?**
48. Hawaiian taro-based dish
50. Pipe bends
51. Kootenay National Park canyon
53. Interjection that expresses encouragement or disbelief
55. William of _____
56. Cash, slangily
57. Writers Quindlen and Sewell
59. Practical
60. Online BC motor injury dispute forum: Civil Resolution Tribunal (abbr.)
62. Hair salon services summary
64. Passes by, like time
66. Eludes
67. Prejudice
68. Math advocate?
69. Thailand, before 1948
70. Eyelid irritation
74. Ancient Semitic language
77. Belly-tightening exercises
78. Female or male
80. French existentialist author Jean-Paul
84. "You'll Never Find Another Love Like Mine" singer Lou
86. Large-eyed lemur
87. Contemptuous interjection

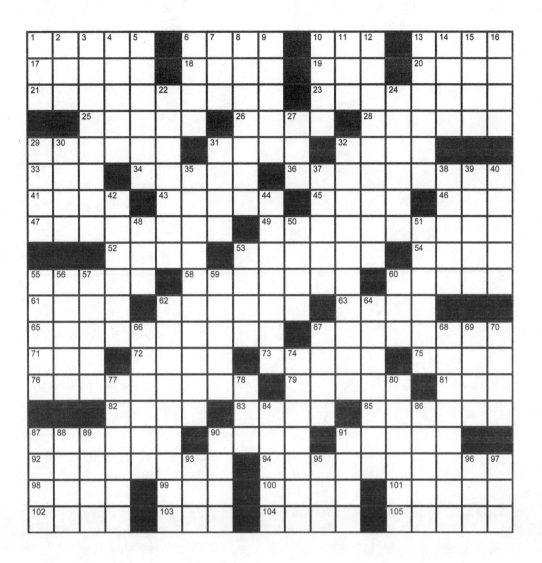

88. Vocal range of Anne Murray
89. Nunavut Quest vehicle
90. Covet

91. Erudite Clue character
93. Familiar lyric for Canadians: "God keep _____ land"

95. Law Enforcement Unit (abbr.)
96. Narcissist's conceit
97. Small dose, for short

SOLUTION ON PAGE 164

Right Place, Right Time

A seasonal excursion

ACROSS

1. Wing-like
5. Give a hand?
9. Cabernet and Chianti
13. Evil org. in *Get Smart*
17. Former Quebec premier Lévesque
18. Gyro bread
19. Pleasant
21. Tiny transports?
23. **Appropriate Ontario place to be on December 25th?**
24. Steam room
25. Sir Desmond _____
27. Valuables storage place
28. Swift Current airport code
29. Not busy, like actor Eric?
31. Rum cocktail: _____ colada
33. Everything else category, for short
35. Glistening fabric
37. Journalist, informally
39. Metal door hinge
43. Devotional desk
46. Approximation phrase
47. Deep fat cooking device
48. Recipient of 3-D: Golden _____
49. Fact
51. Significant life event
53. Shade of green
54. Canadian Association of Petroleum Production Accounting (abbr.)
56. Victoria's Murchie's, for one
57. Labatt can opener
60. **You might pick up some ivy in this Barrie neighbourhood?**
62. _____ feeling
63. Nasal membrane inflammation
67. Country that abuts Algeria
69. Glob
73. Popular with the public
75. Wolf or coyote
77. Troops' munitions, for short

78. Sandwich shops
79. Ancient Roman's wrap
81. A cutting act?
83. Edible taro plant root
84. Unexpected Rogers Cup defeats
86. Wasp punctures
87. 1982 hit from Canada's Spoons: "_____ Heart"
89. Cabot Links starting points
91. Computer Animation Studios of Ontario (abbr.)
92. "Don't _____, don't tell"
95. Early Hudson's Bay Company products
97. Montreal-born stand-up star Mort
99. Peruvian animal
102. **Manitoba town for a white Christmas?**
105. Winter footwear fasteners
107. Fortifications made of stakes
108. As a result of
109. "…'til morning is _____"
110. Extend over
111. Stitches
112. Town northwest of Ottawa: _____ River
113. WWII turning point

DOWN

1. CTV show (2005–08): *Robson* _____
2. Luke's *Star Wars* sister
3. RBC payouts to retirees, for example
4. **Rudolph might have stopped by this 1930s NWT town?**
5. "Brains" of a PC
6. 1994 Oscar best picture winner: *Schindler's* _____
7. Really enjoyed a meal
8. Anise-based aperitif
9. Moved quickly
10. Swelled heads

11. Handsome ship's captain?
12. Narcissist's photo?
13. Netflix martial arts comedy–drama: *Cobra* _____
14. In a skillful manner
15. British singer Murs
16. Bryan Adams single: "I Thought I'd _____ Everything"
20. December 24th and 31st
22. Bundled hay
26. Makes more simplistic
30. British author Bagnold
32. Pearson Terminal 3 electronic board abbr.
34. **Appropriate Cape Breton place to be on December 25th?**
35. Tinned meat brand
36. CFLer whose home games are played at BMO Field
38. Doctrine suffix
40. Colonial India childminder
41. State flower of 45-D
42. Sous-chef's chore
44. Edmonton Arts Council (abbr.)
45. Ogden and Orem state
47. Mrs., in Mannheim
50. "It Came _____ the Midnight Clear"
52. Petro-Canada gas option, for short
55. Plankton particle
58. Son of Hera
59. "It's cold!" interjection
61. Kyoto cravings?
63. Relinquish control
64. Pink-slipped a forestry worker?
65. "I _____ you so!"
66. Top songs of the moment
68. Ocasek of the Cars
70. Protein component
71. Southern Ontario pollution problem
72. Familiar lyric prior to 2018: "…in all thy _____ command"

74. Businesses (abbr.)
76. Computer slot insert
80. Acquire
82. Conk out, like a car
84. These dangle in throats (var.)
85. Bottom of the ocean
88. Murders, like a Mafioso

90. Vancouver area: North _____
92. Cobras
93. Finger clicker's noise
94. Russian peninsula
96. Twist
98. Theatre box

100. Fast-food meal prefix meaning "huge"
101. Not ruddy
103. Roll Up the Rim to _____
104. Slalom turn type
106. Long-running Canadian quiz show: *Reach for the* _____

Same name, different spelling

ACROSS

1. Shopper's sack at Safeway
4. They drop passengers at YVR
8. The scoop, to a spy?
13. "I _____ from the bed to see what was the matter"
19. Rogers Centre pitcher's stat
20. Eastern nanny
21. Type of eel
22. Earth shaking motion
23. Ottawa newspaper name
24. Measles symptom
25. Idaho city
26. Eye part
27. Stone pillar
29. Edmonton's Northern Alberta Jubilee Auditorium, for example
30. Drove
31. Mob members
32. The same, to Brutus
33. **Canadian country singer Carroll**
34. Like aromatic candles
36. In 1909, this insurance giant opened its first branch in Canada
41. Australian marsupials
44. Lamb's mother
45. Some human resources staffers
46. Second wife of Lennon
47. These cover some buildings on the U of T campus
48. System of beliefs
50. African antelope
51. Astronomer Hubble
53. Where the US waged war in the '60s
54. Coconut husk fibre
55. Spine-chilling
58. Ridge on corduroy
59. Shone
62. Like a coddled child, in Chelsea
64. More balanced
66. Small evergreen shrub

68. Michigan-to-Ontario direction (abbr.)
69. Sri Lankan language
71. Building front
74. Without any secrecy
77. Shoe part
81. Once more, in hillbilly-speak
82. Capital of Mali
84. Once _____ a time
86. Jordan Staal, to sib Eric
87. Roughrider to an Argo, say
89. Canadian Blood Services (abbr.)
90. Good news on Bay Street
92. Mischievous one
94. Thrilla in Manila competitor
95. Come up with a creation
98. "Wow!"
99. Scanty
100. Metric length units
102. Pliable protein
104. **Quebec poet and novelist Carole**
105. Tumult
107. Bette Midler played this role on *Seinfeld* once
111. Old distilling device
114. Launching litigation
115. Country in the Horn of Africa
116. Angry Greek goddesses?
117. Canada's Twin Otter, for example
118. Sexy skirt feature
119. Rotisserie part
120. Ancient Greece meeting places (var.)
121. _____ and Caicos
122. Competent
123. 1966 Beatles song: "For No _____"
124. Transmit an email again
125. Seemingly bottomless hole
126. Coloured
127. Parliament Hill place: _____ Chamber

DOWN

1. Broom made of tied twigs
2. Island south of 121-A
3. Yiddish swindler
4. Dances similar to sambas
5. Builds a church congregation?
6. *Tiger King* **big cat activist Carole**
7. Annoyed interjection in a Cineplex Odeon theatre
8. Firmly affixed (var.)
9. Herman's Hermits singer Peter
10. "Lay It on the Line" Canadian rockers
11. Provide comfort
12. Drain clearing liquid
13. 1983 Burt Reynolds movie: _____ *Ace*
14. Guise
15. Zingy comeback
16. Arabian dignitary
17. Opposite of all
18. York University alum
28. Fine thread
29. *The National* audience, say
30. Imaginary
33. **1970s TV variety show star Carol**
35. *Desperate Housewives* star Hatcher
37. Star in Orion
38. John Wayne, by birth
39. Like a feeble old woman
40. Social interaction eschewer
41. **"It's Too Late" singer–songwriter Carole**
42. BC facility: Richmond Olympic _____
43. Like, in Laval
48. Closing section of a musical piece
49. *All in the Family* **star Carroll**
52. Reside
54. Céline or Shania?
56. Canadian history figure Louis

57. Aden's country
60. Downward Facing Dog, for one
61. Angry
63. Glance at a mountaintop?
65. Reach for the top?
67. **1930s screwball comedies star Carole**
70. Nabisco cookies: Chips _____!
71. Unit of capacitance
72. Lissome
73. Statutory day in some provinces: _____ Holiday
75. Glue
76. It burns on Christmas Eve
78. Sun Peaks skier's lift
79. Canadian passport page image: Coat of _____
80. **Rough Trade singer Carole**
83. Vinegary
85. Urgent supplication
88. Frozen mixed vegetables bit
91. Seniors' advancement?
92. Lively
93. "Thou _____ not then be false to any man"
96. Came up with a plan
97. This begins at Lac Saint-Pierre: St. Lawrence _____
99. Like operating rooms
101. Venerate
103. **Ford Mustang named after racing icon Carroll**
106. Sty sounds
108. Blunder by a Blue Jay
109. African country: Sierra _____
110. Lost colour in the wash
111. Yonder
112. In 2018, Alex Gough earned Canada's first-ever Olympic medal in this
113. Cupid, by another name
114. Yarn nubbin
117. "Harper Valley _____"
118. Morose

31

Cooking Up a Storm...

With Canadian chefs

ACROSS

1. *Canadian Geographic*, et al.
5. Baking powder meas.
8. *Eat, Shrink & Be Merry* co-host and co-author Podleski
13. Like a combative medieval slave?
19. Large patch for pulses
20. Excited interjection
21. Maui and Molokai neighbour
22. National skiing body: _____ Canada
23. Coerce a CP train driver?
25. Aroma
26. **Madame Benoît of Quebec who wrote 30 cookbooks**
27. Relatives
28. 1997 Céline Dion song: "Let's Talk _____ Love"
29. Orange juice and champagne cocktail
30. Cellphone, colloquially
31. Waterproofing oil type
32. Pepper plant
33. Foot bone
37. Netherlands natives
42. More dry, in the desert
43. Keen
45. Come home to _____
46. Place to put gloss
47. Ate at White Spot
48. Mrs. Chrétien
49. Canadian comedian James
50. Farm omnivores
52. Unreturnable serve from Canada's Denis Shapovalov
53. Tattoo artist's liquids
54. Like cheap excuses?
57. Firefighters' equipment
58. *Chopped Canada* **judge Capra**
61. Down in the dumps
63. Prepared *Good Times* articles for publication
65. Some amphibians

67. **BC chef Feenie who was the first Canadian to win on *Iron Chef America***
68. Egyptian fruit export
70. Temporarily filling a role?
73. Flips a coin
76. **PEI-based celebrity chef Smith**
80. Enticement
81. Central American wildcat
83. Karate participants' sashes
85. Spanish Mrs.
86. Hold firmly
88. "I'm at the _____ of my rope"
89. Goofed
91. Machine gun steadying device
93. Philosophy suffix
94. Jousting spear
96. Nerve cells plexus
97. Several US states did this in the 1860s
98. Causing the blues
101. Found
103. Atelier stand
104. Fencing blade
106. Nicholson/Cruise movie: _____ *Good Men*
107. Old-style fabric made of flax
109. Made bovine sounds
110. Near the top of the mouth
114. ***The Galloping Gourmet* host Kerr**
115. Obscure, old style
116. Tearful tale?
117. Solution for cleaning contacts
118. Apply chrism to a Catholic, archaically
119. Top number for goalies?
120. Federal party leader O'Toole
121. Very competent people
122. **Lee who was a runner-up on *Top Chef Masters***
123. Get married
124. Golden Globe-winning actor from Ontario Gosling

DOWN

1. *Top Chef Canada* **judge McEwan**
2. Antioxidant-rich fruit
3. Broad smile
4. Like many millionaires
5. You'll see Word icons here
6. Salt dispenser
7. Group of aquatic mammals
8. Blood protein
9. Dangerous, odourless gas
10. 1985 Canadian musicians' fundraising tune: "Tears Are Not _____"
11. Rigid
12. Former flyer: TransCanada _____ Lines
13. Tex-Mex meals
14. Aspects
15. Keep law and order
16. Buenos _____
17. **Olson who hosted *Sugar* on Food Network Canada**
18. *To Kill a Mockingbird* author Harper
24. Cheered (for)
28. Reversion
29. Cantaloupe and casaba
32. Flowered
33. Merman movie: *Call Me* _____
34. Canadian wrestler Wiebe who won Olympic gold in Rio
35. Fork parts
36. Virologist Jonas who developed polio vaccine
38. Braid made from metallic thread
39. US poet T.S.
40. Salon job
41. Velocity
44. Useful car feature in winter
48. "_____ is as good as a wink"
51. Make a sibilant sound
53. Final stage of insect development

O CANADA CROSSWORDS ■ BOOK 22

55. Brain part: Parietal _____
56. Alleged Himalayan beasts
59. Homes for 50-A
60. Subatomic particle
62. Thereabouts
64. Ten years (abbr.)
66. Trace a decorative pattern on your walls
69. In the thick of things
70. Extremely chilly
71. Nova Scotia-set History show: The _____ of Oak Island
72. 1994 Rankin Family song: "_____ Miner"
74. Of bygone days
75. Carried out a military mission

77. This Izzy founded CanWest Global Communications Corp.
78. Deteriorate, like a levee
79. Filled a hold
82. Perfumes with myrrh
84. They fly with the birds?
87. Nice
90. Vancouver church since 1990: Christ the _____
91. Oblique tile edges
92. Freezing cold liquid?
95. Accepts without questioning
97. Pullout couch
99. Send again by boat?
100. Glittery rocks

102. Gangster Al
105. WWI French soldier
107. **Chef and host Long on Restaurant Makeover**
108. Noted Connecticut university
109. Bill of fare from any of the chefs in this puzzle
111. Colloquial moniker for 120-A
112. Soprano's spotlight moment
113. **Crawford who won three battles over two seasons on Iron Chef Canada**
114. US gov. procurement org.
115. Some degs. from U of M
116. Place seeds in the ground

32 A Wintry Mix

TV, music and movies

ACROSS

1. Canadian-born *Matrix* star Carrie-Anne
5. Ontario law enforcement grp.
8. Kitchen utensil for prepping potatoes
14. Big Smoke pollution?
18. _____ vera
19. Standard links score
20. Musical intervals
22. Not on schedule
23. Cover again, through Intact?
25. Social climber
26. Angle on a leaf
27. **Chris Martin's British band**
28. Canada's Snowbirds perform these stunts
30. Telescope part
31. Set out on a ship
33. Pimple, to a teen
34. Type of TELUS charge
38. Newly arrived in the world
39. Votes in an MP again
44. Wide of the mark
45. Lucien Bouchard was the first to lead this party: _____ Québécois
46. _____ to the throne
47. Arabian boat
48. New Brunswick seaport: _____ John
49. Main force of an attack
50. Curly hairdos
52. Salty seafood eggs
53. It follows *printemps* in Quebec
54. Coconut covering
55. Arcade Fire music genre
57. Youngster
59. Wealthy
62. Tracking dog's trail
63. Frothy dessert
64. Light-headed
65. Prancer's pal
66. Old French folks
67. Curt, at First Choice Haircutters?
69. Engineering and procurement company: _____ Canada
70. Sold out a soulmate
73. Fungal foot problem
74. Long (for)
75. Sun worships
76. Arborist's maxim?
77. Belleville clock setting (abbr.)
78. Polish currency
80. Major Toronto artery: _____ Street
82. Burn slightly
84. Chirp heard in a coop
86. Strong cleaning solutions
87. You might take one at Lakehead University
88. Government agency: _____ Board of Canada
89. North African winds
91. Yore anagram
92. Shady section of the Net
93. Southeast Asian people or language
94. Four-season W Network show: *Undercover _____ Canada*
95. Salish Sea island in BC: _____ Spring
96. Attacked from a warplane
101. **Schwarzenegger role in *Batman & Robin***
106. _____ formaldehyde
107. Air Miles program type
110. Irrationality
111. Communism founder Karl
112. On edge
113. Catch a glimpse
114. *The Fountainhead* writer Ayn
115. Buy-in bet, in poker
116. The _____ of two evils
117. High Risk Youth (abbr.)
118. Seeks legal restitution

DOWN

1. Quebec's 24th premier: Pierre-_____ Johnson
2. Margarine
3. Plant pot filler
4. Mail
5. Sumptuous
6. Indonesian knife
7. Profits by exploiting (with "on")
8. Floor cleaning device
9. Alberta Conservation Association (abbr.)
10. Exertion
11. Former Czech president Václav
12. Fairy tale penultimate word
13. Activity for HGTV Canada's Bryan and Sarah Baeumler
14. Like louvres
15. Long skirt style
16. Auditory
17. Hairstyling products
21. **2005 Canadian action film**
24. Broken bone support
29. Garlic bulblet
31. At any moment
32. **British rock band**
34. Hem again
35. Speak like Erato?
36. ***Modern Family* actress**
37. Gentle fellow?
38. Become fuzzy, like vision
39. Modernize a vessel
40. Word on an Irish euro
41. **Suzanne Somers *Three's Company* character**
42. Some Home Hardware purchases
43. Rutabaga grown in Stockholm?
45. Verve, to Vivaldi
46. Dusty Springfield hit: "If It _____ Been For You"
49. 2011 Drake song: "Over My Dead _____"
51. Scrub

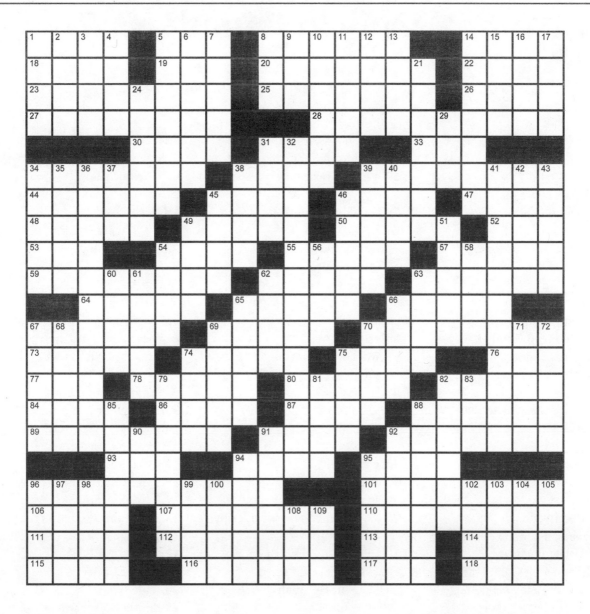

54. Snug space description
56. Bard's contraction
58. Hawaiian dance
60. Run slowly
61. November birthstone
62. Tart cocktail type?
63. Sundin who played 14 seasons with the Leafs
65. Sculptors' compounds
66. MacLellan who composed Anne Murray's "Snowbird"
67. Dance moves
68. Japanese–Canadian
69. Festivals and fairs
70. Healing emollient
71. Avian symbol of America

72. Nerd
74. Vacillate
75. Move headlong, say
79. **Grammy-winning US rapper**
81. Former spouses
82. French author who wrote *Existentialism and Humanism*
83. Irritate
85. Middle Ages weapon
88. Horse for women to ride, old style
90. Canadian game show (2008–15): *Cash _____*
91. Plenty
92. Socks sewer
94. Wins the Grey Cup, say

95. Compress, colloquially
96. Where Russian politicians debate
97. OPEC member country
98. Colour of spring, in Quebec
99. Do drudgery
100. It follows mega or giga
102. Hearing organs
103. Genesis grandson
104. Specific area
105. Curling match segments
108. Canadian cheese maker: _____ Stelle
109. Goose Bay airport code

SOLUTION ON PAGE 165

Only In Canada, Eh?

Native to our land

ACROSS

1. Van Halen vocalist: David Lee _____
5. Quebec's Lévesque, et al.
10. *James and the Giant Peach* author Roald
14. Bitter in taste or tone
19. Office of the Chief Administrative Officer (abbr.)
20. Leave out a vowel in pronunciation
21. Double-reed woodwind
22. Ill-gotten gains
23. **Territorial plant**
26. Gravenstein or Gala
27. Roy Bonisteel hosted this on CBC for two decades: *Man _____*
28. James Barber's former CBC show: *The Urban _____*
29. Mark and Matthew, in the Bible
31. Ancestry.ca data
33. Canadian law since 1969: Official Languages _____
34. Plains peoples' tent (var.)
35. Some *Toronto Star* staffers
39. Street brawl
43. *Blue Bloods* network
46. PDQ alternative
47. Arabic potentates
48. Utah city
49. Showy bloom
52. Call for help at sea
54. This was created by the Treaty of Rome in 1957 (abbr.)
55. One who's counting calories
56. Precious gemstone measurements
57. Obeys, like a good doggy
59. He or she relies on you?
61. States unequivocally
62. Strike out text
64. A witness swears this in court
65. Prognosticator
66. **Algonquin Park mammal**
69. White House office shape
73. "_____ It a Pity"
75. Outdoor living areas
76. _____ donna
77. Most gaudy
82. Water source
83. Piano teacher's session
84. Washed that man right out of your hair?
85. Bar tally
87. Michael Caine movie: *Blame It on _____*
88. Venerable
89. Off-kilter
90. Oceania place: _____ New Guinea
92. Ceases
94. Hi-_____ audio
95. Recipe measurement (abbr.)
96. These experts work with ores and alloys
100. Earlier, on the golf course?
102. Workplace for scientists
103. Dustin Hoffman dressed up for this film
107. American *Walden* scribe: Henry David _____
110. Rowing or running exercise description
113. Real Canadian Superstore deli purchase
114. Rogue wave
115. **Maritimes butterfly**
118. Sign up at U of M
119. One who votes no
120. Bathroom floor installer
121. River in Russia
122. Distorts data
123. He served as prime minister three times: William _____ Mackenzie King
124. Squalid
125. Landmark in the Rockies: Yellowhead _____

DOWN

1. _____ Ontario Museum
2. Dome openings
3. 1974 Bachman-Turner Overdrive single: "_____ Care of Business"
4. Foals' feet
5. Some Esso gas, for short
6. They sometimes marry in Vegas
7. It flows north to the Mediterranean Sea
8. Scandinavian literary work
9. Park toy for two
10. Morose rest period?
11. "Wanna make _____?"
12. Weed removal tool
13. Books that show the bottom line
14. Be demeaning
15. **Fish found only in Quebec**
16. Strong twine
17. "_____ be a cold day…"
18. Colours cloth
24. Tide type
25. Mother-of-pearl
30. Roman goddess of earth and fertility
32. Provokes
34. Mid-morning prayers hour
36. Quebecers drink *thé* in these
37. Soured, like milk in Merseyside
38. All square, at the Scotiabank Saddledome
40. Trifling amount
41. Pizzeria appliance
42. Wrongful act, to a lawyer
43. Drug-yielding plants
44. Fearless
45. Pile of rubble in the Rockies
48. Pub serving
50. **Canada's only endemic breeding bird**

51. Lesley Gore #1: "_____ My Party"
53. Precipitous
55. Canadian Cultural Society of the _____
58. Bale contents
60. GOPers, e.g.
62. 11/24/20, for example
63. Step through a doorway
66. Arthurian legends lady
67. More crafty
68. Tea type
70. Motorcycle helmet component
71. "…mountain out of _____ hill"
72. Crown corporation: Canada _____ Company
74. Nieces and sisters
76. Cribbage player's stick
77. Male undergrads' club, for short
78. Go out on a _____
79. Glossy black cuckoos
80. Kansas or Kentucky
81. Traditional Polynesian cloth
83. Rodeo rope
86. Brief news report
90. Casual or careful reading
91. Cause concern
93. Dumped in a moat?
96. Bird that's no more
97. WWII underwater vessels
98. Like some Tim Hortons orders
99. Put a cork in it?
101. Has a hunch
104. Toyota model reintroduced in 2019
105. Notions from your noggin
106. Canadian dining chain since 1982
107. Short shirts?
108. Nova Scotian singer Snow of "I've Been Everywhere" fame
109. Monstrous figure?
110. Palo _____
111. Melted topping for crackers
112. Capri or Wight
116. Some
117. Shed tears

SOLUTION ON PAGE 166

34 Buzzwords

Newer to the lexicon

ACROSS

1. Bristles
5. Deep cut
9. American Society of Composers, Authors and Publishers (abbr.)
14. Evening, in Rimouski
18. Sundial numeral
19. In this place, in Spain
20. Use a razor
21. _____ 6/49
22. Does not exist
23. Retired to the country
25. Halton Hills ON town
26. Pesticide bath for rams and ewes
28. Left-hand pages
29. Roadway sign
30. Trapeze artists' sources of security
32. **Odd guy with facial hair**
33. Green spaces, in Gatineau
37. Bambi's aunt
38. The National Archives (abbr.)
39. _____ Marx
40. Wicked behaviour
41. Honour given by the government: _____ of Canada
43. Concentration of a chemical solution (var.)
45. Nimble-fingered
49. Balsam secretions
51. Congratulatory action: _____ on the back
53. Canadian actor Cariou
54. Jewelled coronet
55. Statement assumed to be true
57. Friend
59. This used to be mined in Quebec
61. Plays by the rules, say
64. Canadian actor Green, et al.
66. Set on
67. Birthday present
70. **Infrequent food pick-up option prior to 2020**

73. Like a pretentious sculptor?
74. "Far out!"
76. She helps with the children in India
77. Forcefully hit the brakes
79. Most sloped
81. 1998 Nickelback song: "Hold _____ Your Hand"
83. Southeastern BC mountain range
87. Steamer for a vagabond?
88. Part of HRH, for George V
90. Niagara Falls snaps
93. A famed Canadian game tests players on this
94. Top part of a garment
95. Second Cup coffee choice
97. Initial Hebrew letter
99. A giraffe has a long one
100. Old CBC series: _____ *to Avonlea*
102. Seven, on a phone keypad
104. Tuskegee state (abbr.)
105. Be in harmony
106. **Baby platypus**
109. Fast-flowering plants?
112. On _____-to-know basis
113. Orb
114. Publication from Canada's Jean Paré
119. Tarzan's vine
120. Person with a new idea
122. Judges do this
123. Speed skater Gagnon and politician Garneau
124. Seizure sensations (var.)
125. Puff on a joint
126. _____ of Man
127. Popular craft supplies website
128. Loudly laments
129. Tim Hortons food choice: _____ muffin
130. M&M Food Market purchase

DOWN

1. *Rara* _____
2. Yearn for a fairy godmother?
3. Cardinal number
4. Location
5. Irish police person
6. Underground water source
7. Halts a hanging?
8. Rogers Centre single: Base _____
9. Journey to the top of Kilimanjaro
10. **Mom or dad who posts too much on Facebook**
11. Moggie owner's plant?
12. Chevrolet subcompacts
13. Sports pros get banned for using these (abbr.)
14. **People rarely did this until 2020**
15. River critter
16. "_____ you so!"
17. Classical piano piece
21. Tier
24. _____ League
27. Penticton Secondary School (abbr.)
31. Asian weight unit
32. Ontario _____ Association
33. Criminal, to the cops
34. Strongly assert
35. _____ and shine
36. **Urgent environmental situation**
39. Mattel male dolls
41. Middle ear bone
42. Juno Awards genre
44. Prickly plant
46. Gourmand
47. Toronto's Union Station street
48. "Mmm mmm good!"
50. Pen tip
52. Repair a seamstresses' relationship?
54. X
56. Doe anagram
58. Auction offering

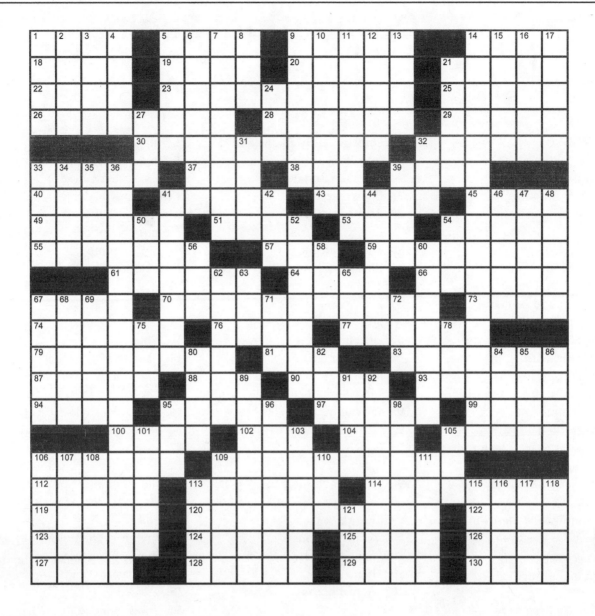

60. Reddish-white metallic element
62. Descended from the same mom
63. Swine enclosure
65. Canadian realtors use this marketing service (abbr.)
67. Extremely windy
68. Book's preface
69. Weirdo
71. Alberta Association of Optometrists (abbr.)
72. Drain of energy
75. Spotify, e.g.
78. 2013 book by an NHL icon: _____: *My Story*
80. Lawn mower storage space
82. _____ Maria

84. For eternity
85. Head vermin
86. See 89-D
89. With 86-D, body of water in Saskatchewan
91. Sweet treat: Bear _____
92. One who chooses
95. *Hawaii Five-O* remake star: Daniel _____ Kim
96. **Super zealous recycler**
98. Oaf
101. As _____ the hills
103. The Toronto Blue Jays won this twice: World _____
105. Supplicate
106. Highest Cannes prize: _____ d'Or

107. Eastern church Christian (var.)
108. Toothed wheels
109. Malady contracted by tropical tourists
110. TV room
111. *Two Women* Oscar winner Sophia
113. Drench
115. Edge of a fedora
116. It drains into the North Sea: River Great _____
117. Lola anagram
118. Bottom of the boat
121. Alberta financial services institution (abbr.)

SOLUTION ON PAGE 166

Destination: Regina

A visit to the Queen City

ACROSS

1. House additions
5. Bursa, for example
8. _____ profundo
13. Canadian Peterson who won a lifetime achievement Grammy in 1997
18. Symbol of Capricorn
19. Continental currency
20. Canadian record label (1974–99)
21. Wild Asian animal
22. **Place for a tour and tea**
25. Durable fabric
26. Old West transport
27. Advanced deg. from McGill
28. Made a request
29. Takes too many drugs
30. Canada's Susur Lee, for one
32. Uninspiring
34. Test at U of A
36. Sternum locale
39. This might be ingrown
41. Quarantine, say
43. Brainstorm
44. Plasters
45. Lobster ova
46. Mineo who starred in *Exodus*
47. Jell
48. Develop
50. Bird that runs but doesn't fly
51. Hellish place?
53. Clubs for Ontario's Mike Weir
54. _____-Raphaelite
55. Lose rigidity
56. Ceremonial spread
60. Ornamental Japanese tree
62. L'Oréal Paris aerosol product
65. Shine, radiantly
66. Gordon Lightfoot hit: "If _____ Could Read My Mind"
67. **The Roughriders play here**
70. Winnipeg Jet, for example
71. "How do you like _____ apples?"
73. Some bagels from 36-D taste like this
74. Ottoman Empire VIPs
76. Op-ed piece
78. Banned pesticide
79. Biblical boat for beasts
80. Bits of phlegm
81. EI, colloquially
83. 2003 Nelly Furtado song
84. Like arrestees who contact a bondsman
87. Former Canadian auto workers union (abbr.)
90. *Mens* _____
91. TELUS product: _____ TV
92. Weathercock
93. Carrie Fisher's cinematic princess
94. Darker than the dark?
96. Sore muscle soother
98. Carpentry joint, in New Jersey
99. Miss Universe Canada contestant's ribbon
100. Full of conceit
102. Honky-_____
103. Access no. at CIBC
104. Richter _____
106. _____-liberal
108. Leery
113. Tsar's decree
114. **"Royal" tourism attraction**
116. Lions' flowing locks
117. Indirect suggestions
118. Not loose
119. Trident prong
120. Trapper's drum?
121. Man of many fables
122. Increases
123. Glance over the headlines

DOWN

1. Ontario poultry farms produce more of these than any other province
2. Pillage
3. Mauna Loa liquid
4. Spike-tailed dinos
5. Wrestling that's big in Japan?
6. 403, in Alberta
7. Some gastropods
8. "_____, humbug!"
9. Nuclear bomb bit
10. Five o'clock shadow, say
11. Carpet type
12. Ontario Centres of Excellence (abbr.)
13. Gamblers assess these
14. Israel monetary unit
15. **Theatre and arts centre**
16. Surveyor's angle-measuring device
17. Stage of sleep
19. Concordia faculty: Engineering and Computer Science (abbr.)
23. Decorate from scratch
24. *And* _____ *There Were None*
28. First, near the finish line
31. **Shoppers' mecca**
33. Zulu spear (var.)
35. Greeted
36. It was founded in 1964: _____ Hortons
37. Stephen Harper cabinet minister Bev
38. Entourages
39. Scolds the boy king?
40. Note promising payment
42. It's found on a staff
44. Cassava root
49. Wander without purpose
50. Susan Lucci's long-time *All My Children* role
51. Vancouver Island place: Port _____
52. Component (abbr.)
54. Medium for Robert Bateman
55. Use corporal punishment
57. 26 letters, en masse

58. Type of rail
59. Terrible time for tykes?
60. Bunch of bits, in computing
61. Excited interjections
62. Utile
63. Prose from Alice Munro
64. 1980s urban professional, colloquially
68. Revolver or pistol
69. Rough up
72. Navigator's aid
75. Some Russian Communists
77. Early name for Toronto
80. Dropped to the bottom of the sea

82. They fly in a V-formation
83. _____-tac-toe
84. Effusively congratulate from behind?
85. Falsehood
86. Musical gift
87. US *Big Brother* network
88. British Columbian's neighbour
89. **Lake for recreation and wildlife**
91. City birds
92. South Pacific archipelago
95. Tag player?
97. Sumptuous
98. Glittery rock

101. Loosen shoelaces
103. Early Scot
105. _____-*majesté*
107. Latch _____
109. Furthermore
110. Suffix with neur
111. Forearm bone
112. Spotted
113. Hesitant interjections
114. Saskatchewan Hockey Association (abbr.)
115. Extra special sense in Spain?

SOLUTION ON PAGE 166

36 Mom's the Word

Relative phrases ☺

ACROSS

1. CBC Radio "Battle of the Books": Canada _____
6. Olden days worker
10. Female choir member's voice
14. Roll of cash
17. **Relative by marriage: Mother-_____**
18. Stare at British nobility?
19. Across-the-river auto transport
21. State of undress
23. Regiment's reverend
24. Megalithic tomb
25. Western Scotland site: _____ of Ewe
27. Farley Mowat's first book: _____ of the Deer
28. **Paul Simon song: "Mother _____ Reunion"**
31. Cellphone download, for short
32. Be abusive
36. Vancouver Island wind?
40. Ontario landmark: Point _____ National Park
41. Reduced Instruction Set Computer (abbr.)
43. Red River Rebellion leader: Louis _____
44. Nova Scotia duck tolling retriever
45. Dunks in water
47. 1960s abstractionism
49. Canadian fashion designer Alfred
50. "Easy peasy," at the gym?
51. Plum pudding description
52. Backs of necks
53. One killed Cleopatra
54. This Italian went to hell and back
55. Cheer syllable
56. Hindu worker caste
59. *Roots* protagonist Kunta
60. Safe to drink
64. Implored
65. Eye surgeon's instrument
66. Moved ancestral remains
67. Arlington National Cemetery (abbr.)
68. Guess Who hit: "_____ on to Your Life"
69. A calendar covers it?
71. Assesses
72. Pillagers
75. Bygone days Romans and Egyptians
77. Subside, at the seaside
78. **Abbey head: Mother _____**
80. Discharges from the army
83. American auto parts distribution org. since 1925
84. Rock garden growth
89. A man might wear this to see *Carmen*?
91. Happening every so often
94. List of tenants
95. Feline, in Frontenac
96. **Nursery rhyme character: Mother _____**
97. 2009 Michael Bublé song: "Haven't _____ You Yet"
98. Big name in pineapple
99. Blood pigment
100. Chairback component

DOWN

1. Clear (with "of")
2. Dine anagram
3. Additionally
4. *Journey to the Center of the Earth* actress Arlene
5. Crossed the English Channel, like Canada's Cindy Nicholas
6. Black widow's web maker
7. As slippery as an _____
8. Species surviving from another age
9. Real Canadian Superstore clothing brand: Joe _____
10. Move more rapidly, on the road
11. Scale note (var.)
12. Rodent catcher
13. **Nacre: Mother-_____**
14. Prepared Christmas presents
15. Ovule protector
16. Physics force unit
20. Furtively get hitched
22. Bathurst Island landmark: Polar _____ Pass National Wildlife Area
26. Cape Breton roadway: Fleur-de-_____ Trail
29. Royal's riser
30. Quebec's Agropur produces this type of product
32. Office msg.
33. Dickensian-era charity
34. Away from the wind
35. **Nobel Peace Prize winner: Mother _____**
37. "Wanna make a _____?"
38. PST or AST: Time _____
39. Frittata ingredients
40. Scotiabank ATM access no.
42. **Where you come from: Mother _____**
46. It's gathered from trees in Quebec
48. Timmins-born 1970s NHL star Mahovlich
49. Dry, like a particular desert?
51. Of sound mind
52. **You can't fight her: Mother _____**
54. Make sulky
55. Canadian jazz great McConnell
56. Transmit unwelcome emails
57. Wrist–elbow connector
58. Reduction
59. NHL stars Patrick and Evander

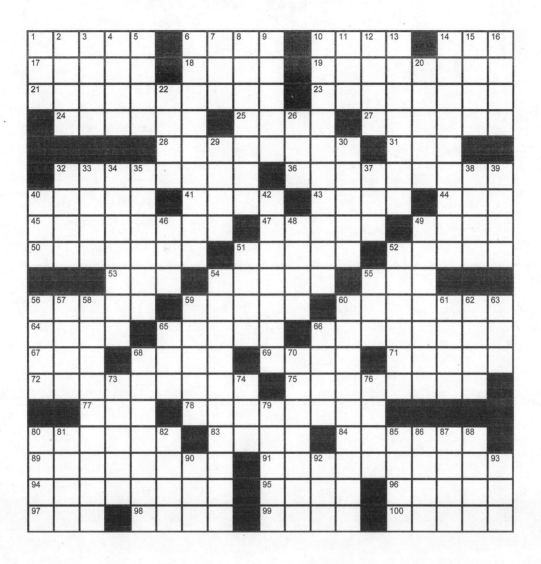

60. Make coffee
61. One of a pair of docking posts
62. Canadian metal queen Aaron, et al.
63. Former OLN show: _____ *Up!*
65. Member of a '50s Canadian pop quartet?
66. Indian princess
68. Nursery rhyme character: Mother _____

70. Common childhood malady
73. Command from 88-D to cancel
74. Exclusive condo amenity
76. UK novelist: Dame _____ Murdoch
79. Geologic era
80. U of A lodgings
81. Fencing foil

82. "Get outta here!"
85. Smokes
86. Toronto Raptor's target
87. Compound for Leon?
88. US space flight org.
90. Everything
92. BC-born ex-Bruin Neely
93. Allow, at Wimbledon?

SOLUTION ON PAGE 166

37 Four-Square

Use mini grids to help solve this one

ACROSS

1. Pendulum's curve
4. Kal Tire shop measurement (abbr.)
7. Every scrap
10. Some Dalhousie degrees (abbr.)
13. Turtledove's sound
14. Permit
15. Round vegetable
16. Roberto Luongo wore this jersey number
17. Fortune tellers' toppers
19. Satyr's pot?
20. Insecticide banned in CDA as of 1990
21. Parliament Hill Liberals, colloquially
22. Adjective for Gretzky
24. Concerning that, in legal language
26. Perfume for a frau?
28. Metric land measure
29. Antecede
30. Rave about
31. Chasms
32. Conflicts between checks and stripes?
39. Destructive weather event
46. Refurbished an engine
47. Sultan's footstool?
48. In a caustic manner
49. Actor Beatty, et al.
50. Snow _____
51. Aquarium fish
52. Conducted the Winnipeg Symphony Orchestra
53. Galoot
56. Kansas city
58. Physics unit
59. Canada's neighbour to the south (abbr.)
60. Interjection of delight
61. _____ Democratic Party
62. Change your hair colour
63. BC roadway: Sea-to-_____ Highway
64. Blasting crew's explosive, for short
65. CBC reality show: *Dragons'* _____

DOWN

1. Seldom-used federal legislation: War Measures _____
2. Make more coarse
3. Right
4. BC region: Interior _____
5. Security system components
6. Tis anagram
7. Zoom or Facebook
8. Farmer's field for livestock
9. BC municipality
10. Señores' shops?
11. Moderately slow, in music
12. Parlour sofas
18. Blessed event for a family
23. Rotisserie spits
24. Canadian comedy troupe: _____ Kids in the Hall
25. BMO charge
26. Canadian Payroll Association (abbr.)
27. Eye, to Shakespeare
32. Swam like a baby?
33. Lothario's activity
34. Join Prince Edward Island to New Brunswick?
35. Spades or clubs
36. Grossly ugly
37. English Language Learner (abbr.)
38. Pigs' place
39. Pull a water skier
40. Gare Centrale, in Montreal
41. Central Netherlands city
42. Compass point
43. Indigenous northern hemisphere person
44. Marine mammal
45. Great West Life offering (abbr.)
54. Pose a poser
55. Alberta-born *King Kong* star Wray
56. "Huh?" in Hereford
57. Bract bristle

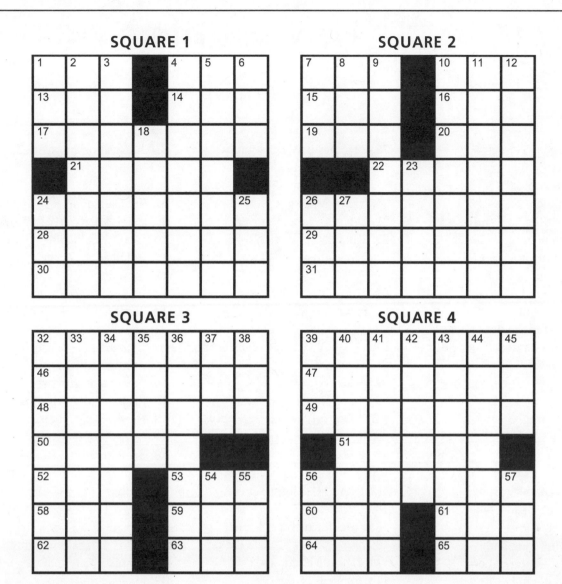

SQUARE 1

1	2	3		4	5	6
13				14		
17			18			
	21					
24						25
28						
30						

SQUARE 2

7	8	9		10	11	12
15				16		
19				20		
		22	23			
26	27					
29						
31						

SQUARE 3

32	33	34	35	36	37	38
46						
48						
50						
52				53	54	55
58				59		
62				63		

SQUARE 4

39	40	41	42	43	44	45
47						
49						
	51					
56						57
60				61		
64				65		

Decode a four-word colloquialism for Canada by using:

- One vertical word from Square 1.
- One horizontal word from Square 2.
- One horizontal word from Square 3.
- One vertical word from Square 4.

Answer:

_____

_____

_____

_____

SOLUTION ON PAGE 167

38

Here vs. There

Words unique to Brits

ACROSS

1. Soldier's civilian clothes
6. Looked at orbs?
10. Grumble
14. Rob at Rogers Centre?
19. Economic org. that includes Singapore and Laos
20. Pierre or Justin
21. Pupil membrane
22. Spicy green sauce
23. **Here:French fries::There:_____**
24. Toronto Raptors, frequently
26. Fall flower
27. Changing the clocks
29. Skylit lobbies (var.)
30. Tart tasting
31. Minuscule morsel
32. Distant
33. Live in Lloydminster, say
35. **Here:Diaper::There:_____**
36. Carlos Delgado, when he was a Blue Jay
38. Domineering dame, say
41. **Here:Sweater::There:_____**
44. Virgil poem (with "The")
46. Casablanca country
51. S-curve, in architectural design
52. Pester your spouse
54. Peterborough clock setting (abbr.)
55. **Here:Soccer::There:_____**
56. Made merry?
59. Less feral
61. Biblical king of Judea
62. Maple Leaf Apps who became an MPP
63. A bit quirky
64. Strong gemstones, old style
67. Collections for Rogers Cup fans?
68. Sign that comes after Cancer
69. Lowlifes
70. Map abbr.
72. This brought cheers for 36-A: _____ hit
75. Becomes harder to climb
77. International Labour Organization (abbr.)
78. It lays large eggs
81. On _____ and a prayer
83. Canadian physicist Robert Boyle helped create this for the Brits in WWI
84. Thin slices of meat
87. **Here:Sneakers::There:_____**
89. _____-di-dah
91. "_____ give you the shirt off his back"
92. Arachnid
93. Notre-Dame Basilica songbooks
94. Colourful Mexican shawl (var.)
96. **Here:Suspenders::There:_____**
98. Snub a bit?
100. Ponoka Stampede ropes
102. **Here:Flashlight::There:_____**
106. Perches
108. Tool for piercing leather
109. _____ bran
112. Diabolical doings
113. Tendrils in the sky
114. Fingering chart for musicians
117. True-blue
119. Highest register for woodwinds
121. **Here:Soccer field::There:_____**
122. Grassland for a gaucho
123. Great jubilation
124. Forget to include
125. Seamless transition
126. Egg centres
127. Geishas' desires?
128. Canadian rowing great Hanlan, et al.
129. Serrated, botanically

DOWN

1. Computer user's shortcut
2. Wedding party chap
3. Canadian "1234" singer
4. Scotch _____
5. Chic fashion magazine?
6. Finishing up
7. Knitter's tale?
8. New Canadian
9. First Reform Party MP Grey
10. Healthy daily pill
11. Indulged excessively
12. More intangible (var.)
13. US space agency since 1958
14. Banff Upper Hot Springs, for one
15. Canadian ice dancer Virtue who won five Olympic medals
16. Prevent, at the bar?
17. Really enjoyed dinner?
18. **Here:Truck::There:_____**
25. Some U of C degs.
28. Beef tenderloin steaks
34. Osprey's relation
35. Sudbury, vis-à-vis Sarnia
36. Drove too fast on the 400
37. Canadian textbook producer: _____ Educational Publishing Company
39. Lifeless, to a bard
40. Moo _____ gai pan
41. Runs
42. Like Cinderella's stepsisters
43. Swiss Chalet serving
45. **Here:Station wagon:: There:_____**
47. Too corpulent
48. Demonstrate concern
49. Coagulate
50. Calgary–Edmonton Corridor town
53. Common conjunction
55. Swamplands
57. Bunny's mama
58. Took up a challenge
60. Reverend's home
65. Nair and Veet
66. Caesar's server?
68. Red Square Vladimir

69. It precedes pool or pit
71. TV remote button, for short
72. Somerset city
73. Not quite right
74. Former name of Thailand
76. These connect with tibiae
77. Slippery surface on a sidewalk
78. Like a massive movie?
79. Ration (with "out")
80. Purposes
82. Grind one's dentures

85. 1998 Barenaked Ladies bonus track: "_____ On Time"
86. Grandmas, in Gelsenkirchen
88. Old-style English measurement
90. Stop who goes there?
94. Hem trousers, say
95. Canadian Monopoly, perhaps?
97. Fall off the wagon
99. Decorative radiator grate
101. Wooden-soled shoes
102. **Here:TV::There:_____**
103. Quarter-round moulding

104. Qatar monetary unit
105. Loud metallic noise
107. Sara, to Tegan, for short
109. Expense or payment
110. Shelf cloud
111. Little bit of laughter (var.)
113. Shrewd (var.)
115. In the centre?
116. Layer cake component
118. _____ Angeles
120. Farley Mowat biography: *My Father's _____*

39

Canuck Vocab

Words from the Great White North

ACROSS

1. Emirs' equines?
6. Home on the Plains (var.)
10. Transmit
14. Nautical call for help
17. Nelly Furtado hit: "…On the _____ (Remember the Days)"
18. First father, in the Bible
19. You do this in church
20. Winnie-the-Pooh pal
21. Component of some school calendars
23. Generate an income
24. PEI's 17th premier Walter
25. Crafty
26. Yukon's neighbour to the west
27. Solving crosswords offers this way out?
29. Wee shot of Scotch
30. + end of a battery
32. Gathered together
33. Bear, in Italian
36. Basswoods
38. **Pita-style sandwich first introduced in Halifax**
41. Ankle bone
43. _____ out of shape
44. Fish related
45. Like weather map lines
48. Little bird's sound
50. Exasperates
51. Thin varnish
52. Judges
53. Montreal-born jazz pianist Paul
54. Gas that's sometimes used as an anesthetic
56. La Belle Province
58. Young men
60. Fine or swindle
62. Tank tops
66. Real Estate Council of Ontario (abbr.)
67. Ingredient for some starchy salads
68. 1940 Disney movie
69. Alberta oil sands deposit
71. *Commedia dell'_____*
73. _____ Regency Vancouver
74. **Place to fill up**
75. US geographic region
78. Seine tributary
79. Aged
80. Book's odd-numbered page
81. Aylmer or Arnprior, in Ontario
83. Officiated at a Canucks game
86. Fired up, like a Calgary NHLer?
88. Fuss or flap
91. Alberta's Heritage Day falls in this mo.
92. _____ Office
93. Chapters or Indigo, for example
95. For
96. Longest river in the world
97. Debussy suite movement: "Clair de _____"
98. Blue-and-white pottery type
99. Turf
100. Like some groves
101. Work units
102. 20th-C. Irish dramatist and poet

DOWN

1. They're attached to shoulders
2. VIA _____
3. *The Full Monty* star Mark
4. Auction action
5. It precedes power or plexus
6. Floor covering for a Japanese flat
7. "Beware the _____ of March"
8. **Office building adjunct**
9. Innateness
10. Drives too fast on the 401
11. Dry _____ marker
12. War on drugs agent
13. Generators
14. Single gem in a ring
15. Needs to pay the piper
16. Bridge coup: Grand _____
22. Israeli airline
28. **Colouring stick**
29. **Tim Hortons order**
31. Done secretly
33. Soul singer Redding
34. Too hasty
35. Dark purple plum
37. The peacock network
38. Chips and _____
39. Like an octopus' squirt
40. Place to live at uni
42. Epsom _____
44. Old Spanish coin
46. "Go team!" word
47. Eugene O'Neill play: *The _____ Cometh*
49. Bird that lays green eggs
52. River mouth description
53. Ship's docking spot
55. They come before xis
57. Hamburger holder
58. Princess who loved Han in the movies
59. Tornadoes and typhoons
61. Place to play poker?
63. *NYPD Blue* star Morales
64. Some small birds
65. Satisfy
66. National Historic Site: Royal Botanical Gardens (abbr.)
67. _____ capita
68. Annual dues, say
70. Tree with red bark (var.)
72. **Case of beer**
75. Combo of songs
76. Annual Woodbine race: Duchess _____
77. Cats for Cochrane and Connors?
80. Commonwealth, for Queen Elizabeth
82. Like an unkempt lawn
83. Emulates Canada's Drake
84. Spending money for a roué?

85. Diabolical

87. Ontario provincial park: _____ Point

88. Musical time signature: _____ breve

89. Adroit

90. Meal morsels

94. Protected place, for a ship

SOLUTION ON PAGE 167

40

What's the Catch?

You'll figure it out

ACROSS

1. In a while, to a nameless poet?
5. Underhill who skated with Ron Duguay on *Battle of the Blades*
9. Tree or pie type
14. This broke the camel's back
19. *Royal Canadian Air Farce* star Goy
20. Fencer's blade
21. 1836 Texas battle site
22. The _____ Rovers
23. Item anagram
24. Cloth made of mulberry bark
25. **Disaster**
27. **Two-hulled boat**
29. Inscribe metal
30. Late night Air Canada flight
31. Nephew of Abel
32. Rose family shrub
34. Dan, to Eugene Levy
35. No Frills buggies
37. Oscar-nominated Canadian film director Egoyan
38. Lean
40. 1958 sci-fi film: *The _____*
44. Eradicate (with "of")
45. Sheath for a yolk
47. Fond-du-_____ SK
49. Untruth
50. Depart
51. Suppress: Keep _____ on
53. Scotiabank Theatre venues
56. Richardson, on HGTV's *Sarah Off the Grid*
58. This kind of guy finishes last
59. Canadian restaurant chain: _____ Japan
60. Greek portico
62. Former Toronto mayor Ford
63. Gretzky won this ten times: _____ Ross Trophy
64. Hospital unit: _____ care
67. Across the pond currency unit

69. Insolence
71. Visibly in awe
72. **See 25-A**
75. Wall panels
79. Tennis competitor's collection?
81. Cummerbund
82. Bury
84. _____ constrictor
87. Newfoundland _____ Club of Canada
89. Enjoys a day at Tremblant
91. New Zealand parrot
92. It precedes Spumante
93. Like healthier crackers
96. Roofing or paving substance
98. W.O. Mitchell novel: *Who Has _____ the Wind?*
99. Performer's phase?
100. Facial spasm
102. Pasture call
103. Former Canadian singing couple: _____ & Sylvia
105. Joke
106. BC Fraser Valley town
107. Shrub bearing red berries
109. Persian Gulf nation
111. Too soon
113. Chef's mushroom
114. _____ acid
116. Shania Twain's first single: "What _____ You Say That"
117. Art piece on Parliament Hill
121. Jamie who skated to Olympic gold with David
122. **Library's collection**
126. **Butterfly larva**
128. Picked out a perp
129. Level, in London
130. US nuclear testing site in 1946
131. Speedy
132. Clock face
133. Bibliographical note abbr.
134. Answer

135. Russian brew
136. Facile
137. Oilers game officials

DOWN

1. *SNL* Trump impersonator Baldwin
2. Roman king: _____ Pompilius
3. Judges' incidental opinions
4. Swimming, say
5. Some Greek letters
6. On _____ with
7. Meal
8. Lanky legume farmer?
9. Woodbine Racetrack entrant
10. Fills with joy
11. **Jeer**
12. Asian domestic servant
13. Our, in Saguenay
14. Femme fatale's alert?
15. Walked heavily
16. Ready for harvesting
17. Pasty-faced
18. Cry of glee
26. Turkey's pace?
28. Bog growth
33. Mosque officiants
34. Show derision
35. Skulls (var.)
36. Sickly
37. Sour
39. Help
40. Implore
41. *Peyton Place* actress Turner
42. Completed
43. Ernie's *Sesame Street* pal
46. Unreturnable tennis serves
48. **Book of Christian principles**
50. Sex drive
52. Cape Breton choir: The Men of the _____
54. Starbursts (var.)
55. 1990s Dan Aykroyd sitcom: _____ *Man*

57. Roman sun god
61. Hydrocarbon derivative
65. Sewing kit stick
66. YXE postings, for short
68. Japanese Expo '70 host city
70. Ottoman Empire coins
73. "May I _____ favour?"
74. Fatty substance in nerve cells
76. Commingle, ethnically
77. Bone related
78. Like Scrooge, initially
80. Preschooler
83. Alliterative farewell?
84. Surname of two US presidents
85. "You might be _____ something"

86. "Instantly" acronym
88. Wake for the day
90. Cutlery set component
94. Grow older
95. Lacking light
97. Nine-season Investigation Discovery show: _____ *Hunter*
101. Deciduous tree
104. Canadian-born *Blood Ties* star Dylan
107. Trickle out
108. French seaport
110. Wolfville NS university
112. Admirer

113. One of the Three Stooges
115. Geeks
116. In a frenetic manner
117. Arcs anagram
118. Ex-QB Drew who played for the Stamps and Redblacks
119. On
120. Kiss and _____
121. Czech, for example
123. Products sold at Murchie's in Victoria
124. US military org.
125. These wriggle underwater
127. Rile

SOLUTION ON PAGE 167

41 Hockey Hooey

Some fun with names

ACROSS

1. Religious belief
6. Capital of Peru
10. 1990s 24 Sussex occupant Chrétien
14. Oakville-born ex-NHL goalie Steve
19. Sound, to recording technician
20. Crucifix inscription
21. Grimm Brothers villain
22. "Rolling in the Deep" songstress
23. Candied spice in syrup
25. Old-style interjection of surprise
26. Freight
27. Lenin or Grant resting place
28. Northern Ontario city nickname: The _____
29. Significant, to a sergeant?
31. **Dances enjoyed by Oiler Gagner?**
32. Tycoon Onassis, et al.
34. Pumbaa's pal, in The Lion King franchise
35. Suffering from SAD
36. Pay a visit
39. One of 12 Biblical spies
40. Engine part
45. Some architectural mouldings
46. Even a bit
47. Palestinian territory: _____ Strip
48. Jamaican tangelo
49. Hang back
50. Condenses, at London Drugs?
54. Winnipeg landmark: Portage and _____
55. Islam religious leader
57. Has a meal
58. Shoe bottoms
59. Crosby of music and movies
60. **Seafood serving for Islander Clutterbuck?**
62. Biblical pariah
63. Tub scrubbing pad
65. "Uh-uh"

66. Her face launched a thousand ships
67. Banana skin
68. Mixes together
71. Readied a new road
72. **Cold medicine for former Blackhawk Eager?**
76. Sat in the passenger seat
77. Uses a crowbar
78. Average links scores
79. Pattaya language
80. Laptop brand
81. Stunned, at the Front
84. Merino mother
85. *HNIC* broadcast
86. Opposite of profit
87. Queries
88. Short Sumatran primate?
90. Elates
92. Subdues (with "down")
94. Calgary Roughneck's game stick
95. Not closed, to a bard
96. There are 10 of these a-leaping
97. Broadway flop, say
98. **Invention certificate for '80s Devil Verbeek?**
102. Disney deer
103. It starts and ends a Three Musketeers motto
104. Skewed perspective
108. Go _____ for the ride
109. CD word
110. *Baroness von Sketch Show* cast member
113. Student's eye part?
114. *Born Free* protagonist
115. Some tunas
116. Right, in Rivière-du-Loup
117. Chemical compound
118. Ink _____ test
119. Channel-_____ aux Basques NL
120. Keyboard type, for short

DOWN

1. Speedy
2. Camry or Corolla
3. The same (Lat.)
4. **Savoury serving for '60s Leaf Horton?**
5. Pig farmer's motorbike?
6. Some floor coverings, for short
7. Rademacher of *General Hospital*
8. GI's prepackaged grub
9. Canadian shoppers' loyalty program
10. **Menial task for ex-Avalanche Sakic?**
11. Prod the hens?
12. Subject of a 2005–06 Canadian government inquiry
13. Flanders, on *The Simpsons*
14. **Birds admired by '40s Ranger Colville?**
15. Garden of Eden male
16. Novi Sad resident
17. 1970s Olympic gymnastics great Korbut
18. Avant-gardists
24. The proof _____ pudding
30. Soul, in Chambly
31. Bodies, in olden days
33. One in a Valentine's bouquet
34. Presses down on
35. Doesn't do much
36. Baby's tummy trouble
37. South African lizard
38. Type of loophole
39. Ring-tailed animal
40. Provide a reception repast
41. *Corner Gas* recurring character Wes
42. One more time
43. Throw, forcefully
44. Slight colouring
46. Close shave
47. _____ Weston, Loblaws pitchman

51. Some tides
52. Serving no purpose
53. Ran with ease
56. Polite: Well-_____.
61. Trendy, in the '60s
62. Even-steven
63. Smell or touch
64. Petite green veggie
66. Flags down a cab in a storm?
67. Employees' extras
68. Town near Calgary: _____ Creek
69. In your area
70. Cause of swollen limbs
71. *The London Free* _____
72. Supports

73. Canadian actress Caroline, et al.
74. Signs of fatigue
75. Vassal
77. Call via Bell
78. Sits for a photograph
81. Caught some rest
82. Good golfers have a lower this
83. UVic res
89. **Break-in at the home of former Panther Niedermayer?**
91. **Computer attachment for ex-Ranger Maloney?**
92. **Pet for former Flame Kostopoulos?**
93. Queen Elizabeth held one at her coronation

94. AB CFB: _____ Lake
96. Dogie catcher
97. Sanctified, old style
98. A first word for baby
99. U of T reunion participant
100. Pith helmet
101. Oklahoma city
102. Canadian _____ of Rights
103. Arabic chieftain
105. Party to
106. Have _____ to pick
107. 15-D progeny
109. Cotillion attendee, for short
111. Santa's palindromic exclamation?
112. Psyche parts

42 Avian Airs

Hits that flew like an eagle

ACROSS

1. Tim Hortons coffee order size
6. One of 206 in the body
10. Yukon tourism slogan: Larger _____ Life
14. Quietly concealed, by the Dalmatian owner?
19. Blender button
20. Get misty-eyed (with "up")
21. It's a long story?
22. Blood of the gods, in mythology
23. Adjust car wheels
24. Opposed to, in the Ozarks
25. Anglican church member
27. Sad
30. Shortens
31. 2004 hit from Canada's Terri Clark: "Girls Lie _____"
32. You might travel in one to YYZ
34. Pyromaniac's felony
35. **Simon & Garfunkel covered this song in 1970**
41. Fruity French brandy
45. Show _____
46. Guitar type
48. Romanian money unit
49. Hollywood screen queen Gardner
50. Spills the beans
53. Deadly snake
54. Some Greek letters
56. Relating to do-re-mi, etc.
58. Walk like a peacock
59. Pageant contestant's ribbon
61. Mamie's White House mate
63. *A Fish Called Wanda* star Kevin
64. Choke
66. Usually
70. United States Athletic Decathlon (abbr.)
71. **1980 Police album track**
76. Strikebreaker
78. Rocky Nunavut island?
79. Despicable lawn layer in Leicester?
80. Chocolate substitute source
82. James Clavell book: _____-*Pan*
83. 1986 Luba track: "_____ in the Darkest Moments"
87. Most awful sausage?
91. Ring of colour in the eye
93. Canada's Julie Payette flew with this US org.
96. I, to Tiberius
97. Love, in Lachine
98. Mountain in Colorado
99. Rearward, on ship
101. Sarah Richardson does this on HGTV Canada
104. Start of a par five
105. The Parthenon was his idea
108. **1984 Prince smash**
111. Chewing tobacco brand
112. Canadian rowing icon Hanlan
113. Medicine Hat-to-Saskatoon dir.
114. Like Cirque du Soleil performers
118. In 2008, 134-A won an Olympic this for team jumping
125. Undeveloped artists?
127. Canadian McCrae's "In Flanders Fields"
128. Manicurist's filing board
129. 1958 hit: "Purple People _____"
130. Prefix with care
131. Pakistani's language
132. Killed with malice aforethought
133. Expanse of grass
134. Canadian equestrian Lamaze
135. Lincoln and Labrador
136. Herbivorous mammal

DOWN

1. Unwanted email
2. Shoe without a back
3. Ovule sheath
4. Smoothly, in music
5. Beatle John
6. Golden Olympic state for Canada's Marc Gagnon
7. _____-mutton
8. Pound with a hammer
9. Salves for healing, old style
10. Liquid medicine dosage amount (abbr.)
11. Former Royal Winnipeg Ballet dancer Evelyn
12. Ancient Greeks gathered here (var.)
13. Super, _____ British Columbia
14. **1976 Rick Dees and His Cast of Idiots novelty hit**
15. Petro-Canada pump number
16. Stairway to the Ganges
17. _____ *with the Wind*
18. Dog bowl scraps
26. Occurs afterwards
28. Musical piece finale
29. Hindu social classification
33. Tease a fisherman?
35. Wanes in intensity
36. Song with a cheerful cadence
37. Alternative to a tsar?
38. Some edible tubers
39. *From Russia With Love* antagonist Klebb
40. Little Newfoundlands
42. Suitcase, in Sherbrooke
43. The first Mrs. Trump
44. Dog-_____
47. Egyptian capital
51. Bogeyman, in a BC mountain range?
52. 1970s Canadian folk singer Rogers
55. Auk's kin
57. Electrical insulation compound
60. Alanis Morissette #1: "_____ in My Pocket"

62. Structural add-on
65. Gift of the _____
67. Self-Addressed Envelope (abbr.)
68. Plot for crops
69. Ambulance acronym
71. Profession
72. Decay
73. Chinese currency unit
74. Achilles' tale (with "The")
75. Cedar Rapids state
76. Canvasback kin
77. À la _____
81. **1968 Beatles *White Album* McCartney solo song**
84. Canadian Taylor who landed the first competitive triple Axel
85. Surprised interjection, old style

86. Dig in your heels: Say _____
88. US campus military program (abbr.)
89. Litigant, in civil court
90. Saskatoon-born NBAer Lyles
92. Solvent, while sailing?
94. Made on a Singer
95. Dull throbs
100. Afternoon break at the Empress?
102. Sophocles offering: _____ *Rex*
103. Bryan Adams hit: "Have You _____ Really Loved a Woman?"
106. Moires anagram
107. Wood fragment in your finger

109. Tangle in a trap
110. In good taste
114. Jungle animals
115. Gullet
116. Johnston who was Canada's first female premier (in BC)
117. Accra currency
119. Traditional tales
120. Sacred Hindu scriptures
121. Muse anagram
122. 2012 Alice Munro offering: _____ *Life*
123. Canadian Opera Company diva's moment
124. Canadian cat in the wild
126. As written, to Octavia

Wild Beauties...

43

Created by Mother Nature

ACROSS

1. Frothed
7. Governor General Johnston (2010–17)
12. Aries symbol
15. Sonny and Cher duet: "I Got You _____"
19. Accept without verifying veracity
20. Overact, on stage
21. Sprang from
23. **Mighty Ontario cascade**
25. Algonquian chief
26. Vodka and lime juice cocktail
27. Carol activity of 10 lords
29. 1960s war country, for short
30. Advanced liberal arts degree (abbr.)
33. Put on weight
35. River in Germany
36. Queen Elizabeth I named this Baffin Island peninsula: _____ Incognita
37. Azerbaijan shares its border
38. Pickle plant tank
39. Rose oil
41. Circulation stoppages
43. Elegant
45. Wrangle in the ring
47. *Silas Marner* scribe George
49. Senior sailor?
51. Lizard type
54. Sore swimmer's malady
58. South China _____
59. Tradesman, say
61. Bird found in every province and territory
63. Leon's or Shoppers Drug Mart
64. Snow or soft hail pellet
66. With the bow, to the cellist
67. Moulded
68. Ontario Waterpower Association (abbr.)
69. **Azure Banff National Park body of water**
72. Prince Edward Island symbol: _____ oak
73. Leaves at a flower's base
75. Short imperial measurement
76. *Nineteen Eighty-four* setting
78. Type of willow tree
79. See 51-A
80. Plant axis part
81. Good times on the TSX
84. Sealtest manufacturing facilities
86. Nest built on cliffs (var.)
88. Virtuous model?
90. Carole or Michael Middleton, vis-à-vis William
92. Pert retort
94. Lump or bump
95. Reverberated
98. Group of concubines
101. Explosive AC/DC song?
103. Solidify, like mousse
104. Photographed a marksman?
105. Hindu people or language
107. In the buff
109. Synthetic rubber
110. Mauna _____
111. "Here!"
113. Junk or jetsam
115. Bother or burden
117. **Trio of peaks near Canmore**
122. Rich, spicy wine (var.)
123. Blow, like Eyjafjallajökull
124. Four-season ABC dramedy: _____ Howser, M.D.
125. Take instructions without complaint
126. Be behind in payments
127. Dos and _____
128. Attach to a tuber?

DOWN

1. Dionne Warwick hit: "Do You Know the Way to _____ Jose"
2. 23rd Greek letter
3. Neighbour of Canada (abbr.)
4. Some street crimes
5. Communicate via the Web
6. Suffix with pachy
7. Wins, like the Canadiens
8. Famed Italian violin-making family
9. Loudness abbr.
10. "_____ all end in tears"
11. Carcross, in the Yukon
12. Breathe
13. At full speed, at sea
14. Milk of _____
15. Sound of a door slam
16. Addresses wrongdoings
17. Censure
18. Serous fluid swellings
22. Harangue an old Hanoverian?
24. Pond scum piece
28. Triumphant exclamation
30. Japanese cooking pastes
31. Working-class citizen in 76-A
32. **British Columbia archipelago once known as Queen Charlotte Islands**
34. Round Indian bread
36. She gained infamy as a World War I spy
38. Fine parchments
40. Greek mythology ruse
42. Set ablaze
44. Noted California valley
46. In a manner of speaking?
48. Summer month astrological sign
50. Goof on a proof
52. Bait
53. Screens in a porch, say
55. **Scenic tip of a Nova Scotia island**

56. Went apace
57. With no _____ in sight
60. Like Alfred Hitchcock films or Stephen King novels
62. Work with Jim Carrey?
65. 1960s US protest type
67. Caulking serves as this
68. Female bear, in Bologna
70. Distasteful
71. Retain
73. Personal trainer's pride and joy
74. Father, Son and Holy Ghost, e.g.
77. Fiddling emperor
79. German Studies Association (abbr.)
82. She wants a cracker

83. Tackle box tying line
85. Mythical city of gold
87. Bard's metrical foot
89. Insurance company employee (var.)
91. 1970s CTV variety show: *The Pig and* _____
93. King and Queen, in Toronto
95. Former name of a Commonwealth Stadium home team CFLer
96. Infantile angel
97. Gravelly voiced
99. Affirmative for 49-A
100. Spouted off
102. Birds' beaks

106. Order more *Chatelaine*
108. Quite competent
109. Wood Buffalo National Park herd
111. School grp. that raises funds
112. Robert Burns poem: "Comin' _____ the Rye"
114. RCMP spectacle: Musical _____
116. Slick, like a sidewalk
118. 1984 Bryan Adams chart-topper: "_____ to You"
119. Psyche
120. Canada won 22 medals at these 2016 games
121. See 103-A

A-simile-ation

In the animal kingdom

44

ACROSS

1. Is feeling unwell
5. Saskatchewan Library Association (abbr.)
8. Parliament passed this in 2014: Fair Elections _____
11. Liable to change one's mind
17. Artery blockage
18. Magazine page space measurements
20. Tim Hortons hazelnut treat
21. Arizona city
22. Equestrian's seated position
23. **Busy critter?**
24. Summer seasons, in Shawinigan
25. Creole cuisine treats
27. Gather at Montreal's Notre-Dame Basilica?
28. Unhappy crowd's sound
30. **Sick Shih Tzu?**
31. Long-time CBC show: *Hymn* _____
33. Too hefty
35. Initial notes, in a scale
36. Filled up at Esso
41. _____ & Perrins
42. Wayson Choy 2004 Giller Prize contender: *All _____ Matters*
44. Weaving threads
45. Hokkaido people
46. **Elated avian?**
48. Old MacDonald's attire
50. Young haddock
51. Pretentious, at the AGO?
52. Bouquet that engages the olfactory sense?
53. Some are precious?
54. Canadian chess grandmaster Yanofsky, et al.
56. **Sly mammal?**
57. Dixie cornbread dish
58. Aspects, in astrology
61. CERB word

63. Calculates a total
67. Adele song: "Rumour _____"
68. Precede in time
69. **Brave big cat?**
70. "If it _____ broke…"
71. Records clerk, say
72. Mafia moniker: _____ Nostra
74. US Rx overseer
75. Bring separate parts together
77. Cyst
78. Clear mist from the windshield
80. American fiction author Philip
81. **Blind flyer?**
82. 1952 Crosby/Hope film: *Road to* _____
83. Quench a thirst
87. "Come up and see me _____"
90. Casino numbers
93. **Angry insect?**
95. Rugby set piece
96. Cascade, in Banff National Park
97. Geological epoch
98. Give over for safekeeping
99. Have feelings of jealousy
100. Deceived, in winter?
101. _____-boom-bah
102. Lacking confidence
103. Red eye cause

DOWN

1. Top spot
2. 2014 Clare Mackintosh novel: _____ *You Go*
3. Become discouraged, in romance?
4. Period of inactivity
5. Kitchen island marble tops
6. Deputy premier of Quebec Thériault (2014–17)
7. Snakebite remedies
8. Scotch production process
9. Give up the reins
10. Bloodsucking African insect
11. Family Day mo. in some provinces

12. 2012 movie: _____: *Continental Drift*
13. **Happy mollusc?**
14. Australasian shrubby pepper
15. Untruths
16. Messes up, morally
19. TO CFL team
26. Uses a sieve
29. Workplace for Canada's Ryan Reynolds
32. Some Greek consonants
33. Earthenware vessel
34. **Ravenous grizzly?**
35. Swiss town that hosts the annual World Economic Forum
36. Took it easy
37. Pertaining to milk
38. Tax shelter for some Canadians: Locked-in Retirement Account (abbr.)
39. Lone ketone?
40. Firecrackers that fail to fire
43. Practises skills
44. Dray driver
47. Metamorphic rock silicate
49. Scotiabank Arena games official
50. Short title for Mike Duffy
53. Dust particles
55. Wager at Century Mile, in Edmonton
57. Equipment item for Bugaboos rock climbing
58. Bangkok resident
59. It does this a lot in parts of BC
60. "_____ She Lovely"
61. Hiding places
62. Tongue-in-cheek?
64. See 102-A
65. **Dead flightless avian?**
66. Unforeseen obstacle in a Yukon village?
68. Italian-made cars
71. And back again

73. 2015 Dora Mavor Moore Award-winning actor Kawa
76. 1960s Canadian skiing star Nancy
77. Tree found in several provinces: _____ birch
79. Runs off to wed

81. Inclinations
82. National Ballet School of Canada co-founder Oliphant
83. Females
84. **Batty bird?**
85. Anagram for Cora?

86. Perceived
88. Very short skirt
89. Slop
91. US folk hero Crockett
92. Terrier type
94. Canadian film director Kotcheff

SOLUTION ON PAGE 168

45 Notable '90s NHL Rookies

Calder Trophy winners with a Canadian connection

ACROSS

1. Southern Africa grassland (var.)
6. Lingerie model's faux pas?
10. Altered shotgun type
18. Middle Eastern leader (var.)
19. Timbre
20. Freshwater flatworms
21. **Selänne whose NHL run began with the Jets (1992–93 season)**
22. German industrial enclave
23. In a preoccupied manner
24. German iris
25. 1981 Iron Maiden instrumental song: "The _____ of March"
26. Quick turn in the pool
27. Theologies, for short
28. Expel
29. He ruled after Claudius
30. Develop after
32. Activity on HGTV shows
35. Ensconced
39. Japanese parliamentary body
40. Beasts that haul burdens
42. St. Patrick's Day mo. in NL
43. Wrote without care
48. Teens' school social events
49. Flow from Mount Pinatubo
50. Infants who arrive early (var.)
51. Like a paltry pate
52. Sea nymph, in mythology
54. 96-A, for example
55. Game invented in Canada: _____ Pursuit
58. Sprightly, like a gymnast
59. International social welfare grp. since 1946
61. Its members include Iran and Iraq (abbr.)
62. Against the current, on the Columbia?
64. Brown or white grain
65. Party hearty
67. Dabbles in, old style
68. *Has Anybody Seen My _____?*
69. Sharpened a blade, say
70. 2019 novel from Irish–Canadian author Emma Donoghue
71. Coiled stovetop part
73. Redeeming quality of a Monaco princess?
80. Bone cavities
82. Anagram of 25-A
83. Cellist's bow coating
84. Cold War country (abbr.)
87. Local Area Network (abbr.)
88. Young guys
89. Growing older and wiser
90. Boiling mad
92. Suffix with narc or psych
93. **Forsberg who started his career with the Quebec Nordiques (1994–95 season)**
94. Card game requiring perseverance?
95. Johnnycake, by another name
96. At first sight, to Caesar: _____ facie
97. Some TTC riders
98. Units of work
99. Black tea type

DOWN

1. US president who rejects legislation
2. Come out from hiding
3. Looked at wolfishly
4. Downfall
5. Has faith in TD Bank?
6. Most stretchy, like pizza cheese
7. Increased the volume
8. Receive a legacy
9. Human being
10. Shovel for PI Sam?
11. Absence of bodily pigmentation
12. Hornets' home
13. Belleville to Ottawa compass pt.
14. **Alfredsson who became a Senators stalwart (1995–96 season)**
15. Treats for Rover
16. Toronto International _____ Festival
17. Author Weldon and actress Wray
31. Increases the ante
33. Monty Python's *Life of Brian* co-star Eric
34. Bruschetta seasoning
36. Loving
37. Quibbler, in Connecticut
38. Pencil ends
41. Coca-Cola or Pepsi, in Pittsburgh
43. Binge, at The Brick
44. Skull related
45. Eyepiece part
46. Priest's linen square
47. "I Wouldn't Want to Lose Your Love" Canadian band: April _____
48. **Bure who served his first season with the Canucks (1991–92)**
49. Permissible, under the law
51. Two-legged animals
53. Surname of a famous Canadian wrestling family
56. Drift without a destination in mind
57. Emits light
60. Description of COVID-19 health care workers
63. Stab of hunger
66. Doorway
67. Slipping or sliding
69. Mother clucker

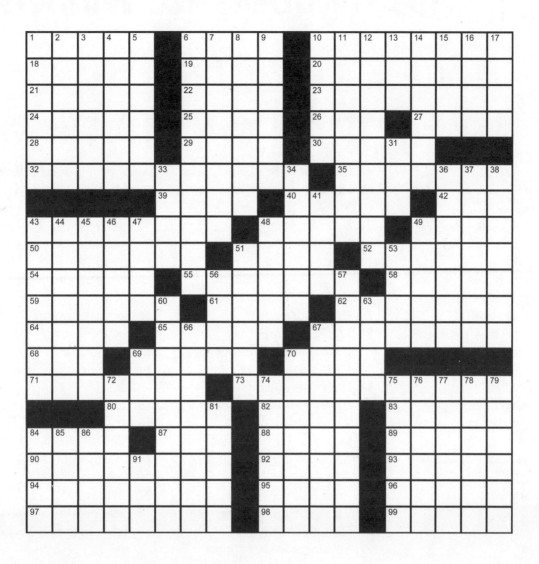

70. Air Canada pilot, say

72. Montreal-born Brodeur who started his career with the Devils (1993–94 season)

74. Tilted

75. Italian after-dinner drink

76. Annual Canadian tennis tournament: _____ Cup

77. "_____ written"

78. Entertainment awards organization: Academy of Canadian _____ & Television

79. Theoretical trace of memory in the brain

81. Celestial beings above Beaupré?

84. It delivers mail to American residents (abbr.)

85. Canadian politician's place in parliament

86. _____ new world record

91. "_____ fly through the air with the greatest of ease…"

SOLUTION ON PAGE 169

46 — 1990s Nobel Prize Winners

Tops in their decade

ACROSS

1. Back end of a bunny
5. Activity for HGTV's Scott MacGillivray
9. 2000 Joni Mitchell album: _____ *Sides Now*
13. They're scrambled for breakfast
17. Arm bone for Luna?
18. Layer of the eye
19. Sword used in Olympic duels
20. Peter, Paul and Mary, say
21. Non-verbal okays
22. Moistens, in the morning?
23. Find fault with
25. Western-style hats
27. _____ fibrillation
28. Donkey's brethren
29. Land, to a lawyer
30. Dalhousie University alum
31. Direction from Rouyn to Val-d'Or
33. And more, for short
35. PC's "insides"
36. Sonny and Cher hit: "The _____ Goes On"
37. Swims in a reef
40. Where Jews pray
42. Circlet for a cherub
44. Most powerful
46. Small, in Saguenay
48. Manouevre for a Canadian Snowbird
50. Greek letter
51. Bangladesh currency
52. **Palestinian leader Arafat (1994)**
54. Brad Jacobs served as this on Canada's golden Sochi curling team
56. Acronym on an ambulance
58. Hamilton-born ex-NHL goalie Emery
59. Like carnivores' food?
63. Strange
66. You might achieve one at Carleton (abbr.)
67. Currency in Belgium
68. **South African politician Mandela (1993)**
72. Neil Young song: "_____ Hank to Hendrix"
74. House addition
76. Henry's second Catherine
78. Darkish pantyhose colour
79. Cosmetics lotion
82. The RCAF and RCN participated in this milestone 1944 invasion
84. Highlands slope
85. Strait in BC's Gulf Islands
86. Reprehensible
88. Sauce for chicken wings
90. Advanced deg. from U of T
91. Crime scene substance, for short
92. River blocking barrier
93. Baby's temporary caregiver
95. CRA deadline mo.
97. Rustling skirt description
99. Voluntary Jewish abstainer
102. Ballroom dance
104. Trig function
105. "_____ I care!"
106. Thick book
107. Kosher store
108. Boat name in *Jaws*
109. Campground shelter
110. Crackle and Pop's pal
111. Pastoral scene poem (var.)
112. Take a surreptitious glance
113. Diabetes Canada, et al.

DOWN

1. Vancouver and Edmonton newspapers
2. Blood mass
3. Sells for less than a competitor
4. Try a nibble
5. **Canadian chemist Marcus (1992)**
6. Happening at some future time
7. Like some CTV shows
8. Federal government prog. for retirees
9. **Canadian physicist Brockhouse (1994)**
10. Like performances by Canada's Étienne Dupuis
11. Somewhat warm
12. Mate of Zeus
13. Addis Ababa is here (abbr.)
14. Northwest Territories' largest lake
15. Cotton seed separating machines
16. Grumpy gardeners, in Gloucester?
24. Vote in an MLA
26. Cul-de-_____
27. Go grey
32. Business attire for him or her
33. Catch a glimpse of an espionage agent?
34. Jazz classic: "Take _____ Train"
36. Bet taker at the track
37. **Israeli politician Peres (1994)**
38. "_____ silly question…"
39. Remain in one place, like Rover
41. Speech problem
43. Shed weight
45. Indian cooking ingredient
47. Semester at Seneca College
49. Poster of a sexy siren
53. **Canadian economist Mundell (1999)**
55. Annual Calgary event cancelled in 2020: Stampede _____
57. Mincemeat recipe ingredient
60. *A _____ of Two Cities*
61. Venetian blind part
62. 40 × 60 cm cake type

63. Murders, Mafia style
64. Mild expletive
65. Genre of CBC's *The Detectives*
69. Certain type of party giver?
70. Sashimi fish
71. Scholarship criterion
73. Not very nice
75. In an extravagant manner
77. Glow

80. 2006 Oscars best picture winner directed by Canada's Paul Haggis
81. **Russian president Gorbachev (1990)**
83. **Israeli prime minister Rabin (1994)**
87. Grazing field, in Felixstowe
89. Harper Valley fundraisers?
92. Cubed carrots, say
93. Capture

94. Greek Muse of poetry
95. Treads the boards at Toronto's Royal Alexandra
96. Loudness measurement unit
98. Dry riverbed in Africa
100. Glass bell sound
101. Small amphibians
103. Stout-stalked mushroom
104. Spinning toy

SOLUTION ON PAGE 169

47 Share and Share Alike

Mountains between neighbours

ACROSS

1. Sudden sharp feelings
6. Crack due to dryness
10. Calgary Co-op store section
14. Calgary Zoo exhibit mammal
19. Mites, for example
20. It's across the Ottawa from Ottawa
21. _____ Bator
22. Sign at a CBC studio
23. Like washed-out highways
25. **Between Yukon and Alaska**
27. Soak up again
28. Receptacle for cigarette butts
30. Data
31. Country lane
33. President Eisenhower, colloquially
34. Bundle of nerves?
36. Jab
39. Delighted
42. Collar fringes
46. Not together
48. 1978 Billy Joel single: "Only the Good _____ Young"
49. 2014 Coldplay song: "_____ Full of Stars"
51. Goal
52. Mandarin orange type
55. Witches' midnight gathering
59. Take _____ to
61. Cheer for FC Barcelona?
62. Riser in a church
64. Ceasefire
65. Chest parts (var.)
66. Central government control political system
69. _____-high frequency
71. Lumber cutter
72. Plague of your existence?
74. **Between British Columbia and Alberta**
77. Cincinnati MLB team
78. Claims against property
80. Truckers' rigs
81. Battle of the boats?
83. Ring of colour, in botany
85. Tendon
87. "There ain't no _____ thing as a free lunch"
88. However, in brief
91. Leaf's central vein
92. Sacred beetle, in ancient Egypt
94. Silenced
96. Sushi fish
97. A ponytail hangs here
99. Lyricist Gershwin
101. Substitute's spot
102. Shoddy goods, say
104. Hadfield and Bondar, once
110. Course of study at Carleton University
111. "Abide with Me," for one
113. Canada provides this to Ethiopia and Haiti
114. Narcissist's trait
116. Event for Canada's Andre De Grasse
119. Provided proof
122. Least ready for picking
126. **Between British Columbia and Alaska**
128. Continuous urging
130. Taunt a hairstylist?
131. It holds old cinematic film
132. Cast a ballot for your MP
133. Extend one's house
134. Tree that trembles in the wind
135. Wonky
136. This month follows Shevat
137. Takes a breather

DOWN

1. Canada's Revell and Wilkes, at the Innsbruck Olympics
2. Highest point
3. California wine valley
4. Tongs
5. Fraidy-cat
6. River Styx ferryman
7. **See 25-A**
8. The entire enchilada?
9. "Guilty," for example
10. Eliza of *Buffy the Vampire Slayer*
11. Bringer of joy
12. Bears' shelter
13. Guts
14. Garden shed tool
15. Taking the place (of)
16. If there's no this, there's no gain
17. "La Vie en Rose" vocalist Edith
18. "_____ I've heard"
24. _____ loser
26. Ontario-born former NHLer McGinn
29. Dog trainer's command
32. Throne room platform
35. Lovers' secret assignations
36. Horse breed: Peruvian _____
37. Gemstone found in BC
38. **See 126-A**
40. Moss for mulching
41. Earls and Milestones
43. **Between Yukon and British Columbia**
44. Wearing flippers, say
45. Blurs
47. Biggest Canadian Brass instrument
50. _____ in "kangaroo"
53. 1939 James Mason movie: *I _____ Murderer*
54. See 135-A
56. Strong-as-an-ox guy
57. It might be 40 watts
58. Canada's William Shatner, for example
60. Céline Dion's *Titanic* song: "My _____ Will Go On"
63. Calculates taxation rates
67. Canada's Jon Vickers was one
68. Copycat

70. Canadian polling firm: _____ Reid Institute
72. Assigned censure
73. More light and bright
75. Rock & Roll Hall of Fame 2018 inductee Simone
76. Per person
79. Popular toy since the 1940s
82. Ergo
84. Alberta Band Association (abbr.)
86. Old-style farm cart
89. 1987 Bryan Adams song: "_____ of the Night"
90. Woodbine attendees' numbers
93. Hillside in the Highlands
95. Annual Alberta event: Calgary _____
98. She opened a troublesome box
100. See 25-A
103. Tre Stelle product
105. Not as loose
106. How the millionaire's home is decorated?
107. Bard's creation
108. More stylish
109. Macdonald and Laurier titles
112. Parent's piehole?
115. Raga instrument
116. _____-tat-tat
117. Affirmatives, on the bridge
118. Early hit from Canada's Beau-Marks: "_____ Your Hands"
120. *Property Brothers* realtor Scott
121. Opera queen
123. Finishes up
124. Tommy Douglas, by birth
125. Viola Desmond banknotes
127. NHLer who plays for OTT
129. Doze (with "off")

48 Instruments of Song

Tunes from the Top 40

ACROSS

1. Politician in some provinces (abbr.)
4. Canadian retailer: M&M Food _____
10. Canada provides aid to this Caribbean nation
14. Clerical garments
18. Deplaned
20. Like cryptic knowledge
21. Slanted type (abbr.)
22. Annual Gulf of St. Lawrence event: _____ hunt
23. U of C enrollees
25. Protuberances
26. Relinquish the reins
27. Buckthorn tree
28. Unsteady on one's feet
30. Waver, near the privet?
31. Swedish money
33. Place pictures on the wall
34. Atlas page box, for example
35. *Deliverance* **theme song**
41. Sever
43. Quebec-born author Hébert
44. Nest on a cliff (var.)
45. 1989 k.d. lang release: *Absolute Torch and _____*
47. Enjoy a day at Sunshine Village in Alberta
50. Former TLC show: *Toddlers & _____*
53. Breakaway religious groups
55. Got an RRSP at TD
57. And so forth (abbr.)
58. Hairstyling product
60. A Roosevelt, informally
62. Ontario's Highway 407 is this: Express _____ Route
63. Keeps in custody
65. Canadian Forces _____
66. With a chill in the air
67. **The Byrds had a big hit with this Bob Dylan tune**
73. Outrigger canoes (var.)
76. Pronoun for a twosome
77. Clinks
81. Gal from Gretna Green
82. In memoriam notices, for short
84. Ophthalmologist's instrument component
87. Janitor's unruly head of hair?
88. Tumult
90. Fragrant rootstock
92. Belgrade nation
94. Ontario place: Sault _____ Marie
95. Stupid, in the thicket?
97. It follows *Hockey Night in Canada*: _____ *Hours*
99. Lees anagram
100. Secret society in China
101. **Linda Ronstadt's first hit (with Stone Poneys)**
105. Calgary Stampede rodeo bovine
108. Seed enclosure
110. Faint
111. Tutu fabric
112. Wine drinkers' glasses
116. Incentive
120. Frequent footnote abbr.
121. Mis-hit at Rogers Centre
122. Treatment of light and dark, to an artist
124. Plexus of nerve cells
125. _____ *meridiem*
126. Somewhat, to newsman Dan?
127. Make booties or scarves
128. Literary adverb
129. Notable historical periods
130. Sense of misgiving
131. Burdened beast

DOWN

1. J. Trudeau government cabinet minister Garneau
2. Answer to a judge's question
3. "When _____ fly!"
4. Staid lady
5. Plan in advance
6. It used to sell records: _____ Victor
7. 18th-C. German philosopher Immanuel
8. Prefix meaning "within"
9. Nuclear _____ Ban Treaty
10. Avid moviegoer
11. Motorist's one-eighty
12. **1986 Billy Joel single**
13. Quebec CFL team moniker
14. Climb up Grouse Mountain
15. English city
16. Scouts Canada award
17. Frequent Canadian precipitation
19. Funny reminder?
24. Indian ladies' garment
29. Brief "notwithstanding"
30. Gate part
32. Bottomless pit
35. Passé
36. Bring together in matrimony
37. Recreate a Civil War battle, say
38. Mighty Olympian
39. Pleasant place on the French Riviera?
40. Air Transat aircraft
42. One of the deadly sins
46. Stretch out an opening
47. Knob on a church organ
48. Underwater plant
49. Do nothing: Stand _____ by
51. Some African chieftains
52. Plural "are," *en français*
54. Saskatoon newspaper: *The _____ Phoenix*
56. Smell really bad
59. CDA finished second to this country at the 1960 Olympics hockey tournament
61. Edugyan who won the Giller Prize in 2011 and 2018

64. Entertain
65. 1970 Guess Who hit: "_____ Rider"
66. Shell's inner surface
68. Agitates
69. On the other hand…
70. Roughly
71. Pipe with a bend
72. Extinct birds of New Zealand
73. Too
74. Very engrossed
75. 1975 Wimbledon winner Arthur
78. Earth-coloured pigment
79. WWI infantryman in France
80. Tic
82. Pizza Hut appliance
83. **1971 Top Ten T. Rex recording**

84. German opera composer Carl
85. List references for an essay
86. They might be addicted to the Internet?
89. Hold dear to one's heart
91. British D-Day aerial attack force (abbr.)
93. Gretchen Wilson won a country vocal performance Grammy for this: "_____ Woman"
96. Munchies
98. Updates the electrical
100. CIBC employee
102. Not feeling well
103. 2020 song released by Neil Young: "We Don't Smoke It _____"

104. Toddlers' spinning toys
105. Austere, at the back of the ship?
106. Lesson receiver
107. Fill with happiness
109. Air Canada magazine: en_____
113. Light brown colour
114. Alanis Morrissette song: "Closer _____ You Might Believe"
115. Seti burial location?
117. Fishy flavour for the cat
118. American historical fiction writer Leon
119. Drunkards
121. US gov. aviation org.
123. "I've found it!"

Illustrious Alumni

49

McGill grads

ACROSS

1. Canada Dry product: _____ soda
5. Dismounted after a Woodbine race
9. Calgary CFLer, for short
14. Bivouacs
19. River in northeastern England
20. Raja's partner
21. Big hit, at Rogers Centre
22. Moulding type
23. Service at Toronto's St. Michael's Cathedral Basilica
24. Blue Jay's glove
25. Mirror reflection
26. Cut more off a log
27. **US songwriter who earned a Bachelor of Music**
30. *Survivor* network
32. Get a move on, rapidly
33. This covers lots of ground?
34. Chemical suffix
35. Have a goal to scale a steeple?
37. Go off the deep _____
38. Parliament passed this in 1985: Access to Information _____
41. Simon & Garfunkel 1970 cover: "El Condor _____"
43. Clock setting in Greenwich?
45. Broad _____ long
47. Retail chain that originated in Canada?
49. Thin clouds
51. Like a German brothers' fairy tale?
52. Zilch
55. Canadian singer/musician Nova
56. Screech
57. Commotions
58. Flying saucers, et al.
59. Rice type
61. Think about at home?
63. Whiles away time
64. Explode
66. Shania Twain song: "Whose Bed Have Your Boots _____ Under?"
67. Genre of Canada's Stephen Leacock
68. Tolkien monster
71. **Basketball inventor who graduated in phys. ed.**
75. 1970s self-actualization program (abbr.)
76. Pen the hens?
78. Bang a "piggy"
79. Eaten anagram
81. North African coast capital
82. Tracing grid
85. Some hot beverages
89. Destination for tourists in India
90. CTV reality show: *The Amazing _____ Canada*
91. Outdoor cushion fabric
93. Tear down
94. AB-born McAmmond who played for the Flames, Sens and Oilers
95. Track shape, in speed skating
96. Submission to Intact Insurance
97. Canadian fashion magazine that went online in 2017
98. Spot's credos?
100. Instrument played at 2-D
101. Shakespeare play: *King _____*
103. Brief sleep
104. Jazz great Calloway
106. Virgil's Trojan War hero
108. Feminine pronoun
110. Close friend
112. Internet acronym
113. Charged particle
114. **Prime minister who achieved a B.A.**
120. All-in-good-fun celebrity bashing event
122. Sky-blue shade
124. Poi source
125. Quaker _____
126. Host of 120-A
127. Contemporary of Kant
128. "Let's go!"
129. Stage set piece
130. Largest city in Senegal
131. Growl
132. Whacks with an axe
133. Vipers

DOWN

1. Straighten bed-head
2. Traditional Hawaiian party
3. Canada's 1972 Summit Series foe (abbr.)
4. Outdoes competitors
5. Ocean squadron
6. Secular
7. Flying, like a WestJet jet
8. Business magnate
9. Actor LaBeouf
10. Tabby's promiscuous owner?
11. Asian childminders
12. BC-raised *Agnes of God* actress Tilly
13. Extreme attention to detail
14. Lace-up lingerie garment
15. Greeting in old Rome
16. **Habitat 67 was an adaptation of his thesis**
17. Unadorned
18. Planted seeds
28. Wallops
29. Regenerated, like an octopus' lost tentacle
31. Some hats have these
36. "Ahem"
38. Baghdad resident
39. Bubbly beverage
40. Wool weight units
42. Split over doctrinal differences
44. **Star NHL coach who graduated in phys. ed.**

46. Some northern Canada people
48. Ottawa landmark: _____ of the Unknown Soldier
50. Purge (with "of")
51. Strong winds
53. Busybodies?
54. Valuable thing
56. TTC commuter's grip
60. With gravy, in cuisine
62. Necklace worn at 2-D
63. Bangkok currency units
65. Precedent-setting legal action
67. Blemish
68. Eightsome
69. Quebec city: Rivière-_____
70. **Columnist who achieved an M.A.**

72. Dofasco makes this
73. Wimple wearer
74. "A stitch _____…"
77. Burton Cummings plays this
80. 1940s Governor General of Canada: _____ of Athlone
82. Subtropical region grasslands
83. Least healthy
84. Ale anagram
86. Round Indian bread item
87. Old Testament book
88. Leak out
90. Juliet's love
92. Document title, on a hard drive
97. Woman's title, in Leipzig
99. Spat
100. Mercenary moneylender

102. Chefs' wear
104. Like some Schneiders deli products
105. Smell
107. Mint family plant
109. It connects truck and trailer
111. Drug for those with Parkinson's
115. Unload shares on the TSX
116. Suppose, in days of yore
117. Rabbit _____
118. On the summit
119. It delivers mail to American homes (abbr.)
121. 11-time Juno nominees: Great Big _____
123. Peaceful, colloquially

SOLUTION ON PAGE 170

50

The Spies Have It

Go undercover with this one

ACROSS

1. The scoop
5. Aussie rockers since 1973
9. Form a mental image
15. Seize
19. 1985 Michael J. Fox film: _____ *Wolf*
20. Montreal-born Caroline who starred in *Sabrina the Teenage Witch*
21. Indian antelope
22. Scowl (var.)
23. Worry about serving goulash?
24. Mongrel
25. Pub
26. Bone in the arm
27. Cheap, to an egg farmer?
30. Delicately built
32. Not factual
35. Blood flow inhibitor
36. New Mexico or New York
38. Soft leather fabrics
39. Keyboarding mistakes
41. Tenets
46. Feeling of deep dread
47. AA or small
48. Indian Ocean arm
51. Soothing ointments
53. Comfy car
54. Niverville or Neepawa, in Manitoba
55. 2008 Jodie Foster movie: _____ *Island*
59. Competed
60. Pillowcases
61. Gently drop bait on the water
62. California NHL city of Regina's Ryan Getzlaf
64. 1980s cop show: _____ *Vice*
65. WWII Canadian soldier's headgear
68. Atlantic haddock (var.)
69. **Spy concerned with stats?**
71. Tried

72. Bun or braid
73. Supports a spine?
74. Went back on your word
75. "Flip the page" abbreviation
76. Join in matrimony
77. Molson lather
79. Dashi-based soup
80. Tugboat horn noise
82. Berry, to a botanist
83. Cut off a chunk
85. Unfettered form of government
87. You are, to a Spaniard
88. Prohibit, legally
93. Diana Krall, for one
94. Perfume compound
96. Church tables
97. Russian–Canadian Evgeny Bareev excels at this
100. Flavour favoured by cats
101. Oblique parallelograms
102. Croatian capital
106. Not content to stay in one place
109. Sword for a French fencer
110. Lacking scruples
112. Noon, in Saguenay
113. Long-time American film critic Pauline
117. Greek letter
118. Andrews Sisters hit: "_____ Woogie Bugle Boy"
119. He preceded McGuinty as Ontario's premier
120. *The _____ Duckling*
121. Long-time hockey rival of CDA
122. Hayseeds
123. Dispatched an email
124. Place for a pig?

DOWN

1. _____ now or never
2. Ottawa Senator Craig Anderson guards this
3. TD Bank charge
4. Advancing ahead

5. Multitudes of ants?
6. Long-time Toronto radio station name
7. **Crime solving spy?**
8. Generated a reaction in the chemistry lab
9. Wholly, to Hadrian
10. *The Mask* star Cameron
11. They help Santa
12. **Spy concerned with secrets?**
13. Sticky paving substance
14. Theory of Relativity scientist
15. Use paste
16. _____ Up the Rim to Win
17. Your cousin's mom, to you
18. Scottish hillside
28. Michael Bublé sometimes records these
29. Stupid stoners?
31. Southern hemisphere constellation
32. CDA trading partner
33. Cloister sister
34. Ewe's young 'un
37. Mahmoud who succeeded Yasser
40. Struts
42. Together, on a bike?
43. Mouth-to-stomach connectors
44. Small number
45. Bay at the northwestern tip of Vancouver Island: _____ Josef
47. See 30-A
49. 500-sheet paper packages
50. Fess up
52. Notice, in Navarre
55. Knowlton _____
56. Indigenous Peruvian
57. Annual folk festival in Ontario
58. Long version of a US freight weight?
60. Aussie terrier
61. Notable primatologist Fossey
63. Caribbean taro

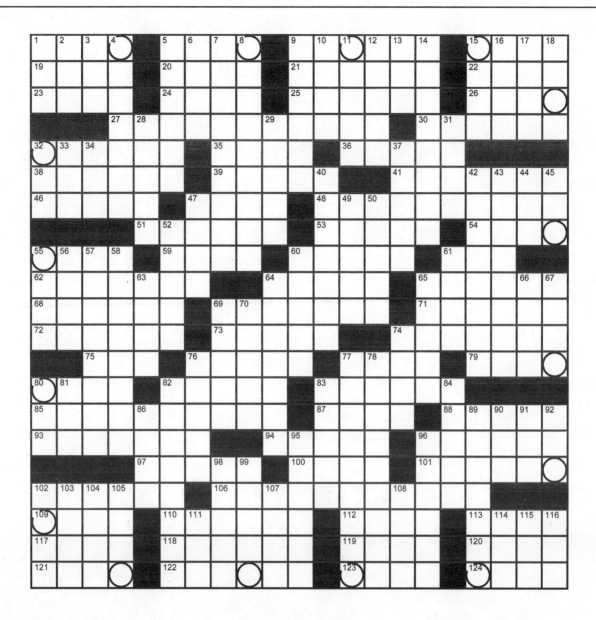

64. Popular 1970s decorative art
65. Céline recorded this type of song for *Titanic*
66. Long time
67. Kerfuffle
69. Calculators made of beads (var.)
70. Some law enforcement officials
74. Sings like Canada's Michie Mee
76. Dull finish
77. Justin and Pierre, for example
78. **Working spy?**
80. Spigot
81. Traditional Japanese sash

82. Southern Africa primate
83. Abated
84. Indian capital: New _____
86. Head pests
89. Buy lots of shares?
90. Plaid cap
91. British coronation crown jewel: Sovereign's _____
92. See 117-A
95. Steps over a fence
96. Mary or Christopher Pratt
98. **Scary spy?**
99. RCMP members' attire: Red _____

102. East Asian ox
103. Calgary Zoo animals
104. Comprehends
105. It's behind you?
107. Service type provided by CP
108. Biblical utopia
111. Barnyard bellow
114. TO attraction for art aficionados
115. Alberta reserve: _____ Island National Park
116. Strong cleanser

Follow the circled letters to reveal the theme: __ __ __ __ __ __ __ __ __ __ __ __ __ __ __ __

51

Streetwise...

In Canadian cities

ACROSS

1. GIs' munitions
5. Advantages
10. Elect your MPP
14. Savoury taste, in Tokyo
19. Forcible government overthrow
20. Showed again, on CTV
21. Big Australian birds
22. Split, old style
23. David Suzuki, for one
26. _____ Bear Lake
27. Terminus
28. Canadian Aboriginal AIDS Network (abbr.)
29. Paces for ponies
30. **"Biggest Little Street in North America" in St. John's**
31. Oscar-winning Canadian documentary: *If You Love This* _____
33. Three-piece suit parts
35. Greek cheers
37. City in Italy: _____ Remo
38. Fork point
39. Opposed to, to Li'l Abner
41. *I've Got a* _____
43. Confined (with "up")
44. Suffix with bed or home
46. Plenty of used cars for sale?
48. Phone button that lets you call back
50. Like some pens and lighters
54. Takes a toke
58. Arborists don't work above this?
61. Gripes
63. Escaped
64. Attempts again
65. Iris components
67. **Long street in Toronto**
68. Flue fleck
69. **Skinny street in Victoria's Chinatown**
74. Grass moisture
75. **Shopping and dining avenue in Edmonton**
78. Intersection sign
79. Nerve impulse cell, in Sussex
82. Introverts
84. Fills a hold with cargo
86. Argued logically
87. Breastbone related
89. White burgundy wine
91. _____ à trois
93. He's smarter than the average bear
94. Waldorf or Caesar follower
98. Some 17th Avenue establishments in Calgary
101. Swapped on Bay Street?
104. In narcissists, they're oversized
106. Fairy's story?
107. Experience remorse
108. Government of Canada staffers, for short
109. Wake up little Susie?
111. Blood poisoning
113. **Entertainment hub street in Halifax**
115. Taters
117. Inside info about drugs?
119. "_____ be an honour"
120. Marilyn's original name: _____ Jean
121. Deterrents
124. Trash, in Tel Aviv
125. Doves' domicile
126. Actor's platform
127. Grain farm bundle
128. Skewered meat serving
129. Canada Council for the _____
130. Models for a magazine
131. Round red vegetable

DOWN

1. Signs an offer
2. Like a bright night
3. Ordinary
4. Ontario Public Service (abbr.)
5. Lists of printer's gaffes
6. Hindu spiritual being
7. **Vancouver entertainment district street**
8. Absorb a loss, colloquially
9. Persnickety moods
10. Like a ridged leaf
11. Skip over
12. Coarse silk type (var.)
13. Direction from Quebec City to Montmagny
14. Basic instincts?
15. Spanish surrealist artist Joan
16. Opposed (to)
17. Golden Olympic Canadian pair skater Duhamel
18. Very focused
24. Preschool teacher's qualification (abbr.)
25. Table scraps
30. Temporarily blocking investment fund withdrawals
32. Not so far
34. Chemical compound
36. Spa procedure, for short
40. Contradict
42. Parapet notch
43. Noted Greek philosopher
45. Loblaws specialty section
47. Scot's hat
49. Sailor's hello
51. Medieval land tract
52. Obligatory, in the old days
53. Volcanic flow
55. Storybook Gardens Ontario city
56. Dan Levy's dad
57. Braised ribs, say
58. Drags a seine
59. Took a picture again
60. Welding gas
62. _____ volatile

66. Ragwort genus
70. Zippo
71. Worked together, like BC Lions (with "up")
72. Canadian shoe retailer since 1972
73. Slangy acceptance word
76. Semesters at St. Francis Xavier University
77. Sea eagle
80. Exploits
81. Pivot
83. McMaster University chancellor since 2019: _____ Smith

85. Pigs' pen
86. **Famed road in Yellowknife**
88. Tartlet fat
90. Some bucks?
92. More long-winded
95. Layers of bone
96. 1983 Anne Murray song: "_____ Good News"
97. Thoroughly against
98. Crown Royal and Molson, e.g.
99. Northern Canada natural phenomenon: _____ borealis
100. See 107-A
102. Belches

103. Extinct bird
105. Fantastic caretakers?
108. Like a peculiar pastry chef?
110. Take by force
112. "The One I Love" US band
114. Classic Village People hit
116. Whispered "Hey!"
118. Architectural moulding type
121. Crime techs gather this
122. In 2016, Canada won four gold medals at these Olympic Games
123. Recede, like the tide

But…

ACROSS

1. Niagara _____
6. Old CTV show: *The Littlest* _____
10. "Hardly"
14. See 10-A
19. 1991 Stompin' Tom Connors tune: "_____ Canadian Girl"
20. *Maclean's* contributor Allen
21. Dry sherry type
22. Yellow-orange pigment
23. **Plant toxic to a dandy?**
25. Crop grown in Saskatchewan
26. City in northern France
27. Gravitational equilibrium of the earth's crust
28. Alberta motto: _____ and free
30. Buddy, in Britain
31. Guy Lafleur wore this jersey number as a Canadien
32. Makes haste
33. Plant with large, prickly heads
34. Regarding, in olden days
36. Big Shania song: "_____ Man of Mine"
37. "From _____ and wide, O Canada…"
38. Depend on
39. Official bird of Quebec: Snowy _____
41. Aussie nominated for Juno International Album of the Year in 2017
42. More foamy
44. Jewish mourning period
47. Unforeseen glitch
48. Group plotting a coup
51. Church service
53. Lethargy
55. "_____ cost you!"
56. First Canadarm maker: _____ Aerospace
58. Vacation lodgings
60. Five Ws poser

63. Anorak or parka
64. New Brunswick Day mo.
65. Fired a logger?
66. Necessitate
68. Cyril Ramaphosa's party (abbr.)
69. **Cherub's fatal flower?**
72. US rockers: _____ Speedwagon
73. Small African antelopes
75. Buckeye State
76. Cauliflower or tin follower
77. British *Theatre of Blood* actress Diana
78. Was painful
79. Sebaceous gland problem
80. Tex-Mex meal serving
81. Sarah McLachlan song: "_____ Give Up on Us"
82. Smooth over rough spots
85. Cereal grasses rot
87. Destinies of some Greek goddesses?
88. Apple variety grown in BC and Ontario
90. TV censor's sound
92. Homer work
95. Snakelike fish
96. Tim Hortons Brier playing surface
97. Viking's letter
99. "For _____ a jolly good fellow"
100. Rogers Centre game official, for short
103. Stairway part
105. On dry land
108. Victoria and Halifax, for short
109. *Rebel Without a Cause* actor Mineo
110. With competence
111. In an orderly manner
112. ET's state of being?
114. Lagoon locale
115. You do this at Swiss Chalet
116. **Italian woman's bane?**
118. Sea near Australia

119. Concludes
120. Bullets, et al.
121. Like a freshly baked loaf
122. Playing cards with three pips
123. Siesta
124. Essence
125. Works by Canada's Al Purdy

DOWN

1. See 80-A
2. Awake for the day
3. Like the scent of some furniture polish
4. Dundee gal
5. Like a certain deadly sinner?
6. Docking ropes
7. Follows directions
8. Canadian's US show: *Full Frontal with Samantha* _____
9. Seniors, say
10. Noisy quarrels
11. Farm storage structures
12. Silly
13. **Lethal plant for some vixens?**
14. As per usual
15. One abuts Canada's west coast
16. **Noxious plant for a serpent?**
17. Yerevan country
18. Thumbs-up response
24. Mythological water nymph
29. 1970s TV marketer: K-_____
35. Luggage handle attachment
38. Hitchcock classic: _____ *Window*
40. Upper and Lower Canada conflict: _____ of 1812
42. Pepper's partner
43. Public persona
45. Diwali participant
46. International News Service (abbr.)
47. Snake's sound
48. Loud insect
49. Lacking muscle strength

50. **Poisonous perennial in Hades?**
52. Hippies' high time?
54. Without any give
56. Went right to the bottom
57. Curly-tailed dogs
59. Reno anagram
61. Everlasting, to a bard
62. Settles on a perch
65. Like a pale chimney sweep?
66. Parliament of Canada proceedings broadcaster (abbr.)
67. Canadian-made Nestlé bar
69. _____-de-camp
70. *From Russia with Love* star Lenya
71. Like a substantial stew?

74. Vedic divine being
77. 14,000 Canadian troops saw action on this
79. "Runaround _____"
80. Arrogance, colloquially
83. *New Amsterdam* network
84. **Lethal shrub for Hero's heartthrob?**
86. Armoured truck sack
87. Came clean
88. 2011 Justin Bieber track: "Only Thing I Ever _____ for Christmas"
89. Lawn care machine
91. Sit-in, for example
93. Seasoning bulb

94. Old photo tint
96. Pastoral poems
98. Web page address, for short
100. Pay period, in foreign commerce
101. 1980s Tom Selleck show: _____, P.I.
102. Kilt folds
104. Offset concerns
106. Paris river
107. Flush and straight, say
108. Settles someone down
113. Nanette's naughtiness?
114. Youth Criminal Justice _____
117. Record co. founded in 1973

Who Am I? 2

A famed Canadian journalist

ACROSS

1. Abandon a skirmish?
6. New Mexico place
10. Military prog. on US campuses
14. Accounting expert's designation (abbr.)
17. Not taut
18. Opposed to
19. Surface _____
20. Traditional song: "If _____ Be a Buckaroo"
21. Secret marriages
23. California university
25. **He's a correspondent on this long-running NBC show**
26. European peak
28. Parliament Hill politicians' meeting
29. Trusty
31. Groovy abodes?
32. Grapefruit kin, in the Caribbean
35. Towering, in stature
36. Tediously repetitious
41. **He is… (with 95-A)**
43. Dip bread in sauce
45. Achieved
46. Green-eyed with jealousy
49. Hollywood star Eastwood
51. Not glossy
52. View
53. Extremely dry
55. Pregnancy procedure, in brief
57. Timely palindrome?
58. **In 2020, he celebrated this anniversary on 25-A**
61. They're smaller than adders
65. Took notice, say
66. Musical symbol
67. Greek letter
70. Empire
72. Used a stopwatch
74. Partially bearded
76. Alcohol or drugs, for a driver
78. Sharp flavour
80. **He's stepdad to this *Friends* star Matthew**
81. Doctors' conclusions regarding symptoms
83. Eccentric
86. Movie projector spool
87. Most essential part
88. Location for 82-D at home
91. Powdered Kraft Dinner ingredient
94. Neat-o
95. **See 41-A**
99. 10-D, for example
101. Architectural style, in Salerno?
103. Israeli submachine gun
104. Hamburg is situated by this river
105. Ta ta _____ ta
106. Cabbies' cars
107. Four-poster furniture piece
108. Incursion
109. Blueprint detail, for short
110. Vote for a councillor, in Calgary

DOWN

1. Kids' winter coaster
2. Soft drink
3. Stem of a tooth
4. Hardship
5. Shakespeare contemporary George
6. Tapeworm genus
7. Tempers by heating
8. National Arts Centre city (abbr.)
9. Mexican agave
10. Carpentry file
11. Oral Rehydration Therapy (abbr.)
12. Serving trolley
13. **CTV morning show he co-hosted (1992–95)**
14. Bit from a Bernard Callebaut shop
15. Lima country
16. Tacks on
22. 14-year Winnipeg Blue Bombers star Stegall
24. Twilled cloth
27. Greeting gift on Molokai
30. _____ Québécois
31. Argue about weather conditions?
32. Stringed instruments, in HI
33. Ontario-born *Miracle on 34th Street* star Lockhart
34. How *Hockey Night in Canada* airs games
37. Wine or tea astringent
38. Go _____ detail
39. Oval Office rejection
40. Milton winter activities facility: Glen _____
42. High school lesson subj.
44. Baby's safe place
47. *The National* content
48. Tommy Douglas was voted this: The _____ Canadian
50. Global monetary org.
54. Unbroken
56. Former federal politicians Jelinek or Lang
59. *Cats* character: Rum _____ Tugger
60. Pile
61. See 53-A
62. Trucker's rig
63. 1986 Madonna #1: "_____ Don't Preach"
64. Insulted, in Ipswich
67. Quebec Christmas figure: _____ Noël
68. In this place
69. Poem celebrating rustic scenes (var.)
71. **His original career path prior to becoming a journalist**
73. Queen who founded Carthage
75. YYZ building

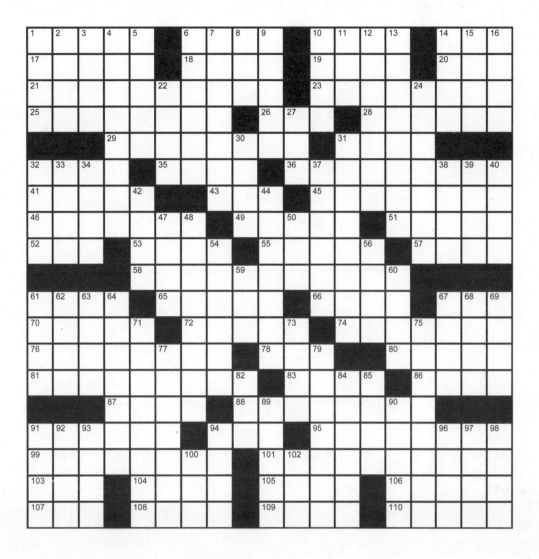

77. Florist's skin condition?

79. Like a hand with outspread fingers

82. Hot tub

84. Cavort

85. *Beverly Hills, 90210* star Spelling

89. Paper's remembrance notices

90. Speak from a stage

91. Great Lakes fish: Silver _____

92. Mental confusion

93. British children's literature author Blyton

94. Took off running

96. _____-Coburg-Gotha

97. Related to hearing

98. *One Flew Over the Cuckoo's* _____

100. Dojo belt

102. Pointy end

SOLUTION ON PAGE 171

Bells and whistles

ACROSS

1. Evidence for Lord Peter Wimsey
5. Former Turkish title
10. 2002 Avril Lavigne hit: "Sk8er _____"
13. Funeral write-up, for short
17. Rick Hansen, to many Canadians
18. Register for a sweepstakes
19. Canoeist's blade
20. Printer's unit
21. Dastardly doings
22. Anoint, in days of old
23. **BC resort town**
25. Feudal system tract
26. Roll up a banner
27. Most luxurious
28. Price Canadian Tire pays for some goods
31. In 1976, Canada signed an economic co-operation agreement with this European org.
32. Mixed nuts nut
35. Binds, morally or legally
37. Final word from the pulpit
41. Some spa treatments
43. Cough up, say
44. Incline
45. Pizza bottom
46. West African trees (var.)
48. 1961 Hockey Hall of Fame inductee Day
50. Margaret Trudeau, _____ Sinclair
51. Early European
52. Governor General, for one
53. Yukon's floral emblem
55. Lamentations, in literature
57. Mottled skin description
58. Take care of business
60. Gore and Pence, for short
61. Capri, for one

64. French vineyard
65. Start of a hole, at the Hamilton Golf and Country Club
66. Mushroom tops
67. "Nonsense!"
68. Very brusque
70. Aggressive animal's sound
72. Nail polish remover ingredient
74. Trickle through the cracks?
75. Some exercises
77. Skimpy top for an equestrienne?
78. Popular card game
80. Denture part
82. Sad
86. Like two _____ in a pod
87. Detritus, at Dofasco
91. **Moscow monument completed in the 1830s**
92. Abstract 1960s painters' style
93. US food franchise in Canada: _____ Bell
94. If all _____ fails
95. Irish or English Breakfast beverage
96. Brink
97. *Metamorphoses* poet
98. Put a piggy in the water
99. Have a debt
100. Property destruction charge
101. Goalie's leg protectors

DOWN

1. Profession of Quebec's Madame Benoît
2. *Hello, Dolly!* surname
3. Large lake that's partially in Ontario
4. **Often unwelcome approval?**
5. Southeast Asian bird
6. Invalidate a marriage
7. Not mono
8. **1980 AC/DC single**
9. Chris Hadfield book of photos: *You _____ Here*

10. Outwardly curving limbs
11. Diamond Head's home
12. Early spring bloomers
13. Canadian eyewear chain: Hakim _____
14. Gallbladder fluid
15. Shoots the puck too far in a Flames game
16. Promiscuous bakery worker?
24. Sarah McLachlan movie song: "When _____ Loved Me"
27. Bends at the barre
29. In the _____ of the moment
30. Pond growth
32. Community Food Centres Canada (abbr.)
33. River in Switzerland
34. AGO exhibit: The Henry Moore _____ Centre
36. African country
38. Director's expensive moment?
39. Foil for an Olympic sport
40. 2009 Lady A hit: "_____ You Now"
42. Allergy assessment procedure
44. Engineering detail, in brief
47. Acclaimed movie director Preminger
49. Some McMaster majors
52. It's sometimes high at the seashore
53. Run from an RCMP officer
54. **Small town visited on the campaign trail**
56. Penny _____
57. **Red, green, orange or yellow fruit**
58. Emulates Canada's Neve Campbell
59. Apple or orange
60. COVID-19, for one
62. War of 1812 skirmish: Battle of Lundy's _____

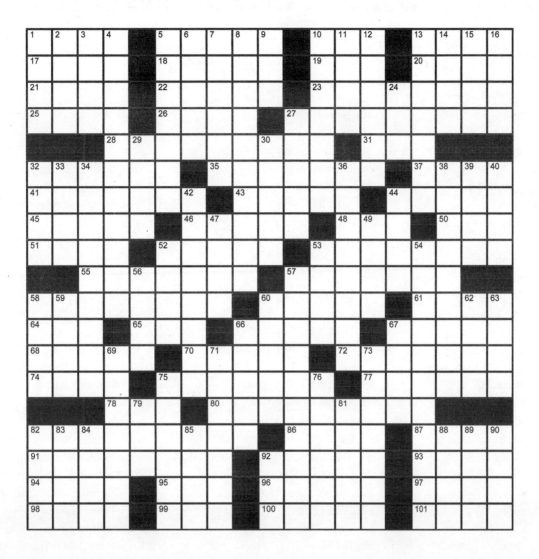

63. Home decor piece
66. Former areas in Italy: _____ States
67. Mossy, organic matter
69. Like some cowboy boots
71. Interstellar gas clouds
73. Castigate

75. Johannesburg township
76. Assegais
79. Natty Englishman
81. Slow, in music
82. Dele opposite
83. Christiania, today

84. Knock down, in Norfolk
85. Travelled via Air Transat
88. Wax-filled light: _____ lamp
89. Corrosive substance
90. Odin and Thor
92. Female reproductive cells

SOLUTION ON PAGE 171

55 Acrophobics Beware...

Of these tallest Canadian structures

ACROSS

1. Rock stars' sound equipment
5. "The Tortoise and the Hare" scribe
10. Acid type in proteins
15. Whisky produced in Collingwood: Canadian _____
19. Early Scot
20. "Time in a Bottle" singer Jim
21. Stylish chapeau
22. Pony up, in poker
23. Blurry
25. Doozy
26. Terry Fox, to many Canadians
27. **Tallest tower in Edmonton**
28. Help a lawbreaker
30. Get a grounded ship back in the water
32. Bombed, at the brewery?
33. Ontario place: _____ Sound
35. *The War of the _____*
36. Eyelid issue
37. Pianist's piece
38. Pale
39. Certain lilies
42. The University of Winnipeg offers a degree in this
45. Perfect place
46. Official Thailand currency
50. *Ghostbusters* Canadian director Reitman
51. Stockholm spending-money units
53. Skin, in Saguenay
54. Manager
56. Flying saucer, say
57. Units of energy
59. Go mouldy
60. Three-masted vessel
61. Jewellery pieces for gentlemen
64. Second printing of a Giller Prize winner, say
66. _____ between the lines
68. **Toronto mixed-use skyscraper**

70. "Shoot!"
71. Ice over
74. Sea near the Philippines
76. Sister of Clio
79. Tiny charged particle
80. Gull-like bird
82. Make seven from three plus four
83. Detached, like a doctor?
85. Snoozes
87. Fortification slope
89. Go from baby bottle to sippy cup
90. Warehouse pallet
91. Cape Breton or Vancouver follower
93. Deceptive
96. Southern neighbour of many provinces
97. Last letter, for Canadians
98. "The Age of Anxiety" poet W.H.
99. Ontario and Quebec do this
103. Supercharged engines
105. Pungent
106. Mocking in tone
108. Where dune buggy drivers drive
110. QEII Highway stopping spot: Rest _____
111. **Tallest of them all in Canada**
112. Canadian C&W group: The _____ Brothers
113. Belgian city
115. Shotgun barrel feature
118. *Doctor Zhivago* leading lady
119. Store supplies for winter, say
120. Angry
121. Tolkien tale creatures
122. US TV excellence award since 1949
123. Aroma
124. Sunflower kin
125. Bills discontinued by Canada in 1989

DOWN

1. Discriminator against the elderly (var.)
2. Tropical waters rays
3. Fussbudget
4. Toy that can travel down the stairs
5. Played a part in *Come from Away*
6. Staal who won 2010 Olympic hockey gold with Canada
7. Justin, to Pierre Trudeau
8. Ontario Chamber of Commerce (abbr.)
9. Explosive devices
10. Oakville golf course: Glen _____
11. Track and field event
12. *Son of Rosemary* scribe Levin
13. Cell type
14. BC coast mammal: Sea _____
15. Canada Post box, say
16. **It towered over Sudbury from 1972 until dismantling**
17. Colonnaded walkway
18. Portable shelter
24. Like costly tea leaves?
29. **Office tower in Calgary**
31. Like cola without fizz
33. Ursa Minor star
34. Unknown author's "name"
35. Hockey great Gretzky
37. Mechanical fastener
38. "These Eyes" group: The Guess _____
40. Cat's cry, in Calais
41. Cook in a wok, say
43. Move rapidly
44. Like electrical plug inserts
45. Egged on
46. Jack-in-the-_____
47. Spadina, in TO
48. **Grand Banks structure**
49. Pines and palmettos
52. NHL icon Bobby
55. Flees

56. Erects, old style
58. Emergency vehicle's warning sound
62. Catch-all abbr.
63. Sis or bro
65. Goa garments
67. Fought it out at the palace?
69. Withdrew, politically
71. Done, in Dorval
72. Swelter in the kitchen?
73. Fluid found in a cyst
75. Killed, like the Jabberwock?
77. Martial art: _____ chi
78. OAS: _____ Age Security

81. Pinnacles
84. Motel alternative
86. Usual night for *Hockey Night in Canada* broadcasts
88. Assist
89. Northern Africa gully
92. Rex Stout sleuth: _____ Wolfe
94. Land mass that's home to five billion people
95. C&W star Brooks
97. Sagittarius and Scorpio are part of this
100. Tyke's owie
101. Brand new

102. Canonical hour (var.)
104. Rogers Centre game equipment
105. Bing Crosby tune: "_____ You Glad You're You"
106. _____ *alia*
107. Leafy salad green, for short
108. Rakish glance
109. Shaving lather
110. Anti, in dialect
111. Shack for sheep
114. Needle's minute opening
116. Title for a married lady
117. Cereal grain

56

Tokens of Affection

For loving the one you're with

ACROSS

1. Enjoy a day at Whistler
7. Maison Birks precious stone weight unit
12. Norwegian "Take On Me" band
15. Temptations hit: "_____ Was a Rollin' Stone"
19. These contain brains (var.)
20. The Brick sells this appliance brand
21. Mrs. Bundy, on *Married... with Children*
22. Berry-bearing shrub
23. **Relevant reading material?**
25. Brain segment: _____ lobe
27. Scored on a serve, like Canada's Félix Auger-Aliassime
28. Prepped a bow, at the TSO
30. **Tea brand for your beloved?**
31. Italian tower town
32. Cookware set vessel
33. Board member
35. Canadian-born James Peebles won a 2019 Nobel Prize in this
39. Receipts from Roots, say
44. This made mortals immortal in mythology
47. RCMP member's red attire
49. Hollywood horror films star Chaney
50. Ringworm
51. Lacking red blood cells (var.)
53. Canadian Mikita who led the Blackhawks in the '60s
55. Toothpaste type
57. YVR flight listing, for short
58. Richard who first explored Antarctica in 1928
59. Toronto theatrical prize: _____ Mavor Moore Award
61. 2006 Giller Prize winner Vincent
63. Whittle down resources
65. Unhappy
66. _____-Cola

67. Aircraft
69. Caters to a crowd?
70. **Gift for Forrest Gump?**
73. "La traviata" composer
75. Contemptible person (var.)
76. Decorative inlay brass piece
77. Long-time prison nickname: Kingston _____
80. Apes
82. Insane or angry
83. Spanakopita cheese
84. Lousy loser description?
85. Dullard shovelling mud?
86. European Economic Community (abbr.)
88. Danish toy maker since 1932
90. Busy, busy, busy
92. Communion table
94. Soft food, say
96. Defeat decisively
98. Supernatural evildoer (var.)
99. Wiring insulator
102. Come before
104. Steep slopes, in Spain
106. Goof up
107. US hip hop group: Salt-N-_____
111. **Flowers with a sweet smell?**
115. Get things going
118. Hit with a hand
119. Agent that contaminates
121. **Peck for a Pennsylvanian?**
124. Peruvian primate
125. Genealogy chart word
126. Related through mother's side
127. Pain relieving drug
128. Desist
129. National tax since 1991 (abbr.)
130. Flies alone
131. Ministers' homes

DOWN

1. Cloth remnant
2. Spring bloomers (var.)

3. These hold horses' traces
4. In its original form
5. No. for good and bad Canadians?
6. Membrane surrounding a cyst
7. New Testament book description
8. *Good Times* star John
9. Sitar star Shankar
10. Regarding, old style
11. Old German coins (var.)
12. Snapchat, e.g.
13. Encouraged the cardiologist?
14. Concurs with
15. National Historic Site in Halifax: _____ 21
16. Sax or clarinet type
17. Small, green veggies
18. Rod under a hot rod
24. Epochs
26. That is, to Tiberius
29. _____-income family
32. Vitamin B6
34. Trudge
36. Dr. Seuss classic: *Green Eggs and* _____
37. _____ Nostra
38. Day of the week abbr.
40. Stocking threads
41. Applied a tattoo
42. US actress Amanda, et al.
43. Marquis de _____
44. Takes into custody
45. Mononymous Irish songstress
46. **My funny Valentine?**
48. Tough task for a giant?
52. Canadian fashion model Rocha
54. Civil rights org. in the US
56. Former Blue Jays pitcher David Wells, for one
60. Float for Huckleberry Finn
62. Alphabet trio
64. Mississauga's region
66. Composition's closing
67. Shoppers Drug Mart bottle (var.)
68. Dresden river

70. Banff landmark: _____ Veil Falls
71. Mount Everest valley: Western _____
72. Former trade agreement: Canada–US _____ Pact
73. Membrane hairs
74. Ham it up
77. **Rhyme from your Romeo?**
78. Hence
79. Garish shade of green
80. Mackerel type
81. Groups of seven (var.)
83. Bobby Orr's jersey number
84. Soft rug type

87. Accords and Civics
89. US Republican Party acronym
91. Small amount
93. Happen again
95. Canadian food retailer: _____ Pit
97. Cuts molars
100. Signalling to an actor on stage
101. Secret storage spaces
103. First Nations group: Woodland _____
105. Note-taking meeting attendee
108. It shares a border between Yukon and Alaska: Mount Saint _____

109. Wallpaper adhesive
110. Many Montreal churches feature these _____
111. Kibbles 'n _____
112. Fail to include
113. Not _____ snuff
114. Wisecrack
116. Russian river
117. Regarding
120. 1993 Blue Rodeo track: "Hasn't Hit Me _____"
122. _____ Kippur
123. Château Lake Louise amenity

57

R Is for River

Canadian waterways

ACROSS

1. Have or hold?
8. Attain a goal
13. Disreputable
20. Description of flight technology
21. Enclose in a cove
22. Former Georgia home city of the Calgary Flames
23. **Stags' Alberta river?**
24. Call the Oilers don't like to hear
25. He gets the jump on unruly bar patrons?
26. U of C dorm
27. Gemstone found in Ontario and Quebec
29. Minuteman III, e.g.
31. Samples a drink
32. Alberta hamlet: _____ La Biche
33. Passé
34. "_____ the thought!"
36. Scale note (var.)
37. Visibly shocked
39. Johnny Cash classic: "A Boy Named _____"
40. Champagne grape
41. Express a viewpoint
43. Lethbridge and Calgary newspaper name
45. Type of lockjaw contraction
47. Dyer's oak dye
48. Cobbler's "Scram!"
50. Like some ancient Germanic alphabets
51. Highliner frozen fish products
52. Old Irish farming peasants
56. Prefix with Georgian
57. Voyageurs' craft
58. Curvy moulding
59. **Franco–Ontarian's colourful river?**
61. Opposite of everybody
63. Elisha who invented the elevator
67. Generous slice, colloquially
68. La-la lead-in
69. _____ oncle Antoine
70. Historic Toronto home: Casa _____
71. Bravery award recipient
72. Guzzles
74. **Fast-moving Saskatchewan river?**
76. Mashhad country
77. Irving Stone novel: *The _____ and the Ecstasy*
79. Confucian ideal
81. Tumour type
83. Trained for a boxing bout
86. Rap sheet listing
88. Second-yr. student at college
89. Gad
90. Desperate plight: _____ situation
92. Kingston Penitentiary, from 1835–2013
96. Like a jittery exterminator?
97. Breadbasket buns
98. Butchart Gardens visitors' guide
100. Clay/ferric oxide mineral
101. Foot piggy
102. Pivot
104. Jointly endorse
106. Brewery product
107. Ensnare
109. Fateful day for Julius Caesar
110. Gloomy Gus, say
111. Fertility clinics freeze these
112. Like safe foodstuffs
114. Bathroom or nursery powders
116. **Noisy Manitoba river?**
119. Canada shares the 49th parallel with this nation
120. Smart _____
121. Banff National Park mountain
122. Saharan stork
123. Forearm bones
124. Gasoline additive

DOWN

1. Average score, at Nova Scotia's Cabot Cliffs
2. Glut
3. Motorcycle passenger's preferred cocktail?
4. Lays a lawn
5. NB, vis-à-vis ME
6. Prolonged military tactic
7. Skedaddles
8. **Rudolph's Saskatchewan river?**
9. Alex Trebek's former role
10. Trifling amount
11. Waste receptacle
12. Free of germs
13. **Bunny's BC river?**
14. Itty-bitty bits
15. Common ailment
16. They're wild for their idols
17. Like acute observations
18. Hit the gas pedal hard
19. Becomes more coarse, in tone
28. Trounce, on the playing field
30. Nile reptile, for short
32. This follows 36-A
33. Yamuna River city: New _____
34. Rack-and-_____ steering
35. Call out a greeting?
38. Gluers' card stocks?
40. Stamp collector's sheet
42. Second part of the Stone Age
44. Busy dynamo?
46. Harmonize instruments
47. Monetary penalty
49. Ostentatious
51. Derrières
52. Whack with a blackjack?
53. Lascivious look
54. Rip apart
55. Bad-tempered
57. Commandeer a leader
60. _____-toothed smile
62. German grandmother

64. Beast in a bullring
65. Islamic officiant
66. Capital of Yemen
72. Suffix with theatre
73. Leisurely walk
74. Chancel crucifix
75. At the _____ of a hat
78. TV drama that featured Ottawa's Sandra Oh (2005–14): _____ Anatomy
80. Shows on CTV
82. Popular sink style
83. Elite police grp.

84. Columbia Valley ski resort in BC
85. It dines on termites
86. Guiding light?
87. **River on the edge of the St. Lawrence?**
90. Bird of peace
91. CFL division
93. GBS aficionado
94. Walt Disney World city
95. Once named, in Nantes
97. **Ontario river that locks you up?**
99. Brosnan who played James Bond

103. CBer's phrase: Roger _____
104. Bacteria
105. Defunct fourpence coin
108. It precedes graph
110. Begged for mercy
111. Vancouver Canuck's jersey mammal
113. Lobster eater's wear
115. American Library Association (abbr.)
117. Volcano output
118. Barbershop styling goop

58

A Prickly Puzzle

It might be a bit barbarous

ACROSS

1. Canadian fisheries catch
5. Mammals that live near Canada's coasts
10. Two-four, say
14. Terrible
19. Bulgarian currency units
20. Ending of an old poem
21. Friendly nation to Canada
22. Restaurant with 670+ Canadian locations: _____ Queen
23. Managing, say
25. 1973 Bachman-Turner Overdrive single
27. Reined in enthusiasm
28. Lions' lair
29. **1968 Jane Fonda sci-fi film**
30. Fructose, et al.
32. Settle a BMO loan
34. It's mined in several provinces
35. Intense pang
37. Liked, like hippies?
38. Spun out on ice
39. Cadge from a vagrant?
42. _____ finish
45. One type of bigot
48. Hamlet, for example
49. Great
51. Data/analytics company operating in Canada: _____ & Bradstreet
52. System log-in components
54. Elvis Presley hit: "_____ Now or Never"
55. To help, in Hochelaga
57. 1958 acting Oscar winner Ives
59. Country bumpkins
60. Shacks that slant?
62. Medieval storage space for mace?
64. **Group of singers**
69. Ottawa's Billings Estate National Historic Site has one
71. Come back with a vengeance
72. Corrosive in tone or taste
73. Data transmission speed
75. Fertile desert areas
77. Bro synonym
80. San Francisco trams
83. Photo, for short
84. Gas cloud in the atmosphere
86. Egyptian goddess
87. Of a metrical foot (var.)
91. Just plain mean
92. Hot beverage in Baie-Comeau
93. Eight-time Grammy nominee Tori
94. Round, green veggie
95. _____ pneumonia
97. Unite at the altar
98. Magical incantation
100. Court game for two teams of seven
104. **Atlas Mountains macaque**
109. Children's chasing game
111. Drumheller AB geological feature
112. Icarus fell into this body of water
113. Top position at *Maclean's*, say
115. Bribe, colloquially
116. YXY postings, for short
117. Of the kidneys
118. Painful skin spot
119. Canadian Craig who won the Cup with the Penguins and Hurricanes
120. Paddock father
121. Old-style hairnet
122. Part of USNA

DOWN

1. Grandfather's timepiece?
2. *The Tommy Hunter Show*, for example
3. Prevent a disaster from occurring
4. **Quebec version of craps**
5. Sowing machine
6. Vancouver-to-Kamloops dir.
7. Passionate
8. She eschews company
9. Logged on, say
10. Coleslaw ingredient
11. Temper concerns
12. Racist's remark
13. Fasteners with looped heads
14. Venerated
15. Allergic reaction mark
16. Replenish your tank at Petro-Canada: _____ up
17. Range in Russia
18. Vega's constellation
24. Lisbon lady
26. Tooth decay
31. Soldiers of Anarchy (abbr.)
33. Cyst fluid
36. Charm a darling?
38. Continental crust layer
39. **Brightly coloured tropical bird**
40. 2005 Michael Bublé cover: "I've Got You _____ My Skin"
41. Not neat
42. It comes before omega
43. Ice fishing shack
44. Bytown law enforcers (abbr.)
46. Spins
47. Marketing and Public Relations (abbr.)
48. 1963 Shirley MacLaine movie: *Irma la _____*
50. *The Hobbit* protagonist Baggins
53. Formal court order
56. Render an opinion
57. Catcalled at a concert
58. Canada Post's American counterpart (abbr.)
61. Canadian-made show: *Highway _____ Hell*
62. Droops
63. Get gussied up
64. **Doll that debuted in 1959**
65. Ovule protectors

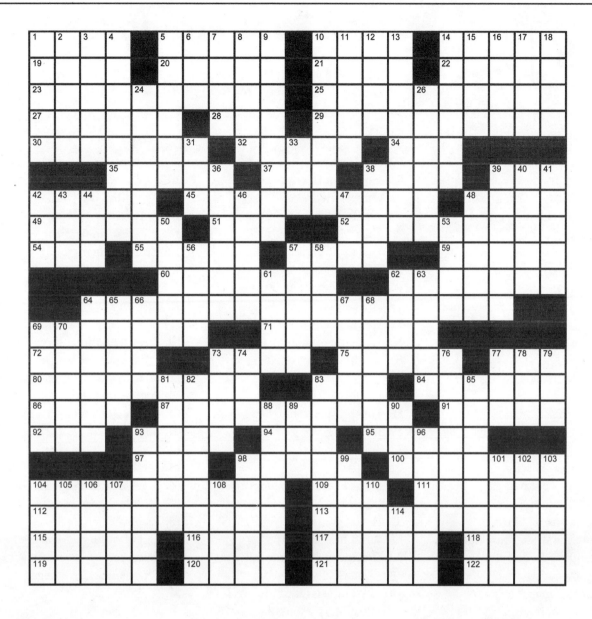

66. Travelled by 77-D
67. Ring tossed in a throwing game
68. Component of RNA
69. Unspoken
70. Cryptocurrency
73. Bikini tops
74. Sap anagram
76. NHLer Daniel Alfredsson was one for many years
77. TTC transport option
78. Final (abbr.)
79. James or Georgian, in Ontario
81. Canada's Yousuf Karsh created portraiture using this

82. Pain relievers
83. Liturgical compilations
85. **Pirates of the Caribbean film franchise captain**
88. Mollify
89. Initial platform element of the Reform Party (abbr.)
90. Swindle
93. Is in store for
96. "Lo and _____!"
98. Harpoon
99. Heavily burdened with
101. Like temporary commissions or committees

102. Blonde, in Brasilia
103. Ran effortlessly
104. "It's not that _____ deal"
105. Got a point off a serve, like Canada's Milos Raonic
106. It precedes "tat-tat"
107. They had a CBC children's show in the '80s: Sharon, Lois & _____
108. Wine region in Piedmont
110. 1970s Canadian pop singer Vannelli
114. Oat anagram

59 Name That Province

Using these official symbols

ACROSS

1. Volkswagen model
6. History, say
10. Vessel often seen in BC waters
15. 1975 Bachman-Turner Overdrive song: "Take It Like _____"
19. Pelvis part
20. Comply
21. Insurer since 1909: Mutual of _____
22. Pedestal part
23. Shine
24. Keloid tissue
25. Ewers anagram
26. Matures
27. Heart contraction
29. **Arboreal emblem**
32. It follows false or fire
34. Suggestive stare
35. Butcher shop purchase
36. Corduroy or calico
39. Entertainer's representative
41. Painful skin ulcers
45. Renown
46. Book of maps
47. _____-wrenching
48. Irony, in literature
49. Former Down Under flyer: _____ Airways
50. Gridiron play
52. Wounded the matador
54. Irrational number
55. Ooze
57. Got off a horse
58. Rattle
60. Musical ensemble's performance
61. Language of 11-D
63. Downtown Calgary gathering spot: Olympic _____
64. Sarah Michelle Gellar played her in two Scooby-Doo movies
66. 1996 Shania Twain hit: "No One Needs to _____"
67. **Provincial fish**
70. Flat float
71. Hey! A word repeated in a nursery rhyme title
73. TV drama starring Canada's Shay Mitchell: *Pretty Little _____*
74. Lassie, for one
76. Royal Dragoon Guards (abbr.)
77. Grassy plain (var.)
79. Highlander's slope
80. Wedding invitation acronym
83. Old Testament book
85. _____ *Andronicus*
86. Lea
88. Lovebird's murmur?
89. Insect organs
91. Some dishwashers, for short
92. Jocular
93. Some Nunavut residents
95. Inspired a loved one's affection
97. Hindu yogi
98. Runs, in the wash
99. Greek war god
100. Electrically charged atoms
101. Part of Miss Muffet's meal
103. **Provincial stone**
108. Covered building entrance
112. Egg
113. Writer Zola
114. Push
116. From days of yore
117. Number of Blue Jays on the field
118. More unusual
119. Nothing, in Nicolet
120. Like a shabby garden?
121. Spiritedness
122. Toboggans
123. Apple tablet
124. Southwestern Ontario town

DOWN

1. Lively dances
2. *Beverly Hillbillies* family member: _____ May
3. Connections
4. New Zealand lizard
5. **Provincial gemstone**
6. Photographer's conundrum?
7. *Dancing with the Stars* network
8. Close an envelope
9. From a certain region of Austria
10. Plant with blue flowers: _____-me-not
11. Middle Eastern dignitary (var.)
12. Speak hoarsely
13. Lab device that measures liquid flow
14. Cried, loudly
15. Attachments for 123-A (var.)
16. Sages who were guided by a star
17. Middle Eastern gulf
18. Face part
28. Ontario/Quebec water boundary: _____ des Chats
30. TV rooms
31. Nanaimo is on this side of Vancouver Island
33. Enrolled at U of A
36. Dues
37. The peak of perfection?
38. **Provincial colours**
40. Surplus amount
41. Red tape related
42. **Provincial grass**
43. Digital document
44. Marsh plant
46. Off-the-cuff remark
47. Co-star of Kermit
51. Capture
52. Growls at
53. Rental from Rogers, once
56. See 114-A
58. UHF word

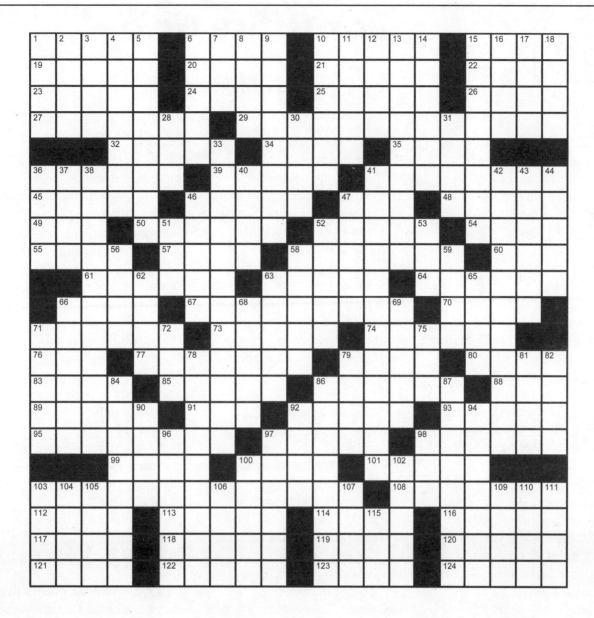

59. Former Governor General: _____ Grey

62. Cobblers' hole-punching tools

63. Makes arrangements

65. Set of two

66. Oscar-winning Aussie actress Nicole

68. Charlie Brown's buddy

69. Frog lover's sycophant?

71. Curtain

72. Ingest

75. Russian writer Tolstoy

78. Based on the number 20

79. One of the Little Women

81. Null and _____

82. Cookware items

84. Assegai users

86. Jefferson City state

87. Floral emblem

90. Garb won in Goa

92. He's overly fond of Chardonnay?

94. Snuggles

96. Alludes (to)

97. Canada's Silken Laumann, et al.

98. Male sib

100. Ran in neutral gear

102. Capsize

103. Southern US cornbread

104. Agatha Christie mystery: _____ *Under the Sun*

105. Ahis

106. Land of leprechauns

107. Spigot trouble

109. Day to beware of?

110. Surrender

111. Quartz stone

115. Goalie who signed with Manchester United in 2011: David de _____

And the province is:

___ ___ ___ ___ ___ ___ ___

SOLUTION ON PAGE 172

60 Box Office *Gold*

Movies that shone

ACROSS

1. A couple of smart actors?
6. Ballroom dance type
12. Trillium prov. upper court
15. 1989 Colin James hit: "Back in My _____ Again"
19. Indian religious dance hand gesture
20. Sat idly by
21. Of the last month (abbr.)
22. Stiletto or sneaker
23. **1981 Hepburn/Fonda dramatic film**
25. Caddy for oolong
27. Utters like Simon?
28. Former W Network offering: *Say Yes to the _____ Canada*
29. Mount Garibaldi climbing tool
31. "Gotcha!"
32. Jittery
34. Accompanying up the aisle
37. Rival pirates' negotiations
40. Unburnt tobacco left in a pipe
41. Coral reef islands
45. Some Hindu people
46. Look sullen (var.)
47. Young boy
49. Smooth and gleaming
50. Court call at the Rogers Cup
51. French nobleman
54. 1974 Top Ten hit: "_____ Tu"
56. Jones who fronted The Monkees
57. Debtor's note (abbr.)
58. Thracian people of old
59. Hamilton clock setting (abbr.)
61. Don Harron's Farquharson character
63. 1977 hockey movie: _____ *Shot*
65. Postscript to a document
67. South American river rodent
68. Rings of light
70. **2008 McConaughey/Hudson romcom**
72. Intimidate: _____ out

76. Famed shroud city
78. More dopey
80. Engage for employment
81. Wearing a covering, like a cook
84. Brit org. that took to the skies on 24-D
85. Register at McGill
87. Colourful garden bloomer: Sweet _____
88. Gulp punch?
89. It follows alpha
91. Hip hop subgenre: _____ rap
93. Average score for Canada's Graham DeLaet
94. Serving on a skewer (var.)
96. Posed for a painter
97. Heavy responsibility
98. Roots
100. Pilsner sold in Canada: _____ Artois
102. Queen Elizabeth's spouse for 73 years
104. Long-time cinematic blonde bombshell
106. Enbridge pays these to shareholders
108. *Tinker Tailor Soldier Spy* scribe: John le _____
109. _____ carte
112. Underwater searching systems
113. Creepy
115. *Return of the Jedi* furry mammaloid
119. Silent bird?
121. **1948 Roland Winters Chan franchise film**
124. UBC teacher
125. JFK is buried here
126. Orange first aid antiseptic
127. Neutral pantyhose shade
128. Dispatched
129. Rush singer Geddy
130. _____ Slave Lake
131. Montreal transit option

DOWN

1. Hebrew Bible prophet
2. Moon goddess
3. Avant-garde, to the fashionista
4. In an ill-humoured way
5. *My Gal* _____
6. Administrative employees
7. Georgian Bay township community: _____ Harbour
8. Swiss peaks
9. Liquidation sale
10. Poultry farm egg producer
11. *Intervention Canada* participant
12. Where to wear a stud
13. Spike on a sports shoe
14. Loss of muscle coordination
15. Tree type
16. *Cheers* barmaid Perlman
17. Smash into others while dancing
18. _____ precedent
24. June 6, 1944
26. Canadian coins that featured a maple leaf
30. This holds a jewel in place
33. Hoist
35. **1986 Brandauer/Snipes drama**
36. **1925 Charlie Chaplin comedy (with "*The*")**
37. From Warsaw, say
38. Pupil circle
39. Solemn ceremony
40. "Blueberry Hill" vocalist: Fats _____
42. *Dreamgirls* star Sharon
43. Biblical son of Jacob and Leah
44. *Say Anything...* actress Ione
46. Western University city
48. They solve cryptic messages
52. Integrated Development Environment (abbr.)
53. Shares a secret
55. Timid
60. Western US flower
62. Instagram, for ex.

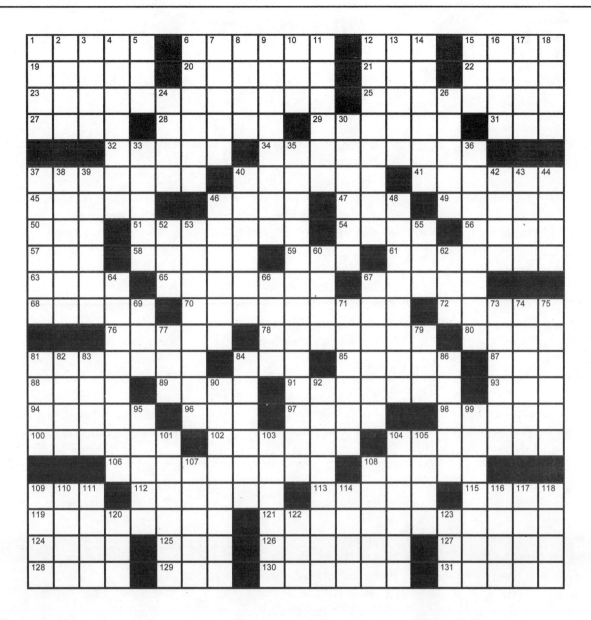

64. 1941 James Stewart musical comedy

66. _____ podrida

67. Adheres to

69. Winnipeg or Brandon newspaper name

71. Share deep feelings

73. "Hurrah!"

74. Blends butter and sugar, say

75. Ontario premier William (1914–19)

77. Civil War "Gray" soldier

79. Ort anagram

81. Requests

82. Surveyor's document

83. Yokel

84. Sooner _____ than later

86. Type of printer

90. Sammy Davis Jr. talent

92. Raki flavouring pips

95. Ecstasy

99. Preadolescent

101. Strong promise

103. Gradually introduce an idea (var.)

104. Canada Post ad?

105. Not worth _____ cent

107. Absurd

108. Hag

109. The War _____

110. Entice

111. "It hit me like _____ of bricks"

114. Cuirass past (var.)

116. Departed

117. _____ and terminer

118. Dawson City National Historic Site: S.S. _____

120. Petite amphibian

122. 2002 Giller Prize winner: *The Polished* _____

123. See 15-D

SOLUTION ON PAGE 172

Who Am I? 3

Name this star

ACROSS

1. Wrist bones
6. Spill secrets
10. Connected computers' network (abbr.)
13. Didn't use the rod?
19. Mountain nymph, in mythology
20. Goosebumps inducing (var.)
21. "We _____ Family"
22. Esoteric
23. **She's promoted this Canadian charity since 1982**
26. *The Picture of _____ Gray*
27. Canadian Conference of _____ Bishops
28. Fairway chunks, at Glen Abbey
30. Ductwork components
31. Office-holders, say
32. Attractive person (var.)
34. South African country
36. "I _____ London…"
37. That man
38. Lisa, to Bart, for short
40. Most gruesome
42. Out like a light
45. Some tropical fish
47. Important numbers for CTV
51. Loud lion's sounds?
52. Set-tos
53. Tennis players' surface (abbr.)
54. 1976 ensemble film: *Welcome _____*
55. Blooming cluster
56. Wearing of a veil, in some cultures
57. National Historic Site in Nova Scotia: Grand-_____
58. **Quebec university that bestowed on her an honorary music doctorate**
59. Chance occurrence
60. Trail behind the crowd
61. Rent cheque recipient
63. Spirited, in Chibougamau

64. _____ for business
66. **Blockbuster for which she sang "My Heart Will Go On"**
68. Boxer's weapon
69. A squirrel might like this squash?
71. Card game for four
72. RBC foyer machine no.
73. Iliescu who once governed Romania
76. **She has won 20 of these Canadian music industry awards**
77. Jimmy
78. Flat-bottomed Chinese boat
81. It follows vena
82. Help a criminal
83. Hr. division
84. Eastern monks
85. Supply wedding reception food, professionally
86. Infrequent meal in Wales?
88. Ohio city
89. In a contrary mood
90. Its feathers are used on hats
92. Royal Air Force (abbr.)
93. Tank for pickle production
94. 504, to Caesar
97. Mists
99. BC university: _____ Fraser
101. As fit _____ fiddle
104. Indian yogurt-based dip
106. Immobilize a pig?
108. St. John's daily: *The _____*
110. Grate remnants
112. **Her first US #1 hit (1994)**
114. Ornamental shrub
115. Move apace
116. English actor/playwright Coward
117. Unit of light intensity
118. Lose something
119. Red Chamber appointee (abbr.)
120. Aching

121. Bread or beer ingredient

DOWN

1. Strep throat bacteria, for example
2. Indo-European
3. Puts one's feet up
4. Walkway at Butchart Gardens
5. Stupid stunts, for example
6. Suit an athlete?
7. East Midlands city, in England
8. Air Reserve Base (abbr.)
9. English Renaissance composer William
10. **She held two concert residencies in this US city**
11. Melodic passages
12. Athlete and Order of Canada tennis inductee Daniel
13. Not happy
14. Ecclesiastical dignitary
15. Veggie patch, say
16. Pours
17. Related via mom
18. Thick in the noggin?
24. Glob
25. Canadian petroleum company: Imperial _____
29. Tim Hortons stick, for example
33. Give way
35. Warmth
37. Roll call response
39. Quiet type of bomber?
41. Mythological giants
42. Landmark between WA and BC: Peace _____ Park
43. Vegetarian burger type (var.)
44. *SCTV* performer, say
46. Calgary Philharmonic practice
48. Religious order newbie
49. Glitzy, for short
50. Bargain event, at Leon's
52. Second Cup cup
53. Gator's kin
56. Criticize a Greek god?

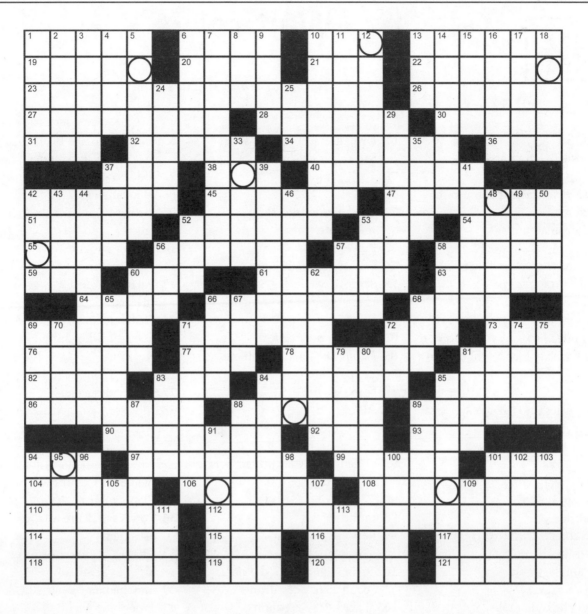

57. It precedes omega
58. Past participle of "lie"
60. Monocle circle
62. Running shoe
65. For the time being, to Caesar
66. Rotate
67. Like slippery slopes?
68. Vancouver Canucks mascot
69. Open, partially
70. Caribbean country
71. Tombstone words
72. Manitoba place: The _____
74. Fall head _____ heels in love
75. Hardly any, in Aberdeen

79. Car service franchise in Canada
80. Exploit the black market
81. Elvis Presley hit: "_____ Help Falling in Love"
83. Oscar-winning actress Sorvino
84. **Number of children in her family of origin**
85. Daddy-long-legs that bothers a bird?
87. Southern Germany state
88. Challenging question, say
89. Convex moulding
91. Kiosks
94. 1970 Pierre Berton book: *The National _____*

95. Metrical feet, in poetry (var.)
96. Feelings, colloquially
98. Drink just a little
100. Actress Oberon
101. Scent
102. Rescues
103. Catkin
105. 1989 Rush song: "Show Don't _____"
107. Very lengthy time periods
109. Scrapbooker's need
111. Articulate through words
113. Go to court?

Use the circled letters to unscramble her name. She is: __ __ __ __ __ __ __ __ __ __

SOLUTION ON PAGE 173

62 · Wait for *It*

Time for some rhymes

ACROSS

1. 1980s CBC drama: *Street* _____
6. Droop, like flowers
10. Beavers' construction project
13. Submissive
17. Orate anagram
18. Son of Isaac, in the Bible
19. Former name for Tokyo
20. Attachment for 66-D
21. Newfangled idea
23. His tomb was opened in 1922
24. Jennifer Jones served as this on Canada's golden Sochi curling team
25. Parts
26. Inquiries into the metaphysical
29. _____ one's time
30. **Gravitational path**
31. Large vase
32. Montreal (1967) and Vancouver (1986) hosted these
35. Tension
37. **Southern Ontario river**
40. Jack-in-the-pulpit plant, for example
41. Price sticker
42. Egyptian pharaoh
44. _____ known as
45. **Cottontail**
48. Overworked horse
50. You might do this on the side of caution
51. Archer who shot an apple on his son's head
52. Quebec flag symbol: Fleur-de-_____
53. Police trap
56. Gave in
58. Lacking lustre?
59. A notable Yoko
60. Signalled a pool shark?
61. Triangle with unequal sides
64. Type of rug or radial

66. Drug users' crises, for short
69. Safari helmet
70. _____ Francisco
72. Feel sick
73. **Canadian donut shop miniature**
75. Prayer ender
76. Day of doom, in *Julius Caesar*
78. Schmaltzy talk
80. Japan Indigenous group
81. **Robber**
83. Prepares potatoes
85. *Happy Days* actor Williams
86. Puppy's bite
87. **Nun's garb**
88. Alone
90. Surveyor's slope-measuring device
93. Canadian Kidder played Lois Lane in this 1978 film
97. _____ Kong
98. In the past
99. Restore citizenship
101. Sibling of Cain
102. Cdn. high school diploma equivalency certificate
103. Lab culture medium
104. Canada's Mucho Burrito chain serves these
105. Bridesmaid's bouquet
106. Molson product
107. Cozy (var.)
108. 2004 Andrew Cohen book: *While Canada* _____

DOWN

1. Luau necklaces
2. Northwest Ireland river
3. CBC Radio show (1937–59): *The Happy* _____
4. Destructive WWII weapon
5. Ronstadt covered this Neil Young song: "_____ a Rose"

6. Henderson Lake BC is this: _____ place in North America
7. Goddess depicted in hieroglyphs
8. Asian language
9. Northern Canada sub-Arctic plains
10. Person under arrest
11. Fully matured
12. Particle of dust
13. Ill-used
14. Generated a love of e-books?
15. Peterson who starred in 1-A
16. Keystone _____
22. _____ *Then There Were None*
27. Everglades avian
28. Mongrel
30. Aristotle compilation: *The* _____
32. Nobility rank, in Britain
33. Dental office procedure
34. Places to drink 106-A
36. Powdered drink mix for astronauts
37. **Electrical current route**
38. Skye, in Scotland
39. Snitched on
43. Woodbine oval
46. Not occupied
47. **TTC word**
49. Italian seaport
54. "Don't get _____ of yourself"
55. The "T" in *ET Canada*
57. Ghana legal tender
58. How an intense light affects you
61. Rough estimate
62. 1977 Robin Cook novel
63. Italian mountain range
65. Damson's relative
66. Japanese garment belts
67. Pet on *The Flintstones*
68. Amaze
71. Eelworm, for one
74. Like a palatial home

77. Kemo _____
79. Charnel house
82. TSX debut
84. Shakespearean term of address
85. Weather Network advisories, say
87. German philosopher Georg

89. Choose
90. Gent
91. Timber wolf
92. Donald Trump campaign trail acronym
93. Canned meat brand

94. This gets carried into the House of Commons
95. On the peak of Mount Rundle
96. Abode in an ash
100. Trip type for a narcissist?

SOLUTION ON PAGE 173

63

Serving Queen and Country

Recent Governors General

ACROSS

1. Not shut
5. All-inclusive holidays provider: Club _____
8. Many cellphones have one
14. Youngish salmon
19. Soften in liquid
21. Respite
22. Rattan furniture maker
23. **Ed (1979–1984)**
24. Out-and-out
25. Suffix denoting "science"
26. Camphor, e.g.
27. Ontario Community Paramedicine Secretariat (abbr.)
29. Buddy Holly single: "Peggy _____"
30. Uses a sieve
31. Asian pheasant
34. Sous-chef's job
36. Toronto Raptors game surface (abbr.)
37. US retailer that closed its last Canadian stores in 2018
41. Rather redundant vehicle?
43. Nigerian dollar
45. Cuban coin
46. Bristly hairs
47. Give a knight a name
49. Rumple someone's hair
52. Like the Gobi
53. Guy's purchase at Moores
54. Roguish one
56. Catafalque
57. Divest of
58. Deodorant brand
59. **Adrienne (1999–2005)**
61. Cannabis pipe
62. 1979 Ian Thomas Band hit: "Time Is the _____"
64. Donkey's sound
65. Horse honoured on a 1999 Canada Post stamp: Big _____
66. Calico horse
67. Landfill rodent
68. Stem clusters
70. 1957 horror film: *I _____ a Teenage Werewolf*
71. Make adjustments
74. Victoria's narrowest street: _____ Tan Alley
75. Suit _____
76. Spiritual retreat
80. Show concern
81. **David (2010–2017)**
83. Day divisions, for short
84. *Star Trek: Deep Space Nine* shape-shifter name
85. Mosque main man
86. Fur on a royal's robe
87. Provided grub
88. Put cargo on board
89. Ex-Vancouver Canuck Sedin
91. Irish _____
92. Topples a tree
94. Moved rapidly
95. Long-time Canadian charity: Easter _____
97. Symmetrical, in olden days
99. Skinned the spuds
100. NATO ally of CDA
102. Bonnie Burnard Giller Prize winner: *A _____ House*
104. Southwestern Florida city
106. Shell's interior layer
108. American espionage agency (abbr.).
110. Geddy Lee's rock group
111. Sharp or savvy
116. More adorable
117. 1971 Jack Nicholson film: _____ *Knowledge*
119. **Roland (1967–1974)**
121. Of an eye part
122. Undivided
123. Poisonous ornamental shrub
124. A Kennedy, informally
125. Allergic reaction symptoms
126. Casino stake
127. Freight weight units

DOWN

1. Russian city
2. Nervously walk back and forth
3. Not fake, in Frankfurt
4. Emperor who might have liked gambling in Reno?
5. Hot dog brand: Oscar _____
6. Summer, in Quebec
7. Detract from
8. Fella
9. Lung membrane
10. Tarnish
11. Canadian North arrival times, for short
12. Raise the flag, say
13. At the back of a boat
14. October astrological sign
15. Timbuktu is here
16. Sometimes
17. **Jules (1974–1979)**
18. Secret assignation
20. Leases an apartment
28. Hip bone
32. Didn't dine at Milestones
33. Rock-bottom point
35. Shoppers' mecca: Toronto _____ Centre
37. Joni Mitchell's "Help Me" album: *Court and _____*
38. Uncanny
39. Half of a 45
40. Canadian sports announcer Black
42. Stag's marsh plant?
44. Garbage
46. Begin
48. Like the most uncouth Blue Jay?
50. Pre-Easter time
51. *Cogito, _____ sum*
54. **Julie (2017–2021)**
55. Former CFL great Lancaster

58. Lair animal
59. Nooks
60. Quebec watercourse: Rivière du _____
63. Early arrival on the maternity ward
64. One of the "Three Bs" in classical music
66. Landmark in the Rockies: Crowsnest _____
69. Bovine's call
70. Municipal districts in some Canadian cities
71. Etching liquid
72. Dalai _____
73. Did a deal
74. Not opposed to

77. Helicopter blade
78. Treasure a loved one
79. Cut the lawn
81. Jiggly dessert
82. Ginger cookies
83. Meeting greeting
87. Social media crowd?
88. Union, in Toronto (abbr.)
90. In an avid manner
92. Schoolmasters' canes, in olden days
93. Rogers Centre pitchers' stats
96. Canada's Christine Sinclair plays this sport
98. Zimbabwe's capital
99. Former title in Egypt

100. Like a diamond fresh from the mine
101. **Jeanne (1984–1990)**
103. Eight-time Juno Award winner Krall
105. Score instruction to be silent
107. Peruse the *Calgary Herald*
109. Some U of T majors
112. Campers' temporary shelter
113. Loosen shoelaces, say
114. High school student
115. Wanders off course
118. National Institutes of Health (abbr.)
120. Oldest St. Lawrence lighthouse site: _____ Verte

64

Cheer-io

Happy days are here again!

ACROSS

1. Severe
6. Canadian social commentary website: _____ News
11. Homey hotels
15. Ontario town near Pickering
19. Open-mouthed
20. California place whose name in Spanish means "The River"
21. _____ polish
22. She was a frosh last year
23. **Fun folks?**
25. Canadian Brass instrument
26. Novice
27. Sailor's shipboard pet?
28. More soaked
30. Small grey birds
32. Went off course, on the ocean
34. Heavy burden
36. Hot spot in Finland?
37. *Downton* _____
40. This has zero measure, in mathematics
44. Flower part
46. Fly high
47. Run of good luck
48. _____ in the woods
49. Vote option, in Vanier
52. Takes notice, at the gym?
54. Astronomical observation instrument
58. Burning cigarette end
59. Second chance, at the photography studio
61. London Drugs pharmacy bottle (var.)
62. Dregs
63. Famous Handel oratorio
65. Bread for a Bangladeshi
66. Canada's Percy Williams won two of these in sprinting at the 1928 Olympics
67. **Cheery Gordon Lightfoot hit?**

73. "Yeah"
76. Travelled by Calgary CTrain
77. The world according to Georg?
81. Actual
82. Not quietly
84. Orbital high point
87. Ontario Chiropractic Association (abbr.)
88. Process of putting into practice
91. Animal world breeding time
93. Drink slowly
94. Defensive trench
95. Old orthography style
97. Accompanying
98. Jabbers
100. Seaplane support
102. Amble along
103. George M. Cohan patriotic wartime song: "Over _____"
105. Edible root
107. Blue Jay Dave Stieb pitched this rare type of game in 1990
109. Rate a movie
111. On _____ of
115. Breakfast treat in Copenhagen?
118. Some Labatt libations
119. Part of the eye
121. **Canadian-invented exerciser that bounces baby?**
124. Okanagan Valley product
125. Extra order at Harvey's, say
126. "What _____ in the neck!"
127. Playground meanies do this
128. Plenty
129. Canada's Dorothy Livesay was one
130. Variety show
131. Noted German artist Max

DOWN

1. Deli counter purchase
2. "Rock of _____"
3. Not usual

4. Paint applicators
5. Alfalfa farmer's prosperous season?
6. Assaying substance
7. Prevalent mammal in BC
8. 1983 Bob and Doug McKenzie movie: *Strange* _____
9. Hibernia
10. 1992 Blue Rodeo song: "_____ Together"
11. Focused on
12. Island northeast of Australia
13. Licorice bit
14. Eastern Europe resident
15. Lost, like a Lab?
16. **Celebratory occasion in Quebec?**
17. Chef's wear
18. An official language of Zimbabwe
24. Do some yard work
29. Foot part
31. Ewe and May, in Scotland
33. African-grown grain sorghum
35. Famed opera house: La _____
37. Type of tea
38. Capital of Idaho
39. Scrubs in tubs
41. Bicycle tire puncture result
42. Fill up a freighter
43. Enjoy a day at Alberta's Marmot Basin
45. One son of Eve
47. NL headland: Cape _____
48. CBC show: _____ *Erica*
50. *Winnipeg Sun* commentary
51. Famed US lawman Eliot
53. Bathsheba's spouse
55. Brilliantly coloured fish
56. Bangkok native
57. Sickens with sweetness
60. _____ *Wayne and Shuster Hour*
64. Racing craft for Silken Laumann

65. Wedding announcement word
66. Montreal hosted these in 1976: Olympic _____
68. Long-time CBC show: _____ Page Challenge
69. Overwhelm the opposition
70. Norse literary collection
71. Greedy pork eater?
72. Ferris _____
73. American novelist Leon
74. Powerful engine, for short
75. **Blessed maternity ward moment?**
78. Nocturnal Indian primate
79. Critical

80. Wishy-_____
82. Not in control
83. Most trifling quantity
84. "_____ Too Proud to Beg"
85. Not much, in Milano
86. Aromatic vegetable
89. Host
90. Barrel
92. Adulterer
96. Bland
99. Springs up?
100. Arrange in advance
101. Delighted sound?
102. One-sixtieth of an hour
103. Fish with a dragnet

104. Three-time Indy 500 champion Castroneves
106. "_____ With Me"
108. 1984 book by 73-D: The _____
110. Tuft
112. Not quite closed
113. See 102-A
114. US rapper: Flavor _____
116. Interval of time
117. Canadian-born actress Elizabeth
120. Brazilian seaside metropolis, for short
122. *Elementary* star Lucy
123. Soften flax

65 Golden '00s Canadian Olympians

They shone in their sports

ACROSS

1. Not suitable at all
6. Marilyn Denis' role on CTV
10. Lights from lasers
15. A lot, to cads?
19. Less dangerous
20. Leer
21. 2010 Olympics opening ceremony flag-bearer Dallaire
22. 2013 Céline Dion track: "Always Be _____ Girl"
23. Firewood delivery
24. Duct drop
25. With a frosty attitude
26. Abortive attempt
27. **In 2008, Canada's men's eight won gold in this**
29. Dresses a queen for her coronation
31. In need of fixing
33. Wrecker's job
35. Street child
36. Dispatching dandelions
37. Is nosy
41. Minute circular shape
43. Piece of glass
44. Tease Scott Joplin?
45. Earned Day Off (abbr.)
46. **In 2006, Klassen and Hughes won track gold in this**
49. **Nestor and Lareau won doubles 2000 gold in this**
51. Large weight unit
52. Chignon, for example
53. Fathers, for short
54. Can't stand
57. Turner's duet with 115-A: "_____ Only Love"
58. Louisiana city: _____ Rouge
61. You might have an ace up this
64. Nobel-winning Canadian author Alice
65. Keyboard that plays by itself
66. Marsh perennial
67. Overlapping fugue components
70. Canadian milk carton unit
71. _____ fertilization
73. Ear-splitting
74. Called up on a CB
76. No voters
77. Consecration ceremonies
79. Senior or junior Bronfman who ran Seagram
80. Conducted an orchestra
83. Former MuchMusic video show host Ehm
84. Mother bird
85. European Democratic Union (abbr.)
86. Royal woman's headpiece
88. **In 2006, Jennifer Heil skied to gold in this**
90. **At Turin, Chandra Crawford won gold in this skiing sprint discipline**
94. 1980 track from 115-A: "Wait and _____"
96. General Post Office (abbr.)
97. Beach play toy
98. "_____ o' the mornin' to ya"
99. Loch _____
100. Camper's light
102. In poor shape
104. Quinn who coached one of the teams in 109-A
106. Items of clothing
107. Minuscule amount
109. **In 2002, our men and women scored gold in this**
114. Fuel for a furnace
115. Canadian music star Bryan
117. Listen to advice
119. Jive or jitterbug
120. Western Asia ethnic group member
121. First thesaurus compiler
122. 1987 album from 115-A: _____ the Fire
123. Nebraska big city
124. Eyelid annoyance
125. *The Guns of Navarone* actress Gia
126. Under-the-skin bump
127. School start mos.

DOWN

1. Russia, from 1922–91 (abbr.)
2. Canada's a member of this international org.
3. Paul Anka song lyric: "Regrets, I've had _____..."
4. 1990s TV actress Gilpin
5. Ontario university
6. BC place: Radium _____ Springs
7. S-shaped moulding
8. Speak in the vernacular?
9. Reptile with a shell
10. Illegally paying for influence
11. Geological epoch name
12. Montreal mates
13. Early '80s Calgary Flame Bridgman
14. Proteinaceous vegetable
15. Ecclesiastical planning council
16. Baker's tray
17. Sum segment, in math
18. Crested Aussie songbird
28. Some mythology beings
30. It joined the Arab League in 1971
32. Pertaining to a monarch's tenure
34. Chinese recipe cooking pot
36. **At Beijing, Carol Huynh won gold on the mat in this**
37. _____ Spumante
38. Bit of acne
39. Former NHLer Linseman, et al.
40. OTT NHL player
42. Not acceptable in society
47. First appearance
48. Wine barrel
49. Starchy tuber

50. Candytuft, by another name
53. Common Canadian tree
55. Shania Twain song: "Come On _____"
56. Overhaul decor
59. Sinuses
60. **Simon Whitfield won gold in this inaugural Sydney event**
61. Construction locations
62. Difficult
63. Indiana town: _____ Claus
64. Student physician
65. Subatomic particle
67. Gin fruit
68. Vacuum pressure measurement
69. Basic
70. Rival of a Stamp

72. *Objets d'art*
75. Appropriate anagram for Caesar's fateful day?
76. Parched, in olden days
78. Fishwife
79. Former Western Canada premiers Stelmach and Schreyer
80. Elizabeth Hay's 2007 Giller winner: _____ *Nights on Air*
81. Goes off course
82. Calendar components
85. Stone Age tools description
87. Motel kin
89. Raises
90. Two-deck card game
91. Spat
92. WPS employee

93. Colourful fish
94. Trousers
95. Dine at The Keg, say
97. Beat on
101. Diacritical language mark
103. Small
105. Hooplas
107. 1982 Juno-winning band
108. Lab vermin
110. Made an appearance
111. Shatter with a hammer
112. Not fake, in Germany
113. Affirmative votes
116. Johnny Carson's band leader Severinsen
118. Deteriorate

'00s Oscars

Best picture winners

ACROSS

1. Scrapbooker's jewellery?
6. Liver-based spread
10. Person using in-line skates
16. Canadian cops' org.
19. Queried
20. They lay large eggs
21. Ex-NHLer Rob who played for three Canadian teams
22. Medium for Emily Carr
23. **Tolkien trilogy winner: _____: The Return of the King (2004)**
26. Compadre
27. OTT publicity
28. One side of Canada: _____ Coast
29. Had a BMO mortgage
30. Herbal tea
32. Sore spot symptom
34. Still snoozing
35. Phantom
36. **Coen brothers' thriller winner (2008)**
42. Some AGO displays
43. 2012 Our Lady Peace track: "Window _____"
44. Poem that praises
45. Pillowcase
49. Move like Tiny Tim?
51. Notable cartel formed in 1960 (abbr.)
53. Tusk material
55. Palindromic animal
56. GPS reading
57. Sound heard at First Choice Haircutters salons
59. Geneva's river
61. Former memory chip device
63. Zinfandel, et al.
65. Unreturnable serves from Canada's Bianca Andreescu
67. Song from Nova Scotian Snow: "_____ Been Everywhere"
68. Written neatly

70. Old-style Uber?
74. McGill staff, en masse
77. Field for 55-A
78. Bakery goody
79. Beauty queen's wrapper
83. Without any accompaniment
84. Post-metamorphosis insect
86. Amniotic sac
88. Blue jeans brand since 1889
89. High point
90. Hemp type
93. Prime minister's pledge
95. Tartans, say
97. Canada's Walk of Fame honouree
99. "I cannot tell a _____"
100. Bachman-Turner Overdrive hit: "You Ain't _____ Nothing Yet"
102. French clerics
103. **British drama winner set in Mumbai (2009)**
109. Bursts of artillery
112. Bartender's liquors
113. Cave, to a poet
114. Style of sunglasses
115. Raga anagram
116. Brief name of Hamilton's newspaper
118. It precedes rock or rain
122. Juno winner Drake's genre
123. **Winning sports drama directed by Clint Eastwood (2005)**
127. Roadie's haul
128. Engenders joy
129. It precedes Tishrei
130. Impish
131. *Royal Canadian Air Farce* actress Luba
132. Topple a tyrant
133. Medically induced state of sleep
134. Canadian birds?

DOWN

1. Stanley Park trail
2. Pale
3. Bee enclosure
4. Travel through space, like Captain Kirk
5. Princess Beatrice's husband, for short
6. Nitpickers
7. Quebec town
8. Bit of hair
9. Kitchener clock setting (abbr.)
10. Molson or Labatt
11. BC sound that shares its name with a Texas city
12. Maid anagram
13. Ottawa-born Blues Brother Aykroyd
14. Hourglass-shaped kitchen gadget
15. Live in Lethbridge, say
16. Aromatic resin
17. Diana Krall plays this
18. Order of Canada painter Sapp
24. One of a pair of equestrian straps
25. Transient person
31. Justin and Sacha, to Pierre
33. Coupes and sports cars
34. Later on
35. Tuber type
36. Stenographer, say
37. Share a thought
38. The _____ Crusader
39. Get back in business, post COVID-19
40. Little dog's bark
41. 1973 Anne Murray hit: "A _____ Song"
46. Former federal Liberal cabinet minister Dhaliwal
47. Illegally off base (abbr.)
48. Same, in Chibougamau
50. Pass into law on the Hill

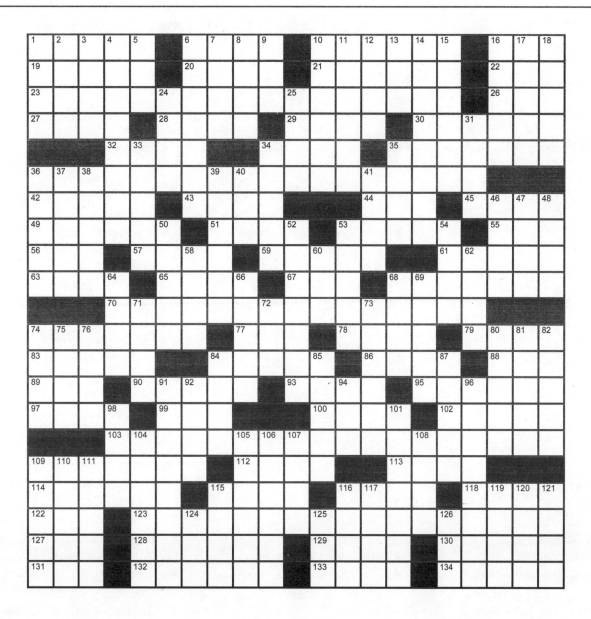

52. **Musical crime film winner (2003)**
53. Not moving
54. Safecracker, in Britspeak
58. Disgusting
60. Eggs
62. Pizza or pumpkin servings
64. Excommunicate
66. Montreal-born *All of Me* actress Diamond
68. The euro replaced this in Italy
69. Devour dinner, say
71. The die has been cast: _____ *iacta est*
72. Nay's opposite
73. Former Alberta premier Notley
74. Lard and suet
75. Frequently
76. Canadian Owners and Pilots Association (abbr.)
80. Suspect's excuse
81. Ceremonial Jewish meal
82. *Steppenwolf* scribe Hermann
84. Tim Hortons beverage: _____ coffee
85. Fertile desert area
87. Colombia land feature
91. River originating in Ethiopia
92. Objectives
94. Israeli city: _____ Aviv
96. Like asbestos removed during renovations
98. Invitation response, in brief
101. Celebrity chef Lawson
104. Hung over the weaver?
105. Bacchanalia
106. Curved, in botany
107. Intend to be nasty?
108. Ocean mammal on a Canadian team's NHL jersey
109. Lamb's neck
110. San Antonio landmark
111. Impertinent
115. California place: Palo _____
116. See 83-A
117. Juicy purple fruit
119. Bistro
120. Heron's kin
121. Unit of force, in physics
124. Place to put a napkin
125. Kwanzaa mo.
126. Former federal Liberal cabinet minister Alcock

SOLUTION ON PAGE 174

67 Palatial Places

Canadian castles, mansions and more

ACROSS

1. Break out of custody
7. Claps of thunder
12. So to speak, formally
20. Brunei bigwig
21. 1940s actress June who was born in BC
22. Installed new software
23. **Scottish baronial mansion in Victoria: _____ Castle**
25. **Baden ON Italianate villa: Castle _____**
26. Unfertilized seed
27. Flexible medical-use tube
29. Florida place: _____ West
30. Bagpiper's hat
31. To-do _____
32. Sneaky scheme
33. Garment repairer
35. Ricky Martin song: "Livin' la Vida _____"
36. Portage, in WPG
37. Dads, in Dorset
39. Settles a debt
40. Long-time Canadian figure skating star Browning
41. Settles a dispute about a crossword?
43. Cone-shaped abode (var.)
45. Here, in Hull
46. Moosehead libation
47. Hamilton Philharmonic section
48. Middle-age _____
51. Humiliate
54. Brown quickly, in the kitchen
55. Start of a refrain
57. Triathlon component
59. Applies extra effort, say
60. Order of Canada endocrinologist Selye
61. Greek mythology queen
62. Long-time soap brand
63. Former Blue Jays manager Gaston

64. Under a _____ of suspicion
66. Battlefield doctor
67. Bible book
68. SK-born Hustak who penned *Titanic: The Canadian Story*
69. Mathematical calculation: Square _____
70. "Toodle-oo!"
71. Carefully nose forward
73. Not masc.
74. Too precipitous
75. Cuckoos' kin
76. Well _____ in
77. State of senility
79. SST boom type
81. Official Alberta tree: Lodgepole _____
82. Jogged
83. Adjective for a dominant male
84. Canines?
88. Potato farmer's spade?
89. Run from the scene of a crime
90. Red-hot cuisine pods (var.)
92. Legal Aid Ontario (abbr.)
93. Scornful Scrooge cries?
94. Jacket type for Ravel?
96. Dubai VIP
97. Comox-born ex-NHLer Neely, et al.
98. Alternative to "Aha!"
99. Tall tree in BC: Douglas _____
100. Chess tactic: En _____
102. Toronto Raptors top executive Ujiri
103. **Gothic Revival mansion in Toronto**
106. **Colwood BC Scottish baronial estate**
108. Having scalloped edges
109. Bouts of chills, in olden days
110. More chichi
111. From Manitoba to Ontario
112. Ministers to
113. Itty-bitty

DOWN

1. Snake mackerel
2. Gloria Gaynor disco hit: "I Will _____"
3. Santa's riders?
4. Not straight
5. Long-running CBC show: *Front _____ Challenge*
6. Cease
7. Sentence segments
8. Breadwinner
9. River that begins in Shakespeare ON
10. Fill-in physician
11. Carries a heavy load (var.)
12. North Sea avian
13. Metal cleats
14. Not as healthy as others
15. English pottery piece: _____ jug
16. Canadian history event: _____ of 1812
17. Writes a *National Post* column?
18. Amend text
19. Cause of ankle swelling
24. More severe
28. Operating room drug
32. **Montreal Italian Renaissance mansion built in the 1860s**
34. Use Just For Men
35. Clare Boothe _____
37. Kilt fold
38. Abandon on a central London road?
40. 2013 CCMA female artist of the year Isabella
42. 1930s screen queen Merle
44. Basset hounds have long ones
47. Models need lots of this?
48. Rani's garment
49. **Montreal French chateau-style hotel/railway station built in the late 1890s**
50. Sweetie
51. Coffee option at Tim Hortons

52. Kicked out of a country
53. Larva-to-adult transformations
54. "Fiddlesticks," to the photographer?
56. As _____ a beet
58. Endocrine node
62. U of T grad's achievement
65. Come second
66. Lunatic
70. Hyperbolic function
72. Car door dings
74. Guess Who classic: "_____ Me Down World"

78. Some Greek consonants
80. Men's collapsible topper
81. Form of civil government
83. 2011 Bieber/Carey duet: "_____ I Want for Christmas Is You"
84. Lack of light
85. Protein that lets skin stretch
86. Some Mexican meal servings
87. Stockings and socks
88. Arid African expanse
89. Previous
91. Recovered from an injury

93. Lawn bowling game
94. Region's plant and animal life
95. US Siouan people
97. Indian class division
99. Diamond imperfection, say
101. Leave agape
102. Filly's mother
104. Paul Rudd plays this movies franchise character: _____-Man
105. _____ insult to injury
107. Tortoiseshell or Russian Blue

68

The Sounds of Music

Let's make some noise!

ACROSS

1. Nuclear missile type (abbr.)
5. Niagara Falls, et al.
13. Sanctuary components
18. Indonesian island
19. Advocate
20. Frog's "ribbit"
21. Mononymous model who hosted *Project Runway Canada*
22. Motion in the ocean
23. Poppy Family member Jacks
24. Abhor examinations?
26. Thaw
27. **Recorder's sound**
29. Pertaining to hearing
31. To be, in Berlin
33. Alice Munro story collection: *Something _____ Been Meaning to Tell You*
34. _____ King Cole
37. 1990 Olivia Newton-John TV movie: _____ *for Christmas*
39. Emerged again
44. Related to soil and crop management practices
47. Wound with a dirk
48. Penultimate Rogers Cup round
49. **Castanets' snap**
50. Shaw Festival production
52. *Animal Farm*, for example
54. Canadian retailer: _____ Renfrew
55. Military chaplain
56. Bolshevik leader Vladimir
57. 16 species of this live in Canada
58. Former PEI premier Binns
59. Bill in a bar
61. Soldier on one side of the Civil War
62. Canadian Marketing Association (abbr.)
65. CanLit, for example
67. Smelling _____
69. *Happy Days* actress Moran

70. Celestial body
73. Rite anagram
74. **Ozark harp thrum**
75. Sinatra signature song: "I've Got You Under My _____"
76. Uses the oars
78. In 1773, over 300 of these were tossed into Boston Harbor
80. Physics branch concerned with motion
83. Irritate
84. Boiling, in summer
85. Mojito alcohol
86. Black, in Beaupré
88. Where CCR got stuck?
90. **Snare drum sound**
94. Not conforming, in Jewish dietary law (var.)
96. 1982 hit from The Clash: "Rock the _____"
100. Roundish
101. Ruin a roast?
104. Canadian auto service chain: Mr. _____
105. Quebec city: _____-Tracy
106. Building's safety regulations
107. US children's books writer: _____ Jack Keats
108. Twitchy
109. Description of lower-level Rogers Cup players
110. Former Russian ruler (var.)

DOWN

1. Footnote abbr.
2. "It _____ Upon the Midnight Clear"
3. **Trumpet's clamour**
4. 1950s movie star Sal
5. Former Spanish currency unit
6. Terminate a forestry worker?
7. Pork-based canned meat
8. Manages okay in a crisis
9. Roebuck's rack component

10. Goddesses and gods
11. The beginning of the _____
12. Hearty recipe: Brunswick _____
13. ParticipACTION encourages Canadians to be this
14. Description of Blue Jays spring training games
15. Put into categories
16. American bluegrass icon Scruggs
17. Hebrides island
25. Reeked
28. Ilia form part of these
30. Fellow Canadian
32. In Nova Scotia, the first Monday in August is this: _____ Day
34. Tortilla chip
35. Gleaming
36. **Flute's vibration**
38. Somewhat warm
40. Written evidence?
41. Tim Hortons option, for short
42. Second-largest bird in the world
43. Yahtzee game piece
45. Month when Canadians give thanks (abbr.)
46. Grocery buggy
51. Bun recipe ingredient
53. Grit
55. Great view from a BC recreational resort?
58. KPH word
60. Entice a trout?
62. **Cymbals' sound**
63. Ontario town named for Canada's eighth Governor General
64. Sense of dread
65. Produces electricity, at Pickering B 7
66. Long-time US newsman Newman
68. Stare, like a Shakespearean king?
69. Ram's counterpart

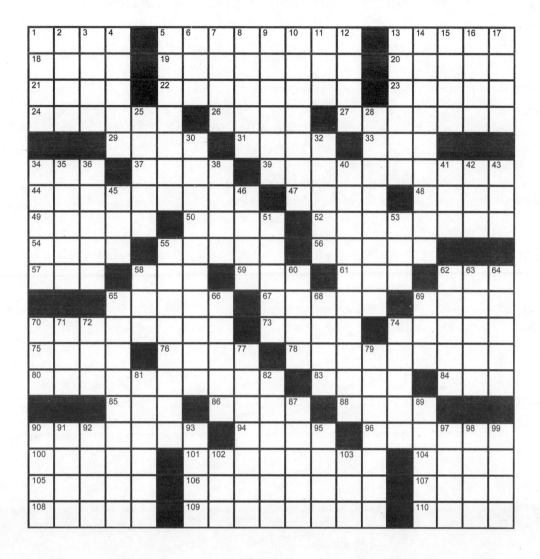

70. Make an inquiry
71. Canada's Ken Read did this at two Olympics
72. Soup can
74. Silent movies star Bara
77. Black sea ducks
79. Walloped the track meet timer?
81. Without any sound

82. Emphatic word that follows yes or no (var.)
87. Scout around, in brief
89. Atoll relative
90. US civil rights icon: _____ Parks
91. Stratford Festival theatre name
92. Acerbic, like the baker?
93. Protein source for vegetarians

95. Government publication: *Canada's _____ Guide*
97. **Kazoo noise**
98. Magician's phrase starter
99. Take in, aurally
102. White or red drink in Repentigny
103. Verse about a doe?

69

Give Me a B...

For these Canadian cities

ACROSS

1. Holds up a bank, say
5. Japanese garment belts
9. Feminine side, to Carl Jung
14. Mark left by surgery
18. Three-quarter length pants style
19. Arne song: "_____, Britannia!"
20. Ethical
21. Tiny hole
22. Canadian movie theatre chain: Cineplex _____
23. Alfalfa or flax, in Saskatchewan
24. Description of some lab work
26. Revelry
28. Seed sheath
30. **City east of Vancouver**
31. Polish city
32. Small speck of land in the ocean
34. Morning, in 77-D
35. Litigate
36. Org. that employs Canadian astronauts
37. Lettuce variety
38. These shed light on the subject?
42. National Non-Smoking Week falls in this mo.
45. Like fens
47. Talk
49. Acid neutralizer
50. In the centre of things
52. Grated potatoes fare: Tater _____
53. Toronto retailer for 68 years: _____ Ed's
55. "Yikes!" in days of yore
56. Less
58. As crazy as a _____
60. Prepare for war
62. **City in the GTA**
64. "When You Wish _____ a Star"
66. 1990s phone company: BC _____
67. National currency abbr.
68. Fermenting yeast
69. Stretch your neck to see a bird?
70. Org. that delivers mail in OR
72. Margaret Atwood offering: *Life Before* _____
75. Fruity cocktail: Mai _____
76. Birds' lofty perch (var.)
77. **Nepisiguit River city in New Brunswick**
81. School type for young ones
84. Beef or pork
86. Farewell word in 77-D
87. Vishnu companion (var.)
88. Fills a sanctuary with perfume
90. Falsehoods
92. Thin wooden board
93. Redress wrongdoing
95. Sydney province: _____ Scotia
96. Sick and tired of Ottawa bureaucracy?
98. Big bird
99. Quebec-born former NHLer Aubin
100. Paronomasia
101. Stylish
103. Catch hold of a crook
105. Pond scum description
107. Khaki cloth
108. Toronto-born Adam who won the Cup with the Rangers and Oilers
112. **Manitoba's second-largest city**
115. Former Saskatchewan premier Wall
116. Inconclusive end of a court proceeding
118. Former southeastern Europe country
120. 15th of May, to an old Roman
122. Composed an email, say
123. Via, informally
124. Releases light
125. Palindromic bread
126. Suffered from an illness
127. Significant periods in history
128. Lions' tresses
129. Surfeit
130. Vintage, say

DOWN

1. Speeders' nemesis
2. Musical entertainers: Manitoba _____
3. **Trans-Canada Highway city in Alberta**
4. Curving in and out
5. Mammal sometimes spotted on BC boat tours
6. **City abutting Lake Ontario**
7. 1969 Nobel Peace Prize-winning grp.
8. Calyx parts
9. Range
10. Shred of silk or wool
11. Interest Rate Option (abbr.)
12. Deadly snakes
13. Shumagin Islands people
14. Sail for downwind directions
15. *Your Show of Shows* star Imogene
16. Damascus resident
17. Lean on for succour
18. _____-a-doodle-do
25. Military training exercise
27. Orange tuber: _____ potato
29. Alex Trebek hosted this: _____ *for the Top*
33. "Because I _____!"
34. Setting for *Psycho*
37. Dog's tooth?
39. Legerdemain
40. Hotel chain in Canada: Crowne _____
41. Allied (with)
42. Window frame part
43. Arabic aristocrat
44. *Pinta*'s companion
46. Pass and peak name in Banff National Park

48. 112-D, vis-à-vis 115-D
49. Verify veracity (with "to")
51. Struck _____
54. Put in place
57. See 129-A
59. Russian Rudolf who danced with Canada's Karen Kain
61. Greek alphabet opener
63. Hypnotic state
65. Golf hole average
69. Long-time late night TV host Johnny
71. Beer or bath bubbles
72. Buttes and tablelands
73. Living and breathing
74. "It'll _____ fly!"

77. St. Lawrence River city in Quebec
78. Disturb
79. Clothing line?
80. Ballerina's tulle garment
82. Containing chemical element Mn
83. Void a marriage
85. Like an imp?
89. Nickname of Pierre Trudeau's second son
91. Canadian fashion designer Alfred, et al.
94. Fixes, on the farm?
97. To some extent
100. Central American canal
102. _____ in plain sight

104. Kempenfelt Bay shores city
106. Supernatural automaton, in Jewish folklore
107. Rude
109. Flower for a string section musician?
110. "Peter Peter Pumpkin _____"
111. Winter ride
112. Homonym for 115-D
113. Western Germany river
114. Indian Pearl Mosque city
115. Take a mouthful
117. "Say It _____ So"
119. Fast & Furious franchise star Diesel
121. Vancouver's "King of Swing" Richards

SOLUTION ON PAGE 175

145

70

Animal Antics

A pack of puns

ACROSS

1. Pillaging or plundering
7. Saffron-flavoured dish
13. French president Emmanuel, et al.
20. Asbestos removal company employee
21. Listen to CBC Radio?
22. Inability to swallow
23. **Fido's mess?**
25. Geological depressions between faults
26. "_____ to Billie Joe"
27. Hippies' drug
28. Alternative choice
30. Voodooism
31. Gall
33. 2013 Drake track: "_____ Love Beyoncé"
36. Early Persian
38. Hampered
40. Island in the Aegean
42. Fall while vacationing?
46. Crossed
49. Patterned fabrics
50. Literary name for the Emerald Isle
51. Provincial capital
52. Forgive someone's sins
54. Without exception, for him?
56. "Sure…"
57. Undisturbed, to Brutus
59. And more, in brief
61. *Corner Gas* actor Butt
62. Jacques Cousteau's ship
64. Computer architecture acronym
66. Weedy vetches
68. Nunavut hamlet airport code
69. **Rudolph's playtime?**
72. Lily, in Laval
75. Calgary Stampede competition rope
76. Portico for Plato, for example

77. Chic
79. Braided lock
82. Hither's partner
84. Russian currency unit (var.)
86. Golden reign?
87. Savoury Asian turnover
89. "Sorry, not possible"
91. Devoted one
93. It's got you covered?
94. Kitty's condiment?
96. Elaborate
98. Texas senator Cruz, et al.
99. Like some McGill buildings
100. Act of contrition
101. Double-_____ tape
103. Therapeutic treatments
104. *Lady and the _____*
108. Über manly
111. Sustenance of the gods
114. You might treat yourself to this at the Empress
116. Bit of baby talk?
117. Weekend tasks, say
119. **Balderdash, to the equestrian?**
123. Smelting slag
124. Of bones
125. Parisians' fishing nets?
126. Elements
127. Comprised of flint-like rock
128. African insect

DOWN

1. Noxious gas
2. House or condo
3. Cellphone predecessor
4. 2014 Juno-nominated Michael Bublé song: "_____ a Beautiful Day"
5. Male peers of the realm
6. Flubs, at Rogers Centre?
7. 1968 Jeannie C. Riley hit: "Harper Valley _____"
8. Northern seas flyer

9. Swathe
10. Jetés at a National Ballet of Canada performance
11. HGTV Canada airing: *Love It or _____ It*
12. _____-lock brakes
13. Big business tycoon
14. St. George's Day mo. in NL
15. Pandemonium
16. **Playboy bunny's antennas?**
17. Gothic moulding
18. Atmospheric event: La _____
19. Window framework
24. Rims
29. *HMS Pinafore*, for one
32. Enliven
34. Innovative thoughts
35. Cardinal, colloquially
37. Remainder
39. Approves of the sermon?
40. CDN army rank
41. Bank of the St. Lawrence, in Quebec
43. Coleridge poem: "The _____ of the Ancient Mariner"
44. Afghanistan neighbour
45. _____-up frustrations
46. Former race car driver from Canada Paul
47. Took an exam again
48. Lithe, like a gymnast
49. **Exterminator's favourite board game?**
53. Pigs' digs
55. Overweight
58. Clamorous
60. Bedouin's desert beast
63. Dolts
65. Sing like Sinatra?
67. Upgrade knowledge
70. Midday
71. More ostentatious
72. Canadian confectioner: _____ Secord

73. Settlement in Nunavut: Rankin _____
74. Cordwood measurement
75. **Most, on the Serengeti?**
78. Sobeys, for one
79. Nearly silent interjection
80. _____ Superior
81. Among
83. Facial protuberance
85. Bay on the western side of Newfoundland
88. Test type for an etcher?

90. Bovine's mouthful
92. Gives notes to a stenographer
95. Rose family plants
97. One of the five senses
100. Ship's accountant
102. Architectural column style
103. Menu, in Montreal
105. Intact Insurance representative
106. Additional social standards?
107. Wild West vigilantes
108. Arizona city
109. Paths for pendulums

110. Resize a photo
112. Sweet chunk sold by 72-D, for short
113. "Nonsense!" in Norwich
115. Geographic region of Canada: _____ Coast
118. "Can't Help Lovin' _____ Man"
120. k.d. lang album: *All You Can* _____
121. Travel via WestJet
122. Rush

SOLUTION ON PAGE 175

Who Am I? 4

She soared for Canada

ACROSS

1. Latter half of a Rogers Centre inning
7. Police officers' emblems
13. Tattled on
20. Cry like Casper?
21. Touch down at Pearson
22. **She is… (with 95-A)**
23. Dudes who are rude
24. Rise, like bread dough
25. Early Maritimes resident
26. Murmurs
27. Places, to Caesar
28. Bathroom fixture
30. Songs for a single
31. Pale, like the chimney cleaner?
33. Owl's claw
34. Tree or shrub name
36. Psi preceder
37. Italy's largest lake
39. Grasp a concept
41. Containing element #76
46. Shania Twain classic: "Any Man of _____"
48. Bogged down in mud, say
50. Livestock meadow
51. **Honour she received in 2018: Order of _____**
52. Undersea "bird"
54. Leave dumbstruck
56. Like narrowly spaced eyes
58. Put the kettle on
59. Elizabeth May's favourite colour?
61. Like one pre-Columbian culture
62. Not in attendance
65. Male children
66. Moniker for Washington Capitals star Alexander
68. Pro _____
69. Costa del _____
70. **Her Ontario hometown**
75. Unit at the gym
76. Paper _____
78. Tippler

79. Liveliness
80. Gastric _____ surgery
82. Meals
85. Sharp in taste
87. Wharf
88. Blacksmith's milieu
90. Wayne _____ Shuster
91. Canada's official summer game
95. **See 22-A**
96. Aggressive knock
98. Marry in secret
100. High-end hotel amenities
101. Student's exam component
102. Body of art?
104. "Halt!" to a salt
106. Montreal CFL team nickname
107. New Brunswick city: _____ John
109. Judge's mallet
111. Zany
113. "The Hockey Sweater" writer Carrier
117. Guide
118. _____ Canadian Superstore
119. Cause exasperation
120. Interested, in the morning?
122. Come out of a cocoon
124. Type style that leans to the right
127. **Alberta city in which an elementary school is named for her**
128. Teapot warmers (var.)
129. Ti to ti, say
130. International alliance
131. Become preoccupied
132. Ancient city in Egypt

DOWN

1. *Top Gear* network
2. Circus tent interjection
3. **Her 1994 book: _____ the Earth**
4. Spasm
5. Chinese tea type

6. Peat _____
7. Poetic songs?
8. These surround pimples
9. Harsh judge, in ancient Greece
10. Generous
11. Cain and Abel's mother
12. Capable of feeling
13. Canadian country and western singer Paul
14. English philosopher John
15. Rhyme scheme triplet
16. The Brick sells these
17. Vigorously, in music: Con _____
18. Too many more to mention abbr.
19. *American Pickers* cast member, colloquially: _____ D
29. Significant pelvic artery
31. Pinnacle
32. *Disturbia* star LaBeouf
33. Manitoba Court of Queen's Bench proceeding
35. Sunday supper serving
38. Nectar for Hindu gods
40. USS *Robert* _____
42. Express scorn
43. Maybelline cosmetic
44. Conceptualizes
45. Felines' forty winks?
47. European river
49. Mends stockings
51. Child of your unc
53. Geological periods
55. **An Ontario university she attended**
57. Cubs' home
59. 1974 hit from Montreal's Gino Vannelli: "People _____ Move"
60. Saharan wanderer
62. Attribute to an author?
63. Short jackets for composer Ravel?
64. Loafers
65. _____-mo

67. Moving company vehicle
71. Yuri Andropov governed this country (abbr.)
72. Omit an "i," say
73. Wild Eurasian goats (var.)
74. Observer, in olden days
77. Bamboo consumer
81. Canadian golfers Henderson and DeLaet, for example
83. Influences
84. CNE city
86. Blue Jays toppers
87. Like Vatican dispensations
89. Iceland currency

91. American country singer Patty
92. **She performed astral experiments on this**
93. Famed physician Jonas
94. Petro-Canada rival
97. 1930s design style
99. Flushes with water, medically
102. Colour clothing for a flower child
103. Princess Fiona, for one
105. Tic
108. BC island community: _____ Bay

110. Cliffside perch for birds
112. Get _____ start
113. Honda Indy Toronto, for example
114. Algerian city
115. Horse farm newborn
116. Gigantic
119. Violent street scene
121. _____ Salvador
123. Group involved in 119-D
125. Michael Bublé cover: "_____ Got You Under My Skin"
126. These, in Quebec City

Classic tales

ACROSS

1. Heathen
6. Makes a selection
10. *The Hobbit* character Baggins
15. Obtains
19. Like a feeble-minded female
20. Indian woman's dress
21. Goodbye word, in Gatineau
22. *Ugly Betty* co-star Michael
23. **Jane Austen novel (1818)**
25. Hold one's attention
26. Blue Rodeo hit: "Diamond
    _____"
27. Plots rented from councils, in England
28. Caviar serving
29. Scalawag
31. Pointe-Claire pronoun
32. Canadian clothing retailer since 1973
33. Said "hi" for the first time
34. German baroque composer
35. Egyptian deity
36. Bruce Cockburn song: "If I _____ a Rocket Launcher"
37. Farm building for fowl
41. Scholars
44. The Blue Bombers did this on 11/24/19
45. Employment opportunity on Edmonton's Whyte Avenue
46. Suncor management grp., say
47. Drops one's guard
49. Children's game
50. Spelling who's married to Canada's Dean McDermott
51. Not so much
53. Newfoundland ecological reserve island
54. Can't stand
57. Influence by flattering
59. Kuril Islands people
60. Sector
61. **See 23-A (1811)**

66. Old-style blow
67. Norway's most populous city
68. Men's or ladies'
70. Horrified
73. Ran from the law
74. Stack
75. Dairy Queen treat: Ice cream _____
76. Southeast Asian language
77. Enter illegally
79. Opiner
80. Styles wet hair
84. Frazier's foe, in a bout
85. Stephen Sondheim musical: _____ *Night Music*
87. The Parti Québécois wants to do this
88. www.nightwoodeditions.com, for one
89. Toronto Symphony Orchestra section
90. Kill a bill, say
91. Medium for some artists
92. Attire sold at Moores stores
93. 1,006 in Roman numerals
96. Shop for a señorita
99. California place: Santa _____
100. Layered, like a rock seam
102. 1971 Anne Murray song: "Talk It _____ in the Morning"
103. 1980s Canadian popsters: Glass _____
105. **William Godwin offering (1817)**
106. BC First Nation
107. Morning wake-up
108. Fair
109. Bodily swelling condition
110. Children's snowy day toy
111. The Knave of Hearts stole these
112. Used to be
113. Former Chicago Cub Sammy, et al.

DOWN

1. Daddies
2. Administer unction, old style
3. Alice Munro collection: *Lives of _____ and Women*
4. Too
5. Subatomic particles
6. Comprised of bone
7. Supplies for Robert Bateman
8. They're slower than gallops
9. Bad actions, in the Bible
10. Like jail windows
11. Dummkopf
12. McCartney movie theme song: "_____ and Let Die"
13. Quilters' gathering
14. Surpass a sergeant?
15. Detective's galosh?
16. Canadian mysteries writer Wright
17. Singer Turner
18. Blind a bird
24. Apathetic, old style
30. Persistent soreness
33. **See 23-A (1814)**
34. Sanders' 2016/2020 campaign slogan: "Feel the _____"
35. Estate, in Spain
36. 36-A, for example
37. 2001 war movie: *Black _____ Down*
38. _____ no good
39. Brown meat in a pan
40. Joule components
41. Pharaoh name
42. Neural transmitters
43. Energy
44. Dewy
45. Exemplary employee's payment
47. Claim by a creditor
48. Slang for "I have no idea"
51. 99 or 86, on *Get Smart*
52. Cry, plaintively
54. Emerge

55. Greater Sudbury is found here: Nickel _____
56. First Choice services
58. Mother of 35-A
59. Beasts of burdens
60. Sibling of Seth
62. Metes (with "out")
63. Flower with sword-shaped leaves
64. Diner breakfast serving
65. Country bumpkin
69. Mother of a girl in Granby
70. Liturgical vestments
71. *The Wizard of Oz* protagonist: Dorothy _____
72. Basket for a Raptor

73. *Winnipeg _____ Press*
74. Tire pressure measurement (abbr.)
77. Former Yugoslavian president
78. The whole enchilada
79. Epistles
81. Vacillated
82. Tea leaf bit
83. Staccato knocking noise
85. Daughter of King Minos
86. You can order one at Second Cup
88. Takes away weapons
89. Stovetop element
91. Like a non-reactive gas

92. Slat on a cask
93. Kilometres, in Kansas
94. Canada's Cindy Klassen won this award twice: _____ Springstead Trophy
95. "Don't get any funny _____!"
96. Canadian mockumentary show: *Trailer Park _____*
97. Shape of a White House office
98. Proofreader's MS mark
99. Lab jelly
100. Black-and-white male duck
101. Canadian cellphone service provider
104. Gem State librarians' org.

73

Inventive Ideas

From clever Canadians

ACROSS

1. Wash off soap
6. On the peak of BC's Fairweather Mountain
10. *RuPaul's Drag Race* episode event: Lip _____ for your life
14. Calgary Hitmen league type: _____-junior
19. Leaves off a guest list
20. Mrs. Dithers of *Blondie*
21. Hero anagram
22. Saudi's neighbour
23. Ibiza snacks
24. Brush's partner
25. "Fine with me"
26. Striking
27. Come from
29. Long-time CTV journalist Craig
31. Greek goddess of witchcraft
32. Goes from brunette to redhead
33. Moon, in Montreal
34. Étude ending
35. Havana country
38. Accept at face value
40. Traditional Molokai feast
42. It buckles you up?
46. A chinook does this above Calgary?
48. **Norman Breakey invented this decorating device**
51. Covered in muck
52. "_____ the ramparts..."
54. City famed for a shroud
55. Pillage, old style
56. Aristocracy
57. Apply rouge, say
59. Señorita or señora
61. Afternoon meal
62. Former Vancouver Canuck Salo
63. Summer meteor shower component
65. Metalworker's fusion
67. Chinese Cultural Revolution chairman

69. 2010 Olympic silver bobsleigh winner Upperton from Calgary
71. American actresses Michele or Thompson
72. CBA member's burden?
77. Attar, for example
80. Fibber
84. No longer in fashion
85. Vascular tissue in plants
87. Very tight
88. Giraffe's relative
89. *David Copperfield* character Heep
91. Purchase every last one
93. Greek letter
94. Wussy ones
95. **Harry Wasylyk created these trash holders**
97. Make weak
99. British dame Myra
100. _____ and crafts
101. Bright garden bloom
104. 1980s Michael J. Fox sitcom: *Family _____*
105. _____ de suite
107. Unseal an envelope
108. Capital of Latvia
110. Coil
113. Timely
115. Psychotherapist
119. Garden soil enricher
120. Complain
121. Subatomic bit
123. Kurt Browning does this on tour
124. Clear a chalkboard
125. Similar to
126. Not fake, to a German
127. 2012 Western Canadian Music Hall of Fame inductee: The Northern _____
128. Female and male
129. Be dependent on
130. Crashes into a Dodge truck?

131. They hold clothing together

DOWN

1. Memorization technique
2. Middle Eastern prayer leader
3. Australasian palm
4. **Sir Sandford Fleming invented this system**
5. Student's writing assignment
6. My Service Canada account user necessity
7. Hit from Vancouver's Doug and the Slugs: "_____ Bad"
8. Brass veneer
9. **Infants' foodstuff developed by Canadian pediatricians**
10. Aggressively push
11. Harness for oxen
12. Close at hand
13. 1963 Farley Mowat classic: *Never _____ Wolf*
14. Relocated to Regina, say
15. Friendly
16. **James Gosling was lead designer of this programming language**
17. "You can bank _____"
18. CNE attraction
28. Rip apart wrapping paper
30. Clumsy
31. *60 Minutes* running time?
34. Bite from a Siamese?
35. Beatles tune: "Here _____ the Sun"
36. Fleshy throat lobe
37. Obscure, in olden days
39. Fleece the sheep
40. Aril anagram
41. Condo complex apartments
43. Fill with gladness
44. Northern Alberta town: High _____
45. Pattern on a radial
47. "Yes," on the poop deck

49. Most hoary, to an old Scot
50. Give a speech
53. "Tom Sawyer" rock band
58. Stein at Kitchener–Waterloo's Oktoberfest
60. 23-year Pittsburgh Steelers coach Chuck
63. Piglet's best friend
64. In lieu of, in texting
66. **Donald Hings invented this two-way communications device**
68. It precedes male or Centauri
70. _____ tide
72. Flu symptom
73. Halos (var.)
74. Mixes things up?

75. Prince _____ SK
76. Question veracity
78. Blackbird (var.)
79. Transient labourers
81. Metrical feet, to a bard (var.)
82. The McIntosh is the "national" this of Canada
83. Goes up
86. Baby hawk
88. Nickname for a Montreal stadium: The Big _____
90. Incomprehensible
92. Sacred song
96. Ancient western Europe region
98. Gladly, old style
102. **Gideon Sundback's St. Catharines factory produced an early version of this**

103. New York state prison
106. Fertile Kalahari tracts
107. He starred on TV with Cher
109. Shallow breaths
110. Billy Joel song: "_____ Always a Woman"
111. Unsullied
112. **Four Canadians developed this cinematic technology**
113. Prod with your elbow
114. Marsh bird by the tracks?
116. Congo people
117. Long part of a wineglass
118. _____ *of the D'Urbervilles*
120. Kidney Foundation of Canada fundraising month (abbr.)
122. Resistance unit

SOLUTION ON PAGE 176

74

Carols of the Belles

Which diva recorded these songs?

ACROSS

1. Just the facts
5. Shows one's feelings
11. Scenic Hamilton roadway: Mountain _____ Boulevard
15. "Yikes!" in olden days
19. Scorch
20. _____ rasa
21. Molten liquid
22. Encouraging expression: "_____ boy!"
23. **"All I Want for Christmas Is You"**
25. When neither a strike nor spare is scored
27. Police snitch
28. Genesis parent
29. Yonge, in Toronto
30. Kempt, in Quebec
31. Animal found in all provinces but one
32. Ground cover
33. Tofino activity: _____-watching
37. British _____
40. Campsite shelter
41. Dolt
43. Enthusiastic
44. North East England (abbr.)
45. Squirrelly one?
46. Mild yellow cheese
48. Hitting a hosier?
50. Sistine Chapel pope selection session
53. As written, in ancient Rome
54. Charon's fee?
55. Eclipses, in competition
57. Verbally expressed amazement
59. Aquatic mammal
60. Like some sounds produced by the larynx
61. Wildflower on a poultry farm?
63. More suitable
64. **"Have Yourself a Merry Little Christmas"**

67. Village People classic: "_____ Man"
71. Rue
72. African country
78. Dress for a ranee
79. Collector's conversation piece
80. Kissing cousins, perhaps?
82. Harriet Beecher Stowe protagonist
84. Ottawa clock setting (abbr.)
86. Low pH issue
87. Australian anteater
88. Cold War combatant (abbr.)
89. Habitual drinker
90. The Jets play on this
91. Mordecai Richler book: *Joshua _____ and Now*
92. Ontario National Historic Site: _____–Severn Waterway
94. The Band classic: "_____ Cripple Creek"
96. King Lear line: "Mend when thou _____"
98. De facto Nauru capital
100. Down in the dumps
101. Observed
102. US or CDN currency unit
103. Moolah
105. Not up-to-date
106. Humiliates
110. Colourful enamelware
113. **"Go Tell It on the Mountain"**
115. Beginner
116. Turn sharply
117. "Begone," to Shakespeare
118. Dust-up over chores?
119. Flowerless plant
120. Appends
121. Former Canadien Savard, et al.
122. Duck type

DOWN

1. Brief philosophical tenets?
2. Well-organized

3. Card game once popular with cowboys
4. Baltimore ballpark bird?
5. Work _____
6. Spice rack spice
7. Ontario Bar Association (abbr.)
8. Soup serving dish
9. Raises
10. This Leo sang "When I Need You"
11. Develop, like a dahlia?
12. Toronto NBAer
13. Needed Narcan
14. Taper off
15. **"Santa Baby"**
16. In and around Toronto (abbr.)
17. CIBC foyer machine
18. *Lost* star: Daniel _____ Kim
24. Word of woe, old style
26. Not very many
31. Southeast Asian pepper plant
34. Fly Air North?
35. Hang around
36. Lawn trimming tool
37. Disguised, for short
38. South Korean capital
39. At a slow tempo, in music
40. Island in Polynesia
41. Ghoulish
42. This country hosted the Winter Olympics twice (abbr.)
45. Arizona Indigenous group
47. **"It's the Most Wonderful Time of the Year"**
49. Soybeans or canola, in Manitoba
51. Playing surface for 12-D (abbr.)
52. Set ablaze
54. Greek salad cheese
56. More timid
58. Ends of swords
62. Like the most frothy nog?
63. Skilled
65. Brakes cylinder
66. New right winger?

67. 1972 film: *Man of La* _____
68. Bow and arrow pro
69. **"Père Noël arrive ce soir"**
70. Be mindful of advice
73. Pacemaker (abbr.)
74. Nevertheless, for short
75. Tree secretion
76. 15-year NHLer Lindros, et al.
77. Canada Savings Bond, at one time
78. Plum pudding description
79. Roughed up?
81. Canada's Raymond Burr played this TV Perry

83. AC/DC has a blast playing this song?
85. Real soulmate?
88. They take off sneakers?
93. Took home pay
95. Hawker (var.)
96. Prolonged state of unconsciousness
97. Environment Canada warnings, say
99. National Intelligence Service (abbr.)
101. Carbonated beverages

102. Justice and Finance, in the GOC
104. _____ Scotia
106. Fraction of a newton
107. _____ bomb
108. Lymphatic swelling
109. St. John's gets lots of this
110. Canadian Taxpayers Federation (abbr.)
111. Corrosive chemical
112. Marion who was the first Canadian woman to run a flying school
114. Haul

SOLUTION ON PAGE 176

Cold Canada

Ready for winter?

ACROSS

1. Scarfs down
6. _____ the minute
10. Private space for women, in the Middle East
15. Treads the boards, at Stratford
19. Quarter-round decorative moulding
20. Quarry
21. Immature seed
22. "Awesome," in slang
23. Petty set of procedures, say
25. Winery barrels
26. Mama's mate
27. **Arthur Sicard invented this useful machine**
28. Nestlé chocolate bar: _____ Kat
29. Fuse
31. Canada's Ron Francis wore this number for the Canes and Pens
32. Bird's perch
33. "Electric" fish
34. *SCTV* star Thomas
35. "Not worth a red _____"
36. Toronto place of worship: Church of the _____ Trinity
38. Theatre mezzanine
39. Ad _____
42. Bond girl Pussy in *Goldfinger*
45. Loose hood worn by monks
46. Ryan Reynolds played this type of character in *Deadpool*
48. Serotonin, for example
49. 1993 hit from 106-A: "Already _____"
50. Vigorous
51. *Legally Blonde* actress Blair
52. Completely similar
53. Extinct New Zealand birds
54. Cost of crossing some bridges
55. Becomes banal
56. Gradually discontinue
58. Partner of aahs
59. Saint John or Vancouver

60. Musical ensemble of four
63. Hurt a brainiac?
67. Grad from U of C
68. Tim Hortons drive-through or app patrons
73. Barry Manilow hit: "Looks Like We _____"
74. Chestnut or cedar
75. Travelling
76. Informal greeting
77. Muslims' faith
78. Moult
79. Crest of a hill, in Britspeak
80. Pinkish colour
81. Treatments for illnesses
83. Sigourney played her in *Gorillas in the Mist*
84. Most willing to play 10-D?
85. Elephant _____
86. Tree trunk
87. General's helper
88. Sidewalk edge, in Ipswich
89. Opening
90. Dy-no-mite explosive?
91. Bonn river
93. Used to be
96. Some fall under your feet?
99. 1978 Alice Munro offering: _____ Do You Think You Are?
100. **Jacques Plante invented this sports gear**
102. Thomas who challenged Henry VIII
103. Willow tree
105. Teetotalling, say
106. Multiple Juno Award winner: _____ Rodeo
107. BC-born MacMillan who voiced Gumby
108. Marketing word for low calorie
109. Give to the University of Manitoba
110. Canonical hour
111. Neatly groomed

112. Did well, in a tennis match?
113. Cleans up powder?

DOWN

1. Long-time Discovery show: *Canada's _____ Driver*
2. Woolly mammal
3. Sign into an Internet account
4. Blemish
5. Señor's topper
6. Displace delphiniums?
7. Ships' front ends
8. TV charity fundraisers
9. Legal hearing
10. **Canada's Arthur Farrell wrote the first handbook on this**
11. Make use of resources
12. Canadian car care firm: _____ Check
13. Hoofed Canadian mammal
14. Text transmission
15. _____ pie
16. Nickelback band member Kroeger
17. Videocassette
18. NL newspaper: *The Western _____*
24. Canada's Catherine O'Hara starred in this: *Home _____*
30. Exaggerate, in Alaska?
33. Pipe bend
34. Dumb druggie?
35. Retinal receptors
37. Be in hock to RBC
38. Temporary break
39. Entertainment news magazine: _____! *Canada*
40. Channel Islands abalone
41. Mountain range through BC and Yukon
42. Struggle to breathe
43. Asian domestic servant
44. Peruvian's preferred bean?
45. South American mammal

46. Dip for taco chips
47. Make a pile
49. Calabash or squash
50. Like a lacklustre tune?
53. Sacred musical piece
54. Quintessential cap for Canadians
55. Shabby, in the greenhouse?
57. Deserving of respect
58. Leered
59. Watch or purse part
61. Nose holes
62. _____ & Martin's *Laugh-In*
63. Wallop, in olden days
64. Chekhov *Three Sisters* character
65. Canadian political commentator Charles

66. Backside
69. Four-sided geometrical shape
70. Ireland, old style
71. Stockholm rugs
72. _____ and pepper
74. "O Canada" word
75. Exercise style
78. River bottom deposit
79. Nickname for a famed NHLer: Sid the _____
80. Lurched
82. Toxic substances
83. Morse code click
84. Arabian folklore beings (var.)
87. Caribou Inuit developed this kind of coat

88. Wearing a Scottish skirt
89. Musician's need: _____ music
90. Motif
92. Excessive speed
93. Magicians' sticks
94. British racecourse attire?
95. Biases results
96. Country's diplomatic reps
97. Part for Canada's Tatiana Maslany
98. Heart of a matter
99. Metal string
100. Big charity bash
101. East Side Mario's reading
104. Source of warmth in Spain

```
STEMS MUNG IONS ETHAN
LINAC EVIL TRET DAIRY
ABASH REPUTEDLY MIDGE
VICTORIA THRILL OLEOS
EATSOUT MAYAN ONN
DES LISSOM TAI UTTERS
    HEN TRIVETS ROADIE
EDGED DIANA EMPENNAGE
ROAM POLLENS SUM GMAN
ANTIPASTI COS NBA
SATNAV STJOHNS EREBUS
    PAM YOU APARTMENT
SCAM RAT EVOKING PATE
LOCOMOTES EXERT STROP
OCELOT DECRYPT DIY
PARENT DAH MISSAL OWL
    TIS BESOT PREPPIE
FLOUR CHOLER WINNIPEG
LIVRE OARSWOMAN CLONE
OMEGA FINE NONE EOSIN
PANEL FLEA SEER STEED
```

1 ▪ Landscape Architecture

```
WHARFS UNREST STOOPS
HEJIRA BROILER TONSIL
ARABIC EGGSFLORENTINE
TAROT MAE KILTER HEED
   STOAT LENS POWERS
STREAMLINED POLES
KOI TATTOO FBI SALAAM
INDIAN INSULAR KYRIE
PIED LORETTA OPS ADS
SCRAMMED RON DAPPLES
   HUEVOSRANCHEROS
PAROLEE OUT INSTANTS
ABA ESL DIARIST LOUT
NICAD SPONSOR DOMINO
STYLET EMS PASSIM SEP
   LEANT PENTAMETERS
SHERPA STAR AISLE
AWAY PISTOL OLD ETHOS
QUICHELORRAINE STROBE
UNFAIR LITTLER ITALIC
AGATES EASELS RESETS
```

2 ▪ Breakfast Buffet

```
ARTS GENOA ALBA AGHA
COOP AMIRS BOAST ROIL
TULIPBULBS BASKETBALL
STEREOS EDEN FRAILTY
   INN TERRY DONUT
PASTS GRATE TOR PESKY
ETAS GAUR STOW MERINO
REB COLES SUNDAE STEW
PULSATOR NIB SITS KEL
SPEAR PINENUT MAMMALS
   ISNT BURGLAR LIES
RASHERS RESEWED LEPTA
URL YAPS ITS FIRETRAP
SEAR CANADA CLEAR UTE
SANEST OUST HOTE SCAR
OLDEN DOG IDEAS BEERS
   CASED POINT POI
ENTHRAL IANS SUBZERO
BAYOFFUNDY MANITOULIN
OGRE EXCON ABORT RUNE
NAES ELLE LAMES ELKS
```

3 ▪ Trivia Pursuit

```
LOWS SCAB SLAW AMBUSH
IDEE TORA LORY COUNTY
SISTERACT YOGA HOLDUP
ANTHROPOID MOTHERLODE
   ADT KIWI TUNIS
BAPS ESK TENS SIN FDE
EURO ORTEGA TAGALOG
BROTHERHOOD ITLL HUNG
EAT ADULT FLOE LOONS
   SABRED ERROR ARRAY
   GRANDFATHERCLAUSE
SPOOR ASCOT OGRESS
TONNE FISH FIBRE CUE
ALIT SORE UNCLEALBERT
ROSETTE STRUCK ONAT
EST YET SWAM SIC ATTA
   SPEAR ALBS CAI
FATHERLAND SECONDBEST
ARIOSE MADE AUNTSALLY
DINNER PILL TRIO LAIR
SLEETS SLED SECS INDO
```

4 ▪ Word Families?

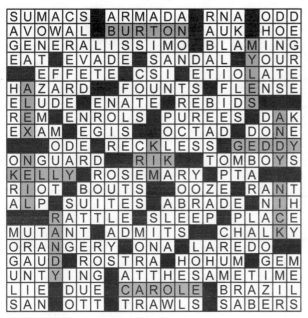

5 ▪ Rockin' Since the '70s

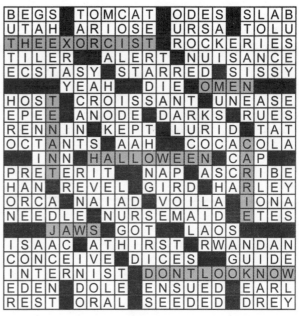

6 ▪ Scary in the '70s

7 ▪ Going the Distance

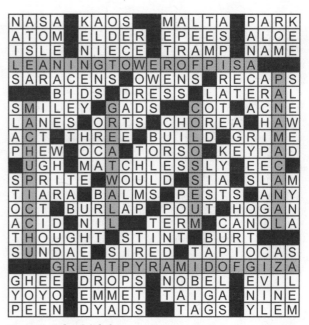

8 ▪ Wonder(s)ful

9 ▪ Sons of Canada

10 ▪ Legendary Ladies

11 ▪ Who Am I? 1

12 ▪ Du You Know the Way…

13 ▪ Historic Canadian Hotels

14 ▪ National Nicknames

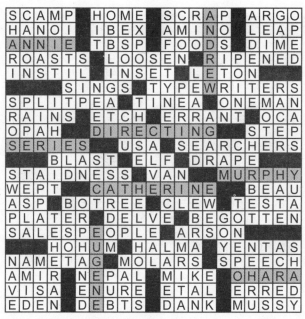

15 ▪ *Schitt's Creek* Cleans Up...

16 ▪ Drink Up

17 ▪ In the Merry Month of May

18 ▪ Ladies & Gentlemen

19 ▪ Lyrical Words…

20 ▪ These Boots Are Made for Walkin'

Answer: All theme answers are original lyrics from *O Canada*

21 ▪ Shiny Stuff

22 ▪ Down Under Denizens

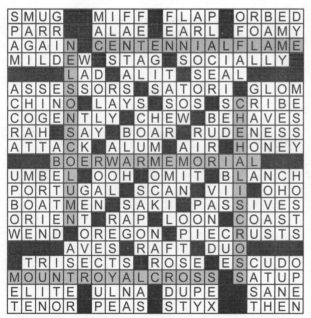

23 ▪ Monumental…

24 ▪ Au *Jus*

SOLUTIONS

25 ▪ Eventful in the '80s

26 ▪ Elegant in the '80s

27 ▪ A Mixed Bag

28 ▪ On the Mat

29 ▪ Right Place, Right Time

30 ▪ His-and-Hers Homonyms

31 ▪ Cooking Up a Storm…

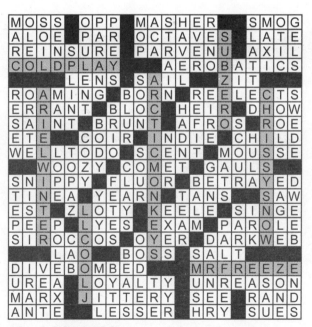

32 ▪ A Wintry Mix

33 ▪ Only In Canada, Eh?

34 ▪ Buzzwords

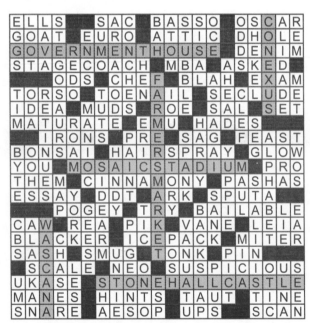

35 ▪ Destination: Regina

36 ▪ Mom's the Word

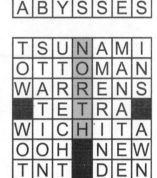

37 ▪ Four-Square

38 ▪ Here vs. There

Answer: 24-D + 22-A + 56-A + 42-D

39 ▪ Canuck Vocab

40 ▪ What's the Catch?

41 ▪ Hockey Hooey

42 ▪ Avian Airs

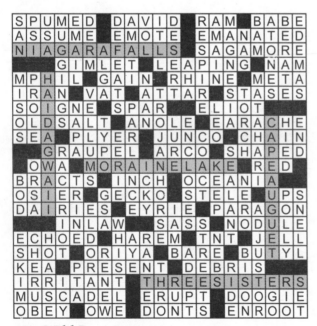

43 ▪ Wild Beauties…

44 ▪ A-simile-ation

45 ▪ Notable '90s NHL Rookies

46 ▪ 1990s Nobel Prize Winners

47 ▪ Share and Share Alike

48 ▪ Instruments of Song

49 ▪ Illustrious Alumni

50 ▪ The Spies Have It

Answer: COUNTERESPIONAGE

51 ▪ Streetwise…

52 ▪ Pretty to Look At

53 ▪ Who Am I? 2

54 ▪ Do You Hear What I Hear?

55 ▪ Acrophobics Beware…

56 ▪ Tokens of Affection

57 ▪ R Is for River

58 ▪ A Prickly Puzzle

59 ▪ Name That Province

60 ▪ Box Office *Gold*

Answer: ALBERTA

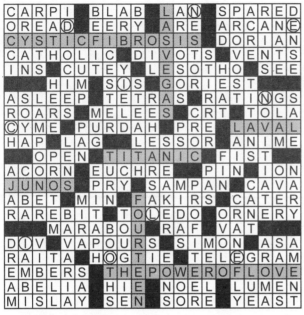

61 ▪ Who Am I? 3

Answer: CÉLINE DION

62 ▪ Wait for *It*

63 ▪ Serving Queen and Country

64 ▪ Cheer-io

SOLUTIONS

65 ▪ Golden '00s Canadian Olympians

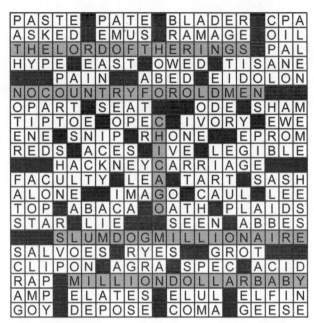

66 ▪ '00s Oscars

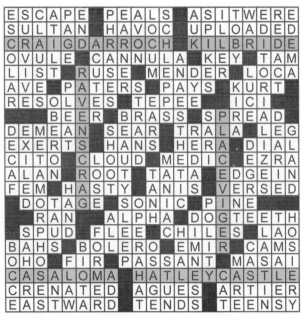

67 ▪ Palatial Places

68 ▪ The Sounds of Music

69 ▪ Give Me a B…

70 ▪ Animal Antics

71 ▪ Who Am I? 4

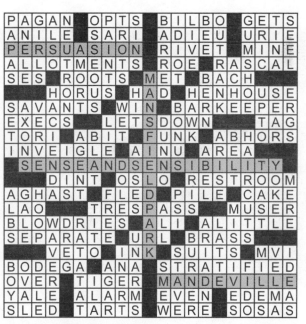

72 ▪ Regency Reading

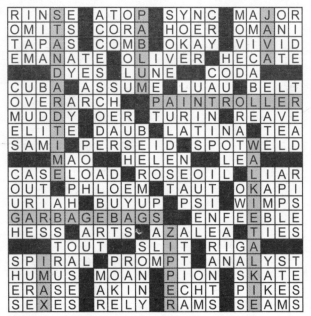

73 ▪ Inventive Ideas

74 ▪ Carols of the Belles

75 ▪ Cold Canada